NO STOPPiNG FOR LiONS

A YEAR-LONG AFRICAN JOURNEY

Joanne Glynn

PIER **9**

First published in 2009 by Pier 9, an imprint of Murdoch Books Pty Limited

Murdoch Books Australia
Pier 8/9, 23 Hickson Road
Millers Point NSW 2000
Phone: +61 (0) 2 8220 2000
Fax: +61 (0) 2 8220 2558
www.murdochbooks.com.au

Murdoch Books UK Limited
Erico House, 6th Floor
93–99 Upper Richmond Road
Putney, London SW15 2TG
Phone: +44 (0) 20 8785 5995
Fax: +44 (0) 20 8785 5985
www.murdochbooks.co.uk

Chief Executive: Juliet Rogers
Publishing Director: Kay Scarlett
Commissioning Editor: Colette Vell.
Editor: Anouska Jones
Designer: Katy Wall

Text copyright © 2009 Joanne Glyn
The moral right of the author has be
Design copyright © 2009 Murdoch

Cover image: Photolibrary.com
Map: Ian Faulkner

National Library of Australia Cataloguing-in-Publication Data:

Author: Glynn, Joanne.
Title: No stopping for lions : travels with Africa / Joanne Glynn.
ISBN: 9781741963731 (pbk.)
Subjects: Glynn, Joanne--Travel.
                 Africa--Description and travel.
Dewey Number: 916

A catalogue record is available from the British Library

Printed on FSC certified paper by Hang Tai in 2009. Printed in China.

In loving memory of the Troopy

CONTENTS

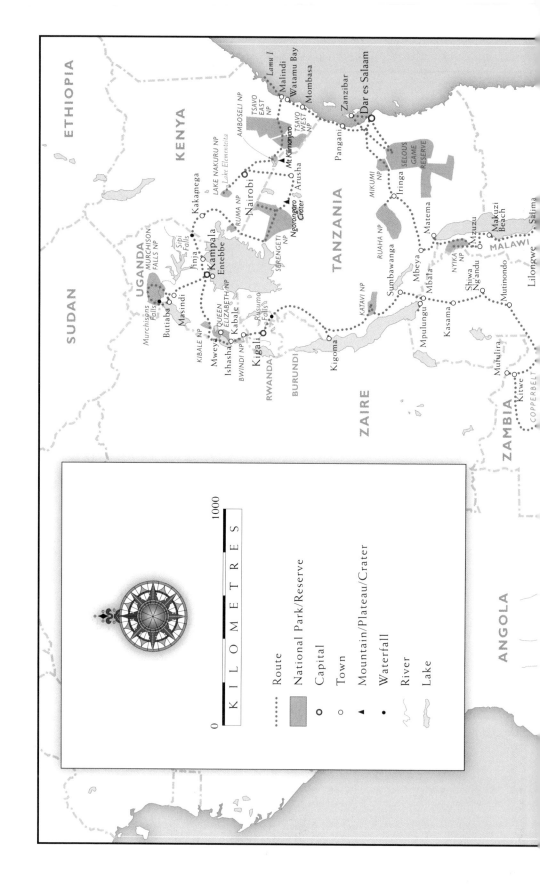

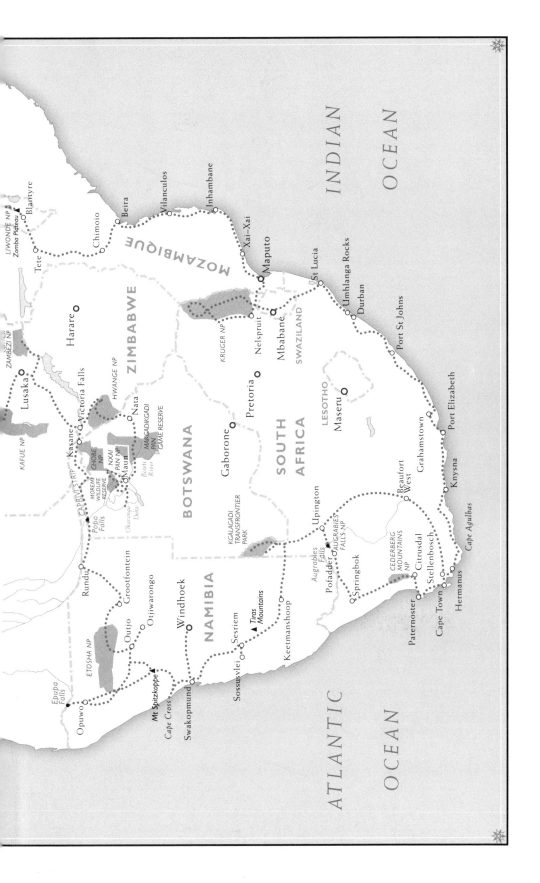

PROCEED WiTH CAUTiON

There is a thick covering of fog over Cape Town as our plane circles. Up here in the sky the morning is crisp and cloudless but below us Table Mountain and Lions Head stick out through a solid white sea like beacons from God. The cabin crew crane their necks along with everyone else as we come down low and slow over acres of shanty dwellings linked crazily by plastic sheeting and electrical cabling. Someone in the row behind us tells everyone within earshot that it's called low-cost housing if there are cement walls and tall spotlights, otherwise it's known as an informal settlement. Either way, this vast recycled jungle has a look of battered permanency, and I can believe that it is not only home to millions of the city's poor and deprived, but that many of the families have lived here for generations.

Immediately after my husband Neil and I walk out the doors of the arrivals terminal they're closed and the airport is locked down due to a bomb threat. Rather than be unnerved by this we take our close call as a lucky sign and motor into the city in a rental car, unconcerned about the confusion on the roads caused by the descending fog. In no time we find ourselves on a fly-over by the city centre, with the harbour on our right and Table Mountain somewhere over there to the left. This is just a guess, given the weather conditions, and we have trouble identifying more immediate landmarks that eerily appear then fade back behind the fogbank. We abandon printed instructions and cruise on through intersections with hardly a turn right or left until there before us is a guarded gate and, wouldn't you know it, it's the right gate.

We have booked a small apartment at the Victoria & Alfred Waterfront, known to all as the V&A. This dockside redevelopment manages to successfully merge a shopping complex, hotels, cinemas, restaurants, a residential precinct and marina with Cape Town's working harbour of wharves and historic buildings. It's a city within a city and a little removed from the buzz and racial mix of the streets outside, but it's skipping to its own rope and has a reputation for being safe, with security guards and key cards keeping the riffraff out. As soon as the fog starts to lift we're out exploring, wandering the wharves where fishing boats with interesting sailors are returning for the day and big blubbery seals heave and flop onto wet wood jetties right at our feet. The air is clear and the water sparkles, and it feels as though this day and this city are glowing with approval for the boldness of our journey.

For we have embarked on a twelve-month road trip that will take us to all the places in Central and East Africa that we've ever wanted to visit, to familiar landscapes as well as new horizons. I plan to watch the sun set over a Namibian desert and follow wildebeest through the Serengeti; Neil wants to track

African wild dogs in the Selous and canoe down the Zambezi. We'll drive as far north as Kenya and as far west as the Congo and we'll go with the breeze, following the seasons and taking as much time as we please. The only deadline we have to make is to meet my sister, Viv, who'll be joining us for a month in Botswana, and the only time limitation is our return air ticket, dated twelve months away.

There is, however, an anchor to this adventure: at its heart is a search for something from Neil's past that has danced and wafted through his memories since childhood. He was born and raised in Northern Rhodesia, later to become Zambia, and now he hopes to find a farm there that was the family home for the latter part of the 1940s. His parents, probably suffering from a false sense of ability, upped stakes from the Copperbelt in the country's central west and leased an existing cattle farm in the remote far north, close to the Tanzanian border. Itembwe was in the middle of nowhere, beautiful but isolated, miles from the nearest farm and three hours' drive from the closest town when the road was passable. A paradise and a pipedream.

Neil and his brother were youngsters, his sister not yet born. Also along for the ride were Neil's uncle, aunt and cousins — two girls much his own age who became more like sisters in this secluded playground. For the adults it must have been a hard, unworkable existence; for the children it was a world of adventure.

Neil's memories are full of special stories. There was the time he and his brother negotiated with a *medula*, an old man, to buy a highly venomous Gaboon viper, but their mother wouldn't cough up the threepenny price tag; there was the gun boy, who sat in a tower with a 303 popping off marauding baboons in the ripening maize fields; lions taking the cattle; Neil's father shooting the lions; the children being sat on the backs of shot lions and sables for photographs while vermin abandoned the dead bodies like passengers from the *Titanic*; payday, when the native workers and their families lined up to receive their wages and allocation of mielie-meal (maize flour) and chunks of bush meat if game had been shot. Then there was Janson, their brave but foolish bull terrier who walked on three legs after being bitten by a baboon. A storybook life that the rest of us could only read about.

Itembwe's main farmhouse was a whitewashed Anglo-Colonial affair dominating one end of a small valley. Proud and imposing, it looked down over maize fields and was surrounded by rocky slopes and *miombo* woodlands where the leaves turned red and gold in late winter. Sweeping stone stairs led up to the deep verandah, and this was fronted by a row of graceful white columns. It is this house, or its remains, which Neil now hopes to locate, armed only with a name and a handful of old black-and-white photographs. We're also armed with a small list of contacts, as before we left Sydney we corresponded with an acquaintance in Zambia who was able to suggest likely sources of information. In a land of limited telecommunication, personal visits will be the only means of gathering the necessary leads.

We decided to purchase a four-wheel drive in Sydney and have it kitted out there to our specifications before shipping it to Cape Town. We felt that we needed to be familiar with the vehicle that was not only going to be our transport but also our home and shelter. Neither of us had driven a four-wheel drive off-road before, so we took it on weekend courses and trial runs where the only disappointing performances were from ourselves. A lot of thought went into the choice of model and make. We knew that what was needed was a vehicle strong enough to withstand the rigours of bad and dusty roads; it had to be able to be fixed anywhere, by anyone; and we couldn't afford to have fancy computers or special tyres that couldn't be replaced. It had to have enough room in the back to take an extra water tank, a wardrobe compartment, drawers for cooking equipment and spare parts, assorted chairs, tables and a tent, and it had to be big enough to carry a sleeping capsule on top. The Toyota LandCruiser 70 series fitted the bill, and although we didn't order the troop carrier model, somehow we were referring to it as 'the Troopy' even before it left the factory.

Now, in Cape Town, we wait for it to be cleared by customs. It's just two days after our arrival, three days after it was unloaded, when the phone call comes through from the shipping agents. Neil races off but a small problem arises when the agents inform him that they only take cash for payment. Neil goes to an ATM in the centre of downtown Cape Town to withdraw thousands of rand; he's just inserted his credit card when a thin black hand snakes over his shoulder and snatches it. The card gets passed to an accomplice who quickly swipes it on a scanner hidden in the folds of his big heavy army coat then takes off at full speed. Neil races after him but is stopped by an onlooker who indicates that he thinks Neil must be crazy to try to catch a thief in this city of desperadoes. Because he is conveniently outside a bank Neil is able to cancel the card promptly, organise for a replacement and withdraw enough cash to release the Troopy. He's surprisingly calm when he returns to the apartment — he looks pleased with himself and relieved to have the Troopy once more in our possession — so I dismiss the incident as the first of many we're bound to encounter in the months ahead.

The Troopy looks shiny and new and raring to go. It sits in a parking bay beneath our bedroom window and we keep looking out to check that it's still proud and safe below. We notice that passers-by stop to look too and this is our first inkling that the

Troopy is not the norm in these parts as we'd thought, but an object of desire.

Our last city days are spent on final shopping for gas cooktops, toasters and fold-up chairs. I convince Neil that camping equipment is so cheap here it'd be a shame not to benefit from the savings. I buy an electric jug and a hairdryer that will plug into a car's cigarette lighter but only read the small print once I've ripped off the packaging. The jug takes eighteen minutes to boil, and the hairdryer is given such a short cord that I'd have to have my head down by the gear stick to use it. After so many months of detailed planning back in Sydney, Neil is amused that I can still find something that we simply have to have.

We're keen to hit the road but our laptop has a dial-up problem that will have to be resolved first. Although we anticipate that we'll only be able to log on in Internet cafes in major cities, access to the web is a critical component of this trip. Not only will we need to visit itinerary and accommodation websites to plot our progress, but emails will be the only real contact we'll have with friends and family. The laptop itself will be invaluable as we will need to regularly download photos from our three cameras, and both of us intend keeping an electronic diary of our progress.

Neil spends endless hours going round and round with helplines in South Africa, then Australia, but nothing seems to work and he becomes more worried and frustrated. On the third day he's up throughout the night to Dell Asia Pacific trying to find what should be a straightforward solution. He's become obsessed with solving the problem and it dominates our days. He knows that it has to be resolved before we leave civilisation behind, but we don't want to delay our departure because of it. He's a dog with a bone.

Thank goodness for generous relatives. We've arranged to have dinner with Neil's cousin and his family, dedicated Capetonians. Tim's wife went out of her way to smooth the path for us before we arrived in town and their local knowledge of the ins and outs of officialdom here has been invaluable. Neil and I choose a restaurant nearby but, oh dear, what a bad choice. Neil makes us all laugh when he lifts up the pasta on his plate in one dry, undressed clump that looks like a bird's nest but tastes worse. He's starting to relax but a worried furrow appears on his brow when someone suggests that this substandard food could be the norm from now on.

Another cousin, here on business from Melbourne, pays us a visit. He listens to Neil's dial-up woes, wanders over to the laptop and solves the problem in a few minutes. After days of tackling a mountain, Neil was unable to see that it was only a molehill. He is mightily relieved and shouts us lunch. At the restaurant he relaxes into his chair and cracks a bad joke, and only then do I realise how much pressure he'd felt. While I'd looked at the stolen credit card and dial-up problem as annoyances, just the first anecdotes from a big adventure that was going to be full of challenges and surprises, Neil had been bearing the burden of having to overcome them.

Listening to our lazy conversation over coffee, I'm struck by how easily I've fallen into the African way of referring to Europeans as whites, and black Africans as blacks. I was bought up to think that this sort of verbal discrimination was derogatory, so it's been surprising to find that the terms are, in general, just words used to describe each other and don't intend slur or racial prejudice. In conversation with the cleaning lady back in our apartment, she'd asked whether our maid at home is black or white, and once she got over the shock of discovering that we don't have a maid, proceeded to inform us that, in her opinion, whites do not make good cleaners or good dancers.

We're on-line again. The first email through is one from the guys at the camping centre where we'd shopped, expressing interest in buying the Troopy from us when we finish the trip. We respond with the promise of first option. Then there's an email from a contact in Zambia in the travel business who has finally come good with some form of third-party insurance for the Troopy for seven of the countries we're to be visiting.

Trying to arrange insurance before we left had been a major hurdle. No one in Australia would insure the Troopy for travel outside the country, and because it was not going to be registered in an African country, nobody there would issue any form of comprehensive insurance either. Neil resorted to contacting brokers all over the world, from Lloyds of London to a shonky outfit in Switzerland who did come up with a policy — one that would cost $25 000. So we made the decision to travel without comprehensive insurance and to arrange third party as we went along. We knew that this was payable sometimes at border posts and sometimes included in the vehicle entry pass, so now with this Zambian insurance we believe that we have just about every country covered. At last, everything is in place to head out into the wild beyond and we're both jumpy with excitement.

COLLiSiON COURSE

Neil's wandering spirit was given wings by his parents' sense of impermanence. They had met and married in Northern Rhodesia and their children were born there, but there was always the notion that they'd be 'going back home' to the United Kingdom. The family did return once, young Neil and his brother decked out in navy blazers, khaki shorts and little pith helmets, but the trip was short-lived. It may have come to an unsatisfactory conclusion for the family, but it seems to have taught Neil at an early age that moving around was the norm. Later on he could accept long train journeys to and from school and travelling about during short school holidays to stay with the families of friends. He learnt to take border crossings in his stride and to understand the vagaries of African bureaucracies and the mysteries of official paperwork.

It seems he was always travelling. After his family's move to the farm he and his brother, aged six and seven, spent the school week boarding in a hostel in the nearest town, three hours away. Both the school and hostel were run by his aunt, who by this time had left Itembwe and moved with the girls in to town. When life on the farm became unviable the rest of the family moved back to Mufulira in the Copperbelt and there were a couple of years of stability before the boys' secondary education had to be addressed. When Neil was eleven the two boys began their travels to school in South Africa, which involved a twice-yearly train trip of five days and four nights and meant that they were home for only seven weeks of the year. This wasn't unusual; each term saw a mass migration of children from the two Rhodesias heading to and from boarding schools in the provinces of South Africa. These trips were legendary, particularly when the boys were older. Whole trains, sometimes co-ed and sometimes segregated, passing through four countries and picking up unsupervised students who were oblivious to border crossings or authority as they concentrated on one thing: the opposite sex. The kids lurched from boredom to hormone-driven mania, and the days were filled with attempts to satisfy both. Neil tells great stories of hot tubs in the public baths of the Bulawayo station, saving his meal money by eating only watermelon for the whole journey, jumping train at one station to lie in wait for the girls' train to pass through, and developing a skill for hypnotism which made him a hero even after one episode went terribly wrong when his subject, as the race driver Sterling Moss, crashed and 'burned alive'. This particular time Sterling Moss, who had driven the racetrack of his imagination with great skill many times before to the amusement of his schoolmates, took the scenario into his own hands. Unprompted and out of Neil's control, his car first spun off the track, then crashed and burst into flames. Sterling writhed and screamed that he was burning, and Neil found himself powerless to snap him out of it until the very last minute, when Sterling stiffened then went still. For a second the others feared that he'd 'died', but to Neil's relief he had fallen asleep and woke up shortly afterwards, apparently none the worse for his near-death experience.

Neil's first real job was back in Northern Rhodesia with the Standard Bank and he was sent to their branch in Kasama, the main town of the country's north. He'd think nothing of hitchhiking 500 miles (800 kilometres) to work, taking a shortcut through the Congo and waiting days for a lift. Sounds heroic now, and today it would be foolhardy bordering on impossible, but those were more halcyon times. Once, having been dropped off near a village, Neil had to shake the hand of every inhabitant after the headman had gathered them in a deferential line. Another time, in the middle of the bush and miles from any white settlement, any other white person in fact, he sat down to an extraordinary three-course meal with the visiting district commissioner, attended by white-gloved servants.

He moved on to work for BP Southern Rhodesia in the country's capital, Salisbury, and while there he was called up to do National Service, a common requirement of many countries at the time. This was followed up by fortnightly territorials, and photos taken on one such training exercise show an almost unrecognisable Neil, as fit as Phar Lap and as pumped up as Rambo. He was transferred to Shell BP in Northern Rhodesia, now independent and called Zambia, but the grass of the outside world was too green to be ignored and the next year he resigned and headed for Europe. After twelve months of backpacking around there, living life to the full, finding new friends and working just long enough to finance the next leg, he thought he should knuckle down. So it was back to Africa and the University of Cape Town to study economics. More fun and games and new friends, and lectures in subjects that turned out to be pertinent and dynamic. Although the regulated life of a student was not for Neil and he threw it in after the first year, his study of African history and African government and law turned an interest into a passion and he left with a life-long interest in Africa's failings and fortunes.

Then it was back to Europe and work in a factory in Münster, ostensibly to learn German — but something odd was happening. Neil was feeling the opposite of restless for the first time. The notion that this life couldn't go on forever was lapping at his feet and he sensed that it was time for commitment, to put a stake in the ground. He had learnt enough to know that newly independent African countries such as Zambia would go through long and hard periods of adjustment in which the quality of life and opportunities for young white males would lessen considerably. South Africa was relatively stable then, but Neil found the regime of apartheid abhorrent and he couldn't see himself living there with any conscience. So instead of returning to Africa he went to Australia via the United States and an old girlfriend.

It was the time of Poseidon, when Australia was experiencing a mining boom and stock exchange floors were a hotbed of soaring shares and instant fortunes. Neil walked into a Sydney stockbroking firm and asked for a job. He chose this particular one because Neil made up part of their name and perhaps because of this cheeky reason he got the job as an operator on the stock exchange floor. He made big money, and good friends on the rugby field, and it didn't take long for him to decide that Australia was where he wanted to be; he became a citizen as soon as he was allowed.

Between then and when I met him three years later Neil had flown to Perth in a light aircraft, been stranded in Fiji during a cyclone and backpacked around New Zealand. The old need to be on the move was always there, but he compromised by staying put at the stock exchange and getting his light aircraft licence so that he could at least go flying on weekends.

In comparison, my upbringing was very pedestrian. I'd grown up in a New South Wales country town, Mittagong, at a time when a trip to Sydney with Mum, dressed in our Sunday best, took two and a half hours in a sooty steam train. We'd emerge at Central Station to the smells and sights of an altogether different, more glamorous life. It was escalators and lifts, and lunch at David Jones' sixth-floor cafeteria. La de da. Our family went away twice a year for school holidays, always in the car except very early on, just within the reaches of my memory, when it was by flying boat from Rose Bay to Grafton. May school holidays were spent on the south coast, Uludulla and later Batehaven, from where we'd go for drives inland in search of cheese and in-breds. In the September holidays we'd drive up to Mum's family home, a property outside Grafton, where we'd ride horses and collect bush lemons and watch proudly as Dad, originally a city boy but an ex–Light Horseman, mustered cattle with the best of them.

These commutes to holiday destinations were a necessity, a means to an end, and sitting just beneath the excitement there was boredom and bickering. Bedding stacked high under our feet in the backseat, our turns at the window being timed to the second, and stupid games that I never won. One successful year Dad bought all the kids a carton of Life Savers each and we spent the hours swapping rolls, making necklaces and rings with them, and having competitions as to who could keep one in their mouth for the longest time without chewing. I remember these trips as endurance tests but they must have cast the seed of adventure too. Back home it was a different matter: the car was our magic carpet, our escape from the mundane.

There were seven of us in the family, and on Sundays we'd all pile into the Ford Customline and go for drives around the district, exploring fresh landscapes and old back roads. Sometimes on a Saturday someone bored would say the magic words *let's go for a drive* and Dad would back her out and we'd be fighting for a window seat before he could say *where to?* Sometimes Mum would stay at home, overcome by the business of having five young children, and we'd bring her back souvenirs of our trip — a big brown feather, a waratah (not picked by us, honest), and once, a dead wombat we'd come across bloated by the side of the road.

Dad was an avid bushwalker and would take us up tracks on Mount Alexandra, behind Mittagong, where he taught us orienteering along with his love of the bush, and of photography too. We all had cameras, and we were very proud of Dad's movie camera, really an 8 millimetre cine camera. The older kids made home movies in which the final scene was always my younger brother on the ground in the last spasms of death. We all had bikes as well, and it was nothing to ride for miles, way out beyond the airstrip, to creep through the old cemetery or to check for zebra finches in my brother's bird traps.

My dolls were dressed in kilts and grass skirts, and my books were picture books of bullfighters in Spain and maharajahs in Rajasthan. I'd save copies of church missionary booklets and stare at the photos of New Guinea natives with albinos among them staring back flat-eyed and unsmiling. In high school I loved geography but had no time for history. It was the here and now I was interested in, and who all those people out there were and what they were thinking.

I'd been in Sydney for two years and was about to sit my final radiography exams when I met Neil in a pub. He was the blind date for my flat-mate and in my ignorance I thought that his unfamiliar accent was from somewhere in the United Kingdom, like the rugby mates with him. This accent plus his unusual phrasing was a bit of a turn-on to a country girl who'd never been outside her own country, rarely even her own state, and when the flat-mate declined an impromptu visit to Luna Park my hand shot up in a flash. We still have a strip of photos taken that night: three couples crammed into an instant photo booth, me looking startled after the uncharacteristic number of beers I'd downed earlier in an attempt to appear sophisticated and worldly. We fell into bed on the second date, fell in love on a Queensland beach and were married within a year.

Early married life was not quite the bed of roses I'd imagined. Living blissfully together was overshadowed by the banalities of keeping house, sticking to a budget, watching Saturday rugby games with other new and uninterested wives. Before the wedding I'd sit in my car outside Neil's flat under cover of darkness just to catch a glimpse of him; now I saw him every day, all the time. Where's the romance in that? Before, I'd spend ages on my clothes and make-up before seeing him; now he'd come home to find me in hair rollers, with cucumber slices on my eyes. Neil wanted rugby training nights and I wanted flowers. He wanted to travel; I wanted to shop. The one thing we both wanted was each other, it was just that we didn't know how to compromise or to share.

Neil did, however, know what to do about it and twelve months after our honeymoon we both quit our jobs and headed overseas for six months. This first trip outside Australia was a bombshell for me. It was one thing reading about these places, but actually being there, surrounded by strange languages, different customs and unusual smells, not to mention the volumes of people, was the first time in my life that I felt truly intimidated. France was our first stop and after flying into Charles de Gaulle airport we caught the train in to the George V Métro stop. I was ready to come home after my first mumbled, laughable attempts at *'Ou est rue Vernet, s'il vous plaît?'* And Neil did laugh. It was his reaction as much as my inadequacy that upset me, and I've hated that part of Paris ever since. My confidence improved as we went along but unfortunately my linguistic skills didn't.

We had many arguments in these first months of our holiday as I came to grips with new environments and experiences. I suspect that I was hard work, becoming despondent when I couldn't make myself understood and sulking when Neil's strict adherence to budget deprived me of a souvenir or a second bottle of Coke. On top of this, being together for 24 hours a day for weeks on end was trying on both sides, and small things like ordering beans and bacon over artichokes and bacon turned into a battle of wills. But gradually, without being conscious of making compromises, we began to consider the other person and settled into a comfortable alliance. Or maybe we just got tired of disagreeing.

By the time we got to Africa four months later I believed myself to be a seasoned traveller. We arrived in Nairobi, took a room at the Norfolk Hotel and ordered something to eat. After some time I answered a knock on the door and, whoa, got the fright of my life as all I could see in the gloom was a plate of sandwiches and a row of white smiling teeth. I was going to have to get used to seeing black faces in dark places.

As soon as we'd landed in Nairobi there had been an immediate though subtle change in Neil. He became less of a cajoler and more of a teacher; he wanted to show me something special of his and share with me its wonders. I thought him confident and in control in Europe, but here he was comfortable, at home with his history, and the new rapport we'd acquired in Europe made it easier for him to convey this to me.

Our funds were getting low so we set off from Nairobi for Arusha in Tanzania using local buses, Neil and I sitting grandly up front in first class. However, not everyone appreciates the concept of user pays, and the Maasai we picked up along the way squashed into the front section with us. I remember it being close and uncomfortable, but that was a small price to pay for the excitement of sharing space with such extraordinary people. One lean, beautiful youth couldn't take his eyes off the inappropriate red and yellow raffia sun hat I'd carried all the way from Sydney, while I constantly stole glances at his smooth chocolate head, stretched earlobes, and rows and rows of bright beaded jewellery. Then, not yet out of Kenya, we were passing through a lightly wooded area when a face appeared over the treetops — a giraffe! In the wild, just hanging around! I could hardly believe it; this was the Africa I'd only ever read about and imagined, and the moment is one that is still with me after all these years.

When we returned home we were on a tight budget and fell into the habit of driving out to Sydney's airport on weekends to watch planes come in and fly out. This free entertainment only stopped when we ourselves began to fly off to destinations new and far away on a regular basis. At first it was a Christmas in Noumea, then five days in Vanuatu, then a return visit to Italy one year kindled a great fondness for the country and we found ourselves making an annual pilgrimage there, bracketed by stopovers in Asia. We discovered that as soon as we were in the air we fell into the companionable state of mind forged in Europe and cemented in Africa on that first trip, and that in itself became an incentive to pack our bags and head off. On the canals in Venice, in the streets of Hanoi, it would all come together again and we'd experience the world from a world of our own. Kurt Vonnegut describes it as a nation of two, and that's how it often feels on our charmed journeys through foreign lands.

Now here we are in Africa, and the prospect of twelve months together in constant co-existence fills me with excitement and optimism.

NO OFFENCE TAKEN

We leave Cape Town after lunch, having squashed everything we possess into the Troopy. It's just an hour or two's easy drive to Paternoster, a Cape Coloured fishing village up on the west coast, and the contrast with Cape Town is dramatic. It's isolated and starkly attractive, with whitewashed low-lying buildings on a treeless inlet and flat blue surf stretching along the bay. The day is almost perfect as we walk along the beach to fishermen cleaning and salting their *snoek*, and I see more of those disconcerting very pale fox-green eyes I'd noticed in Coloureds on the boats in Cape Town. In fact, apart from a handful of white locals and a similar number of tourists, all we see are the distinctive flat, round faces of the Cape Coloureds.

The predominant population group in the Western Cape Province, Cape Coloureds have an ancestry originating in the mid to late 1700s when breeding and intermarrying existed between the local Khoisan peoples, the Dutch settlers and the slave labourers they brought to South Africa from places such as Madagascar, Malaya and Indonesia. From what I've seen they are a modest and hard-working people who enjoy life and keep to themselves, but under apartheid and then since independence they have become increasingly marginalised, and their rights and livelihoods are constantly being reviewed. Just before our arrival the South African government withdrew all fishing licences then re-issued them to blacks as part of Black Empowerment, a move that takes even more rights from the Cape Coloureds who have traditionally been the fishermen of the Cape. Adding to their woes, the crayfish season has officially ended and here in Paternoster they can be seen hanging around town trying to sell illegal catch for a bit of income.

At our little rented beachside house we sit on the verandah and watch the sun set over the natural rock breakwater with a glow bright with purples and pinks. Young children come to the door and ask shyly if we'd like to buy long chains of beach-bleached shells, and dogs trot back from the water's edge, wet and sandy and looking pleased with themselves. We befriend a lean black dog we've watched on the beach; it's his beach, and he's been out there all day chasing off seagulls, moving long stems of kelp around and escorting other dogs along his stretch. Beach Blackie we call him and he only ever runs or trots. He belongs to everyone and no one, but for the time being he's ours.

Neil buys Beach Blackie a rissole at a Pick n Pay supermarket. It's eaten with surprising delicacy and in return we're given protection for the rest of the day. Things turn from cute to ugly in no time as he stations himself up on the front deck for maximum visibility and barks loudly at anyone, black, white or Coloured, walking past our door. He growls at cars driving past and when there's another dog in the backseat BB practically attacks the vehicle. One driver shouts and waves a fist in our direction. BB comes back to us jaunty and eager for praise, and we don't have the heart to reprimand him. But someone else must have taken the problem into their hands because BB suddenly disappears and we don't see him again, not even on the beach.

We don't need to say it but we're both totally relaxed and happy to be here, and tingling at the prospect of happening on a hundred more special places like this in the months to come. We rouse ourselves and wander down the beach for dinner in a converted old beach shed where the highlight is a commercial hash brown dead centre in my smoked salmon salad.

We head west to the Cederberg, an area of soaring rock formations and deep, fertile valleys where we've read mountain leopards still roam, protected by a conservancy of local farmers. On approach the road passes through Citrusdal and, not surprisingly, this pretty town in a lush valley is surrounded by green citrus orchards. At a stop in town to pick up diesel and provisions a white down-and-outer eyes the Troopy, approaches us and says, 'Hello, welcome. From the United States?' When we say, 'No, Australia,' he responds apologetically, 'Oh forgive me. No offence.'

It's a beautiful drive through the Cederberg Mountains, and the lodge we've booked is dwarfed by the folds of a valley of spectacular scenery. Already there's a feeling of isolation, that the land holds dominance over the scattered human population. In the evening we walk along a creek bed in the fading light accompanied by Stompy, a large floppy mastiff whose face is in a permanent smile after a run-in with a porcupine, and he's still with us at dinner where I'm served an avocado cocktail with a Jatz biscuit in the middle. At this rate I'll be off salads for the rest of the trip.

On the way out next morning we drive past the rockiest olive grove I've ever seen to look for the ancient San (Bushman) rock paintings said to be hiding in a sandstone alcove nearby. We walk along what's barely a path through scrubby vegetation and when it stops at a rocky overhang the paintings are right there before us, clear and unprotected. Animals and what appear to be hunting scenes are depicted, but what is remarkable is the clarity of the work. With few tourists to this private gallery, the drawings are so well preserved they could be the recent works of a homeless vagrant. Walking back to the Troopy we see in the dust large cat spoor, which I *know* must belong to a mountain leopard. Neil and I are debating whether this could be true or just fanciful — that we might be on a path that a leopard wandered along the night before — when it hits me that we're here. It's not a daydream or someone else's story anymore, it's us walking in the footsteps of leopards and living life large.

Still in the Cederberg, we check into a camping ground where we'll spend a couple of days before continuing northward towards Namibia. This is to be our first attempt at camping and we couldn't have chosen a better spot. A place called Algeria, it's in a valley between towering peaks, with a little river flowing through it and manicured grassy lawns. We have the whole camping ground to ourselves, which is just as well under the circumstances. The rangers in charge of the ground direct us to the best site under oak trees, and they offer to give us free of charge any provisions that we may be lacking, our being novices. The generosity of strangers here is so unexpected.

It takes us some time to erect the tent, an hour of laughter (and not always from us) interspersed with bouts of dissension and dispute, but by 5 p.m. it's stable, we've had a shower and are sitting around a roaring fire in the dark with a glass of wine, waiting until it's late enough to eat. We're going to have to think of something to do to fill in these chilly, dark hours before bedtime.

With our thermals on we climb into the sleeping capsule and pile blankets and sleeping bags on top of us. At every little noise we stir and whisper 'What's that?' but it turns out to be just some sort of little beast scavenging in the dead oak leaves around the Troopy. The loudest noise, which gives Neil the biggest fright, is from the zipper when I open a peephole to check outside.

On the road out we pick up a local who's hitching a ride. He's a young Coloured man, jogging into the next town 15 kilometres away to visit his sister. When we ask him where he'd like to be dropped off he politely says 'at the tree' and, sure enough, as we approach the town there is just one tree on the side of the road. Later on we pick up an old fella, another Coloured, who has a big backpack and two bags of oranges. He's a little under the weather and after he establishes that we can't speak Afrikaans he stops chattering, sings a bar or two then falls asleep. Just in case he's listening subliminally we play some Ladysmith Black Mambazo tracks. This male group has developed a style of performing which combines *a cappella* singing with choreographed dance steps, and their worldwide appeal lies in the primeval beat of Africa that permeates their music. If they don't get a reaction from our friend, nothing will. Well he doesn't move, so when we get to his turn-off we wake him up, bail him out and leave him on the side of the road looking dishevelled and dazed. But he rallies enough to give us the thumbs-up and he shouts out 'Good ride!' as we drive off.

I'm impressed by the etiquette shown by drivers on country roads here and we've quickly become used to flashing our indicators in thanks when a car pulls over to the far left of the road as we overtake. In actuality it's most often us pulling over for vehicles which, as they draw close, flash their intention to pass us, travelling at a leisurely pace, then, once in front, flash again. Sometimes it goes to ridiculous lengths, when we then flash acknowledgement of their flash in return. Such a degree of consideration engenders a sense of camaraderie that I find infectious, and once or twice I've annoyed Neil by adding my own touch such as a double flash or a wave preceded by a flash then a quick beep.

The further north we go the straighter the road becomes and the sparser the vegetation. We're aiming for Springbok, 600 kilometres north of Cape Town and just 120 kilometres from the Namibian border. Springbok lies on the only main road between the two and it's the only town of note for hundreds of kilometres in this thinly inhabited corner of the Northern Cape. We book into a guesthouse and have dinner in a steakhouse off the main street. Being Saturday it's a big night out and the bar plays old Elvis and Stones tracks. There are kilo steaks on the menu and blond blue-eyed men in the bar. Here English is very much a second language and we get the feeling that we're being looked on as a curiosity, with our Australian accents and small appetites.

I've started a list of animals we've spotted and so far there have been plenty of ostriches, a mongoose and some wild donkeys, and today heading into Springbok we see a springbok. I don't plan on getting out of the Troopy when we get to the next big town on the map, Pofadder.

The plan is not to drive into Namibia at the nearest border but to veer north-east and visit two of South Africa's semi-arid national parks, Augrabies Falls and Kgalagadi Transfrontier Park. The latter occupies an isthmus between Botswana and Namibia in the most northerly part of the Northern Cape and if we're lucky the proposed border post linking Kgalagadi directly with Namibia will be open for business and we won't have to backtrack down out of the park to enter Namibia.

Augrabies Falls National Park surrounds the waterfall of the same name and we find a surprising number of tourists in a place we'd thought would see few visitors. We've booked a SANParks (South African National Parks) cottage for the night and at dusk we sit out on the *stoep*, or porch, with a tumbler of cask wine, thinking about what we'll have for dinner. There's a flat metal disc on a stand embedded in the paving and a sneaked look at the other cottages reveals that this is used as a barbecue, known here as a *braai*. I notice that others down the row are already stoked up for the evening meals. Wives are slicing vegetables and wrapping potatoes in foil, and their partners are dragging out the esky and uncorking the beer and brandy. We look on in admiration and resolve to become this organised in future. By the time we get up the next morning the *braais* are already cleaned and scrubbed shiny by staff and I'm beginning to see why barbecuing is so popular here.

Unlike any waterfalls I've seen before, these ones are below ground level and are conveniently just a short walk past reception out into a rocky treeless terrain. Here the Orange River has cut a deep ravine through the desert and huge volumes of water are forced through a narrow s-bend, culminating in the final drop. Not particularly high, but powerful and magnificent, and this isn't even after rain. There are fall-proof viewing platforms built scarily out over the ravine and we stand back from the edge and the spray, mesmerised by the thick brown blanket of water below.

Early next morning we take the Troopy on an early morning game drive, our first, but the game is disappointing. Maybe we were expecting too much, hoping for the list to be overflowing with sightings after a couple of hours, but apart from a family of giraffe who materialise out of the red rocks then disappear again, and klipspringers, like baby dainty deer, picking their way through the early heat, the park appears empty. Driving along a track between ridges and shadows we find ourselves with the full moon of the previous night high and bright in the sky to one side, and the new day's pulsing sun rising large and hot on the other. I feel all at sea in this landscape of strange phenomena and unfamiliar sights and I am starting to see that there's a lot more to safariing than just animals.

Roughly 100 kilometres upstream on the Orange River lies Upington, an economic and traffic hub of the Northern Cape. It's said to be the hottest town in South Africa but it looks cool and green as we drive around the suburbs looking for accommodation. We soon discover that this is because of extensive irrigation, and the town sits in the middle of a narrow but long strip of fertile land of citrus orchards and vineyards. Driving in, we passed areas like large barren paved car parks where grapes are spread to dry to supply raisins for the European market, but beyond, the empty land stretches to merge with a rainless, cloudless sky.

Neil finds an electrical store and falls into conversation with a gentle, tall Coloured man who refuses payment after correcting a small problem with our laptop. He likes Australians. His younger brother was an Australian sports aficionado and followed every rugby, tennis and cricket match with such fanatical dedication that his family buried him with an Australian scarf around his neck after he was killed in a motor accident. This story is told to us with great tenderness and we leave the store sorry that we didn't have anything vaguely Australian that we could have handed on to be put on the grave.

Next Neil takes the satellite phone in for repairs to a shop around the corner and the proprietor, who's never worked on a satellite phone before, takes up the challenge. He pulls it apart, does a bit of re-soldering and, Bob's your uncle, the on/off switch now turns off. When Neil asks him how life has been since the end of apartheid, he answers that, for him, a Coloured, apartheid is just beginning. And by the way, he tells Neil, the roads aren't safe so don't ever give a lift to anyone.

We find a camping store and get talking to one of the proprietors, a closed, quietly dour Afrikaner. After a while he relaxes in our company and tells little stories of life up here in a lonesome corner of the country. Then, after he and Neil get talking about the fall of apartheid and the introduction of Black Empowerment, he surprises us by stating that he's always believed apartheid to be immoral and he confides with embarrassment that there are still fellow countrymen on surrounding farms who beat their workers. People are not always what they seem. Neil negotiates with him a trade-in on our recalcitrant tent and we leave stocked up with a fancy blue and yellow lightweight number, new air-mattresses and state-of-the-art headlamps.

That night we drive back to the B&B from a restaurant in town through a strange sparkling light. The hostess tells us that it is the beginning of a desert mist and that we can expect it at this time of year. She is curious about our trip and we spend a half-hour or so chatting to her about our plans and adventures. Although she can sympathise with Neil in his wish to locate the family farm, she hints that she thinks it's a lost cause and that he must be slightly crazy, dragging his wife into the dangers of the bush.

Afterwards Neil asks me, for the hundredth time he says, to stop interrupting him when he's telling a story. Justifiably, he finds it more than annoying and the fact that I keep doing it is more annoying still. I know that I do it, and sometimes do try to restrain myself, but I tell him that I get so involved in his story that I just have to add to it. He's not buying that excuse. I try to find a more valid one but the truth is I can't, so we leave the subject with a threat and a promise hovering over the issue like the settling mist outside.

My determination to be a glamorous traveller is waning. By the third day out from Cape Town I cut back to a bit of lipstick; by day five it's just a quick smear of sunblock and lip salve. In Upington main street I catch sight of my get-up reflected in the Pick n Pay window: zippered safari trousers already shrunk, baggy T-shirt and a sleeveless padded vest affair all in shades of khaki, beige or brown, teamed with my good Italian buckled court shoes now down at heel and dusty. However, unable to detect the dark roots in the reflection I think my hair is still looking pretty good.

THE CHEETAHS MADE ME DO iT

Kgalagadi Transfrontier Park is one of the few national parks in South Africa that allows for the free movement of wildlife, the fence on the Botswanan side having been taken down. The closer to the park we get, the more ostriches and gemsbok (known as oryx outside South Africa) we see, and road-kill appears in our path and on the verge. Somewhere north of Upington we come across what I've been looking forward to seeing: a donkey cart, known locally as a Kalahari Ferrari. Driven by a young boy and loaded up with brothers and a mother with a bandanna-clad head, it moves at a good pace along a worn track parallel to the road. The landscape changes from rocky, tussocky desert to red sand, and we leave the tarred road behind and hit heavy corrugations. There are few trees and even fewer signs of human habitation so we're surprised when a little family of children jump out on the road in front of us, dancing madly and waving us in to stop at a little lean-to of a stall they've set up to sell simple carvings and jewellery. One wears unruly hair and a lap-lap; all he needs is a bone through his nose and he'd be the spitting image of the drawing of Neil done by a good friend, an artist, as a going-away present.

It is the policy of SANParks to maintain the ecological balance of Kgalagadi by limiting the number of visitors, and for the same reason the camps are kept small, which makes it difficult to get accommodation. Months ago we'd reserved a combination of camping sites and cabins, taking anything available, and we'd been lucky enough to score tents in three wilderness camps.

We register at Twee Rivieren, the gateway to the park, then set off for Kieliekrankie Wilderness Camp. Almost at once we see lots of game: gemsbok, sleek fat antelope with beautiful markings and elegant sexy horns; red hartebeest, which look like they're compiled from the body parts from many different animals and whose horns don't seem to know in which direction they should be growing; black-backed jackals; herds of springbok; and the snooty kori bustard, a big handsome bird strutting around with its nose in the air. We're both excited to be here and immediately fall in love with this park.

Just after we reach camp two elderly couples arrive and we meet for the first time the ugly rich Jo'burger. One wife with voluminous black hair is decked out in over-sized silver earrings, gold front tooth, diamonds on the soles of her shoes. A lineless, smileless, plump face. Polite and pleasant, one husband manages to get over in a short conversation that he owns 40 Mercedes and lectures me on the dismal state of the Union; the annoyances and inconveniences caused by the current regime; how hard it is to enjoy the fruits of a lifetime's hard work; honest hard-working whites paying too many taxes and supporting the rest of the population, who are always wanting time off to go to the funeral of a brother or sister or granny. Do we have the same problem in Australia with Aboriginal staff?

Neil and I sit on the terrace wrapped in blankets to guard against the rapidly dropping temperature and drinking red wine. It's a landscape of red dusty sand, stumpy blue tussocks, afternoon greys. No sound at all, then a single jackal bark from one side, answered by the hoots and hellos of his family from all over the place.

When we leave the next morning at 9.45 we are reprimanded by the camp officer for not observing an important park rule — visitors must be checked out of camps by nine o'clock each morning. We fear expulsion or at least a fine, but drive off with just *9.45 a.m.* underlined on our access permit.

Nossob rest camp is our next destination and on arrival we read that the temperature the night before was –5°C. We're allotted a good site and the new tent goes up without a hitch, although we can't quite work out what the extra toggles on the pins are for. We settle in and manage to have a meal cooked and eaten before scavenging jackals pass through the camp. Later, a lion roars and grunts at regular intervals and the sound cuts across the night and echoes around the tents. I'm getting to like this life, but I can tell by the way he starts at scuffling sounds and stumbles on the guy wires that Neil still has a way to go.

After an 8.55 a.m. departure we drive out heading northward and come across two male lions said to be brothers snoozing right on the verge. Any closer and they would be hit by a car coming around the corner. As it is, the tail of one flips out over the road every now and then. On a later drive we see two more males — or could they be our brothers? — reclining in the scant shade of a thorny bush. They stretch and yawn and look particularly dopey — dishevelled teenagers after a big night out. We go on a guided evening game drive and see a lone brown hyena, head down, plodding around his territory with determined resignation. With his beautiful flowing brown coat he looks like he's just come from the hairdressers rather than a cramped and dusty den. We're told he does this 5-kilometre lap of his territory every evening. The guide is excellent and bears out our suspicion that the information gleaned from a good guide more than makes up for a lack of sightings. All the other passengers are old devotees of Kgalagadi, some having visited the park many times, while one family comes back year after year. The wife tries to describe the attraction and, half embarrassed, settles on 'mystical'. I can see what she means, as I'm completely charmed.

The road to Gharagab, the remotest of the wilderness camps, passes close by Unions End. This is the confluence of the borders of South Africa, Botswana and Namibia and may as well be the ends of the earth. As soon as we near Gharagab we sense that this is a special place. Four timber and canvas cabins look out over rolling Kalahari dunes and low thorn-scattered savannah, totally quiet and perfectly still. The loudest noise is the squeak of the floorboards and the brightest light is the sun reflected in the waterhole below. The tap water is so salty that it leaves a crust on dishes and glasses. We love it. At night a beautiful gecko whose white spots glow luminous in the flash of the torch keeps the insects down in the kitchen. He moves into the bedroom when we go to bed and we sleep soundly knowing that he is there protecting us from the only wildlife which we fear that night — mosquitoes.

We move on to Bitterpan camp where we're greeted with the news that a puff adder has just been relocated from beneath a chair in the communal kitchen. We later see the camp officer out the back cautiously kicking over a log then jumping back, rifle ready. From then on I open every cupboard cautiously and look under every chair before sitting down. After dinner we go down to the huge saltpan in front of the camp with a spotlight and the only other guests, a young South African family. All we spot is the silhouette of the camp officer skulking about with a torch in the bush behind our cabins. In the morning he tells us that he was looking for a young leopard that has been sniffing around. He adds that when this camp was being built the lions were so plentiful and so menacing that a fence had to be built around the perimeter of the site to keep the workers safe. There's no fence now, no security at all except for our armed ranger to protect against fierce predators and confused puff adders.

After nightcaps with the South Africans, Neil is packing away our glasses and wine cask when he makes a worrying discovery: by a miscalculation we appear to be drinking more than we'd intended. He's read the small print and it appears that the South African casks we've bought are not 1.5 litres but 2 litres, and it's been taking us the same amount of time to polish one off.

Leaving Bitterpan the Troopy nearly runs over a beautifully marked puff adder, just coming out onto the road to sun itself in the morning warmth. We're halfway to the next camp when we have to pull over so that I can remove a tick embedded in Neil's neck. At least it's not a puff adder.

Our last night in the park is spent in Kalahari Tented Camp, another unfenced wilderness camp. It's peaceful on the terrace of tent number 12 and we sit and watch for birds, not wanting to move, but as evening approaches we pull ourselves away and go out for a game drive to the Dalkeith waterhole. There are giraffe up the gully and springbok on the ridge. We scare off the only other car there then pull up beside a clump of acacias and look around for some action. This is what people told us we should do on safari: park by a waterhole and just wait for something to happen. We've only been there five minutes when off to the left we notice movement. Neil suddenly grabs my arm as he realises what he is seeing: two cheetahs, moving in cautiously across the dry riverbed. They are totally focused on the springbok and pause mid-step for minutes at a time, working to an ancient agenda. When they reach long grass they move a little quicker, low and camouflaged. Thirty minutes have passed and they've covered just 20 to 30 metres. We lose sight of them behind a tree then see in the rear-view mirror that the giraffes are behind us, wanting to get to the waterhole but sensing danger. It's action on all sides but we realise that we'll have to leave at once to get back to camp before sunset, the cut-off time. As we drive off we go past the cheetahs, only their heads visible above the long grass, but our engine has scared the springbok and they run away. We hightail it back to camp and arrive just as the attendant is marking his clipboard with a big red cross against number 12. Neil starts on a long-winded excuse for why we're late: the waterhole, the grazing unawares springbok, the interminable time it took the cheetahs to move across the *vlei* — they took too long! The attendant listens for a time then says, 'Sshh, I understand. It is the fault of the cheetahs.'

On the road out next morning we take the Dalkeith fork but there is no sign of anything by the waterhole, let alone two big fat cheetahs and the remains of a springbok. We later meet up with the Bitterpan family, who tell us of their morning drive and of a leopard with a jackal kill in a tree overhanging the road. This is on the alternative fork in the road to the one we took. They have news of our cheetahs, too, who apparently did get a springbok early that morning and, again, by the other road. It just goes to show that it's the luck of the draw when it comes to watching game.

A policeman pulls us over on our last afternoon game drive. He does a radio check on the Troopy and reminds us of the speed limit. We're in trouble again; apparently you must carry your entry permit with you at all times when on the road, and ours is back in camp. Neil tries to distract the officer with a discussion about the state of South African roads as opposed to Namibian, which seems to work because we get off with a warning. This encounter dampens our enthusiasm for a time and makes us realise that we're not exempt from the rules and laws that apply to those around us. We may be free agents but we're not free to do as we please.

Even though big wooden gates and new immigration buildings are in place at Mata-Mata, the hoped-for border crossing into Namibia through Kgalagadi is not yet operational. Apparently the diplomatic and bureaucratic to-ing and fro-ing requires many more months of important meetings and workshops at beachside locations. Now we must exit the park and head south to the closest border post, half a day's drive away at Rietfontein.

A BUCKETFUL OF DASSiES

We experience our first border crossing today when we reach Rietfontein. Still on the South African side, our firewood is confiscated because *it's not allowed into Namibia — see that sign?* The sign says no maize or maize products are allowed into Namibia. But it's cold and there are no trees around so leaving the wood is the least we can do. Once in Namibia the roads and scenery immediately improve. One minute we're driving through a landscape of red mesas and brown buttes that look like the badlands in spaghetti westerns, then over a ridge and it's plains of grasslands, silver like vast fields of snow.

Keetmanshoop appears out of the desert and we find an Internet café. Also street boys, asking for sweeties. We're warned that they'll scratch our car if we don't give them any, but they appear in awe of the Troopy and not only do they leave us alone, but they direct us to the OK Bazaars supermarket.

Quivertree Forest rest camp is a few kilometres out of town and we arrive just in time for the three o'clock cheetah feeding. The owner's daughter arrives at the gate of the enclosure with a bucket containing two freshly dead dassies. These are the cutest little mammals when alive. Also known as rock rabbits or hyrax, their true name, they look like a cross between a rabbit and a guinea pig. They make good eating for larger carnivores — cats in particular seem to fancy them — and these cheetahs go wild when they see the contents of the bucket. We're told to keep well back, then the daughter opens the gate a crack and chucks a dead dassie to each of the cats. They're so preoccupied with tearing their meal apart that we're allowed in with them and encouraged to pat them. No way. I'm all for keeping wild animals wild and keeping all my body parts.

The campsite is over a rise on the periphery of the quiver tree forest. Just before sunset we wander through the trees, which are famous for supplying the wood for Bushmen's quivers, and we see the old family patriarch and his wobbly dog appearing over the rise from deep in the forest, a rifle in one hand and a trio of dead dassies in the other.

The roads in Namibia are impressive and Neil in particular enjoys driving on them. Mostly gravel, sometimes compacted gravel and mud known as *murram*, and rarely tarred, they are straight and flat and only present a problem in the unlikely event that there's another vehicle in the vicinity. This becomes visible from kilometres away, a long white vapour trail advancing steadily towards us until it whizzes past and we're forced to pull up immediately or at least slow to a crawl, so thick is the dust. Once, when it settled, we were surprised to find ourselves in a different landscape altogether, one all soft and dreamy. It wasn't until I wound down the window to take a photo that we realised the Troopy had been coated in a fine white powder.

We're heading for farm accommodation in the Tiras Mountains, a stark, rocky range on the edge of the Namib Desert, but here the landscape is flat and a thick ribbon of dust hovers over the road in our wake. We divert off the main road to drop off a hitchhiker at the farm where he works and the slight detour takes us past the first high red dunes we've seen so far. If this is an indication of the famous landscape at Sossusvlei, I can't wait to get there. In photos and documentaries this long sweep of a valley appears to be from another planet: smooth, stationary dunes, the highest in the world, a moonscape made up of surfaces and shadows which change from intense red to soft lilac as the day progresses and the sun bleaches the light.

We turn off onto the farm road — barely a track — and we're concentrating so much on keeping to it that we nearly miss seeing a family of wild horses moving quickly across a dune. These are the famous wild horses of the Namib and something I'd just been reading about. Their total adaptation to the harsh conditions of the desert is legendary, and romantic too, and it's even more intriguing that they have an uncertain history.

It's well known that they've been around since 'German times', and one theory is that they are the result of cavalry mounts let loose by the German Schutztruppe and/or South African forces during World War I. Another story has it that they are the descendants of breeding stock belonging to an eccentric German baron who left his stud to go off and fight in the war. The neglected horses were forced to fend for themselves and found their way to permanent water in the Garub region. Then there's an Australian link, as it's thought possible that thoroughbreds from a ship bound for Australia from Europe swam ashore after being shipwrecked off the mouth of the Orange River. Only the strong survived, and it is their genes that have created the hardy feral stock of today.

Whatever their history, I am excited to have caught a glimpse of them, especially since Frau Hundin at the main farmhouse tells us they've only recently appeared here. The farm's campsite is in a dramatic setting, nestled in amongst large boulders at the end of a narrow valley, and there's a welcoming party of one smiling Labrador who stays with us until we go to bed. When we go over to our bathroom, tucked in against a smooth rock face, we discover that there's no hot water, as promised. Neil braves a cold shower but the temperatures outside are too low for me to contemplate taking off any layers, let alone risk standing under an icy jet. That night the wind picks up to a gale and the tent is blown over. We're snug in our sleeping capsule but feel that it would be safer to de-camp to the shower block. We drag stretchers and bedding over, lock ourselves in and get a decent sleep, even though the farm's workers are stomping all over the roof and rattling the door throughout the night, trying to fix the hot water.

The next day we abandon camping and move to a little stone chalet built into the rocks. It's tiny, little more than a room with two beds and a tree growing up through the middle, but it has a wonderful peaceful air and we sit on the *stoep* like dassies facing the sun, drinking coffee, trying to get warm. This is something that I'm only just getting used to: the fact that it's winter and it's cold, but every day the sun is shining and there is no chance whatsoever that it might rain. Even Neil has taken some time to readjust to the predictability of the seasons and I've seen him looking concerned and wary whenever he spots clouds massing on the horizon.

The farm's main industry is breeding emus and we're invited to wander around the yards and enclosures. On an afternoon walk we come across a wild female ostrich who has wandered in from the dunes in search of a mate. She's spied a nesting male and flutters and flirts and tries all sorts of fancy dancing to attract his attention, but she seems not to have noticed that there's a tall wire fence separating them. On his side the male seems to be excited, but it's not clear whether this is because he's falling for the seduction or is just annoyed at her distracting him from his brooding duties.

People speak about 'overlanders' with a mixture of affection and dread. They can be found all over Africa, travelling in big, heavy passenger trucks that stop for no more than 24 hours at a place before whooshing off to the next. There's usually a determined driver gripping the wheel, and tired or sleeping faces at the big picture windows.

We're about 20 kilometres out of Sesriem, the access point to Sossusvlei in the Namib-Naukluft Park, when we see in the wing mirrors the telltale dust trail of a large vehicle gaining on us fast. It passes in a cloud of gravel and dust, and a few kilometres further on we see it take a curve in the road (an unusual thing in itself) on two wheels, sliding on the loose surface but with no noticeable deceleration. When we get to Sesriem campsite the overland driver is in the office, cajoling the ranger into giving him a particular site. His life must be one long journey of deadlines and hassles. We are allotted our site, which is large and private, under a big tree on the periphery of the grounds and thankfully a good distance from the overland groups that are settling in at the extreme ends of the camp. We hear loud male Australian voices from one end and a mixture of European accents drifting over from the other.

It's dark and we're sitting around our campfire watching a giant cockroach — or is it a grasshopper? — move slowly up the flap of our tent. The air is crisp but warm and a full moon ripples through fields of silvery grass beyond the camp wall. We're surrounded by people but we may as well be the only ones wrapped in the heart of this empty desert. Then we hear voices and through the shadows come dreadlocks and smiling faces. Two girls introduce themselves as Sonje and Gigi and wonder if we might take them with us into Sossusvlei in the morning as their rental car is not a four-wheel drive and can't go as far into the dunes as the Troopy. Of course we agree and an hour before sun-up the next morning the four of us are in the Troopy, lined up at the park entrance along with many overland trucks and four-wheel drives, waiting for the gates to open. We're soon away, and take off on a very good paved road for the hour's drive to be at Sossusvlei for the rising of the sun over the famous red dunes. The girls are great company and we learn that they're from Brussels and both employed to promote the use of Flemish in the households and boardrooms of their country. Neil comments that they'd be pushing it uphill, but their young enthusiasm chooses to ignore this Doubting Thomas. We have to go faster and faster, well above the speed limit, to make it on time, and the girls cheer every time we overtake another car. When we get onto the four-wheel-drive section the Troopy alternately stalls and skids in sand drifts, but the girls love it. Only Neil and I know that he's never tackled anything like this before and I can see his knuckles white and tight on the steering wheel. As soon as we reach the car park we all bail out and race towards the east, ploughing through sand and dry saltbeds, and just as Gigi reaches the top of the tallest dune the sun emerges and the world goes red.

On the return journey the girls urge Neil to accelerate through the sand drifts and as we slide alarmingly off our track they whoop and laugh and high-five each other while Neil and I sit tense-backed in the front seat. Later on when we are saying our goodbyes we notice their rental vehicle. Only halfway through the holiday but already the little sedan is scratched and coated in thick dust, with missing hubcaps and a torn and hanging side mirror. They've collected dings from rocks and hit chickens as they've flown around the Namibian countryside, and taken a 600-kilometre detour to drop off a local to whom they gave a lift.

The road north east to Zebra River Lodge in the Tsaris Mountains ribbons along wide sunburnt valleys and between rocky peaks and mesas. There's not another person in sight, not a vehicle on the road nor a farmhouse to break the landscape. At the lodge we receive a very nice welcome from four dogs and three cats and a manager who promises to give me a Reiki massage later on. We're served lunch, despite arriving at 3.30 p.m. This is something Neil remembers from his early days of travelling through Africa, that there's always a meal waiting for you and no one's put out if you arrive late. Unreliable vehicles and unpredictable conditions make deadlines irrelevant, and communication can be patchy with mobile-phone coverage limited to populated areas, so everyone is used to expecting you when they see you.

That night we eat with interesting guests: an American family (daughter working in *Malooorwi*), and a very urbane German. Neil and I have our first real disagreement after Neil takes a dislike to the smug daughter. When she says that she could help us with our travel plans because she's lived in Africa for three months Neil transparently tries to trap her by asking if the border post at Sumbawanga is currently open. Then when he senses victory he proceeds to lecture her in detail on the significance of the northern borders, and the history of Central and East Africa in general. He's being petty and trivialising her knowledge and her enthusiasm for a continent that he himself is enthusiastic about. The others are bored and I'm embarrassed. As soon as we get back to our room I tell him to cool it, that before our trip is over we're going to come across many more like her who see themselves as Africa experts and who believe that their experiences are unique and their knowledge all encompassing. But Neil is incensed that this parvenu, who can't even pronounce Malawi correctly, thinks she can tell him, Neil, about the place where he was born and raised. It has slipped his mind that he has never visited Malawi. I tell him that I'm not prepared to spend the next eleven months listening to his lectures then feeling obliged to apologise for his boorish behaviour the next morning. We go to bed angry with each other and irritated that each one's point of view is being ignored by the other.

Next morning it's all forgotten as Neil wakes me to look outside. A heavy mist has blocked out the early sun and the scene looks like an old black-and-white photo. The table and chairs on our verandah hover unrooted and unreal, and all sense of perspective is lost as trees and a windmill loom in silhouette further away. When the mist lifts we go for a long walk up over the mesas looking for mountain zebras, but only come across a big barking black baboon, warning us away from his mountain. It's amazing that animals can survive and flowers bloom in this most severe of landscapes. There are very few trees, just some low clumpy acacias and a lone quiver tree standing like a portrait on the horizon, but we come across a flourish of pretty pink flowers growing from a rock face, and pincushions of tiny white ground cover nestle in the shadows of a dry riverbed.

The kitchen hand and general dogsbody of the lodge is Mac, a nineteen-year-old black Namibian and hospitality student getting hands-on experience. Well spoken and motivated, if he represents the emerging Namibian youth, the country is on the right track. Why should I be surprised that he can intelligently discuss his long-term goals and has worked out a plan to achieve them? Have I, under the surface, been assuming that young blacks are ambitionless and unable to articulate their hopes and intentions, let along have any in the first place? I've always believed that my father's open-mindedness embedded a strong sense of social justice in his children and that I inherited his latitude and respect for all. But this attitude I'm taking is not open-minded at all; I'm mistaking a lack of First World education for simple-mindedness, and a difference in culture for a lack of one. It's just as well I've met Mac early in our travels and been forced to question these prejudices before falling into a bigger trap. After meals when his duties ease, Mac, the German and I talk about food and cooking. Mac is hungry for knowledge and loves to hear stories of our favourite dishes and new-to-him ingredients. The German tells of eating truffles in France, and I try to explain why I think prosciutto with melon is the perfect pairing. I promise Mac a cookbook and he jots down his contact details, saying that eleven months is not too long to wait for it.

We move on northwards to Barchan Dunes, a farm that offers accommodation I've been wanting to stay in ever since I saw it on the Internet. Called KuanguKuangu, it's located a kilometre up the valley from the main house in a lonely, lovely spot. The design is inspirational, with the kitchen and bathroom open to the stars. We eat at a table under a solitary thorn tree and look down an ancient valley of yellow grasses and purple peaks. For hot water, Neil lights the donkey heater, and for food, I cook on an outdoor gas stove. Hannetjie, the chatelaine at the main house, is an excellent cook and on the first night Neil and I walk down the valley for dinner. They serve springbok fillet — 'seared for five to eight minutes only' — and a lovely yoghurt and chocolate dessert, an old German recipe that Hannetjie graciously translates for me. Her husband used to be an engineer on the Windhoek municipal council before Black Empowerment replaced him, but it's obvious that his heart has always been out here in the empty valleys and hills of his homeland. He takes us on a drive around his farm, mainly looking for his baby gemsbok and the elusive mountain zebras. The former he farms for meat, while the latter are protected wildlife and have the run of the range.

Going through the Namib–Naukluft Park on our way to the coast, with nothing else in sight and desert on either side, the first car in an hour drives past and throws up a huge rock that hits the Troopy's windscreen. We're momentarily deflated, seeing a big tennisball-sized crack on our pride and joy, then we perk up a little when we convince each other that this battle scar adds something; the Troopy no longer looks like a brand new cadet but a war-weary general of character and experience.

A SERiES OF UNFORTUNATE MiSTAKES

Swakopmund is roughly halfway down the coast of Namibia, just north of the commercial port of Walvis Bay and due west from the country's capital of Windhoek. It's trendy and smart and very much the holiday destination for Windhoekers, with its cafés and boutiques, and overseas tourists fill the streets and hotels. Driving in for the first time you can't help but be amazed by its position slap in the middle of desert, where dunes roll right up to the sea. Over the next few days we settle into town life in a house rented from a Windhoek family. Town water is a little salty but okay to drink, and there's a garden hose so Neil tops up the Troopy's drinking-water tank reasoning that the salt and the metallic taste of the new tank will counteract each other.

I go to an overworked, rude dentist to get a wobbly front crown glued back in and Neil goes to the post office to try to phone the United States about the satellite phone, which is still giving problems. The repairs done in Upington were short-lived and the on/off switch has jammed in the on position. Neil is once again preoccupied with solving a technical problem and spends most of his time trying to contact the right people overseas and organising the posting to America of the offending phone. He becomes grumpy and forgetful, and when he starts to leave things in cafés and repeatedly walks off leaving the Troopy unlocked, I become apprehensive. We'd always said that the only way to take this journey was to treat it as an adventure. We'd done as much forward planning as we could and hoped that we'd anticipated most things that could go wrong. If problems started to grow into obstacles it would be time to re-think what we were doing. Well, now it is time. After a coffee and a walk on the beach the decision is made to forget about pursuing the satellite phone problem any further; we'll just work with the phone as it is, which means keeping it continually plugged into the Troopy's battery so that it's always charged and ready to use.

We have the Troopy serviced by a particularly pleasant German–Namibian who, we later learn, called up his friends to come and admire the Troopy. He tells us that it would be much easier to sell the Troopy in Namibia than in South Africa and asks if we'll agree to give him first option to buy when we're finished with it. We agree in a flash. Apart from the window crack the car still looks brand new but I hate to think what it will be like in ten months' time.

On our last afternoon in town we take a two-hour flight over the desert to Sossusvlei. This is the sort of flying that you'd never get away with in more regulated countries, and Neil is rapt. We're 30 to 40 metres above ground, zooming down gullies, between red dunes, flashing by ostrich and gemsbok at eye level. Then circling over Sossusvlei and the valley that we'd driven down days before with Sonje and Gigi. Then dive-bombing seal colonies and abandoned diamond mines before scooting back up the coastline where the sea breaks directly onto high golden dunes. What an amazing place.

The house we've been renting is on a corner opposite the beach and it's exposed and windy cold. It comes with a night watchman, a young thin man who curls up like a cat on his polar fleece to keep warm and who always waits for us to greet him in the mornings before going off duty. Neil has insisted on giving him a meal every night. It started with half a pizza, but by the last evening I was making enough chilli con carne for three. His plate and cutlery are always left washed and neatly stacked by the side door.

We wake up on our last morning in Swakop to the famous fog. It's very eerie: everything is grey, black and white, and even though they are going slowly, oncoming cars appear from nowhere then disappear again, lost in space. Landmarks are invisible and road signs unreadable, and it takes us twice as long as it would normally to find our way out of town.

On the way up the coast road to the seal colony of Cape Cross, we detour in to see the famous sand golf course at Henties Bay. It's built on dunes with fairways of sand and greens of grass, but with the coastal fog still hanging around, it's a deserted and slightly spooky scene.

The Cape fur seal colony is something else. No fog, but the smell is unmistakable: a mixture of urine, wet fur and rotting carcasses, as mangy black-backed jackals slink around preying on the young and infirm. We're tempted to stay a night at the beautiful Cape Cross Lodge but settle on lunch after hearing the cost.

To get to Spitzkoppe, our next destination, we must retrace our steps to Henties Bay and now we notice for the first time little piles of rocks and empty bottles at intervals beside the road, always on the western side. It becomes apparent that these are individuals' markers indicating the turn-off to their favourite fishing spot down on the shoreline, and they are the only sign of human presence in this barren, misty landscape. At Henties Bay we turn eastward and it's not long before we can make out the red Spitzkoppe peaks hovering on the horizon, even though we're still a couple of hours drive away.

Up close Spitzkoppe is just like the postcards: a towering mass of orange-red granite peaks sitting like an island in the middle of flat semi-desert, reminiscent of Kata Tjuta in Central Australia. The only accommodation available is in the campsite run by the local community, and this is spread over a large area among the outcrops and gullies. Neil begins to have doubts about the Community Campsite when the man at reception is vague about our site's facilities. He tells us that there are no showers because either the bad boys in the village have taken the fittings, or there is not enough water in the village to supply all the sites. We later determine that there is just one workable shower with a rusty collapsing tank for the entire grounds, and the en-suite toilets are literally that: a toilet bowl hidden in the rocks, no plumbing or pit attached. Dinner in the restaurant that night? No, because the ladies in the village need time to prepare.

We find our allotted site number 2 and it's a wonderful spot, right in the heart of a deep chasm between two towering rock faces. It's so isolated and the landscape so overwhelming, that it's all a bit surreal. We pitch the tent where we'll get the best view, bang in the middle, and over a glass of cheap South African wine and with a CD playing, we wait contentedly for night to descend. It seems like only yesterday that we were sitting in Algeria trying to think of something to fill in this languid time of day, but now alone and under the stars we listen to Maria Callas throw herself off the parapet while we talk animatedly about where we've been and where we're heading.

Next morning a slight breeze comes up, which turns into a gale whooping down our chasm and dismantling the tent and sending the toilet paper in a ribbon all over the site. It's dawning on us that you don't automatically choose the best-looking site to set up camp, you have to consider things like wind flow and weather conditions and seasonal variations. A combination of this realisation and the wind whistling incessantly around my ears makes me irritable and I harp at Neil, who is trying his best to retrieve clothes and utensils scattered all over the place. He points out that we have two options, we either stay or we can leave, and the simplicity of this is enough to diffuse my exasperation. Then clip-clop up our track comes a young boy with his donkey cart to sell us a ride. We settle on three photos for six pens instead and decide that this place isn't so bad after all.

Neil negotiates with reception for a move to a cabin and this turns out to be very rudimentary. It's like an old Australian bush slab hut where sun and wind creep in through the gaps between the slabs, and there is no glass and no secure fastenings over the windows. No wonder the ladies looked confused when we asked for a key to the door. We entertain ourselves by making up stories about the young European woman in the next-door cabin living, so it would seem, in near poverty with a black man. Is this the secret that seems to be hovering over the camp, making the locals guarded and a little standoffish?

The ladies have been in the kitchen all day preparing our dinner. We are to be the only guests. At seven o'clock we go to the restaurant, order a beer each and are immediately served a plate piled high with packet macaroni cheese and potato salad, and three little chicken wings and one thigh between us. That's dinner. Over the dregs of the beer we debate the fate of the remaining three thighs and one wing as we take in a month's supply of carbohydrates. The ladies are very pleased with themselves and have already started preparations for our breakfast.

The following morning we're back in the restaurant for breakfast and the ladies are becoming decidedly friendly. We have fried eggs, which come from the kitchen one at a time, and freshly baked bread that's the best we've had to date. Steaming tea comes out in a big aluminium pot, and it's just as well we take it black because there's no milk. Well, there was milk — we saw the ladies pouring the last of it into their tea in the kitchen when we first arrived.

Further north into the Namib Desert in Damaraland, just 70 to 80 kilometres east as the crow flies from the notorious Skeleton Coast, is Twyfelfontein, Namibia's first World Heritage site. Here, an enormous number of engravings and paintings by hunter–gatherer communities, said to be more than 2000 years old, cover an absurdly small area of rock face. There are several theories as to their purpose but this uncertainty seems to add to the enigmatic draw of the place, and we had resolved early on to see it for ourselves. Now we're heading for Doro Nawas, a lodge within striking distance of the site.

The main building of the lodge sticks up brown and forbidding from a single rocky outcrop in the middle of a floodplain rugged with rocks and dry yellow grass. On our approach the staff appear at the entrance, hands shielding their eyes to focus more clearly on the beautiful machine humming up their track. They trot down the steps and greet us with a cool drink and a joke, and the drivers, mightily impressed, jostle for the privilege of taking the Troopy around the back to the car park. We're shown to our chalet, which is glamorous and large, and it has a large bathroom with an isolated toilet, which is just as well because both Neil and I have picked up some sort of bug and have diarrhoea.

On our second day there we go on an afternoon drive looking for desert elephants. The guide, Barnabus, is greatly intimidated by a South African bird expert aboard and stops answering our questions after the birder constantly corrects him, but one thing he does tell us is that there are no predators in the area. So driving back to camp after finding the elephants we are startled when a big dark cheetah appears going like the clappers parallel to our vehicle, in pursuit of a springbok. This follows hot on the heels of a near miss with an incoming light aircraft after Barnabus, unaware of its approach due to him being rattled by the birder, drove across its path at the start of an airstrip. In all the excitement my crown again becomes loose.

Driving through the countryside, past villages and small homesteads, we've commented on the number of abandoned *bandas*. These simple thatched dwellings are always well built and look to be weatherproof, so we've speculated as to why squatters haven't moved in, or at least purloined the building material in a land where any possession is precious. Barnabus provides the answer by telling us that these dwellings are usually not abandoned, but temporarily vacated. As villagers move around seasonally with their goats or to tend crops, shelter is needed in different places and at different times, and it's accepted by all that any *banda*, whether currently occupied or not, is private property.

Over the next three days Barnabus shows us many weird and wonderful things, including the amazing welwitschia plant, a prehistoric leftover which grows only in the Namibian desert and can live for hundreds of years, just one spongy leaf which splits and furls into a low, convoluted mass sometimes metres wide.

We leave Doro Nawas with an early start for Grootberg Lodge via the town of Otjiwarongo, where I have an appointment with another dentist. We've been on the road for a couple of hours when Neil realises that we've forgotten to visit the rock art site at Twyfelfontein, so wrapped up were we in old plants, loose teeth and even looser tummies. But it's too late now, so we press on to Otjiwarongo and locate the dental surgery. What a difference in practices. Here everyone is chatty and helpful and genuinely trying to help. My recalcitrant tooth is stuck back in with extra strong glue then off we go.

It's late by the time we get to the wild and desolate Grootberg Plateau, and almost dark when we come to the turn-off to the lodge. Their road is one of the worst I've ever driven on, a contender for an advanced four-wheel-driving course, but the position of the lodge is spectacular. It's perched on the very edge of the Klip River Valley, which includes elephant, zebra and rhino among its wildlife. If we were to stumble out our chalet door in the dark without a torch we'd be in danger of falling into the valley to join them.

We've been trying to pinpoint the cause of our diarrhoea and the lodge's manager confirms our fears that the water we put in the Troopy's tank in Swakop is contaminated. Apparently garden water there is recycled waste water. He very kindly offers his staff to drain the tank, slush it out then refill it with his clean mountain water. I self-prescribe and get us on a course of antibiotics, Imodium and lots of water, mountain water. Apart from a daily walk through the surrounding bush we stay in the comfort of the lodge, content to take it easy. The manager takes to joining us when he is free, and over the next few days we learn about life in such an isolated location, and about the people who inhabit the region.

The two main ethnic groups up here in the far north-west are the Herero and the Himba. They're relative newcomers to Namibia, both descendants of Bantu-speaking people who moved across from East Africa about 150 years ago. The group split and the majority, known today as the Herero, moved southward to the central plains of Namibia where they settled and became successful cattle ranchers. The ancestors of the Himba remained in the north and lived a semi-nomadic life as herdsmen, following their goats and cattle in search of water and pasture. Their way of life is much the same today, as their harsh homeland has always been inhospitable and isolated from the rest of the world, and an undesirable option for colonists and commercial farmers. On the other hand, the Herero have had to compete first with indigenous people, then with the Germans when they colonised the country. The Herero were greatly influenced by the Germans and the most obvious sign of this is in the traditional dress of the women. Reacting to the prudishness of missionaries, they moved from wearing very little at all to an adaptation of the clothing they saw on the Europeans — full, voluminous skirts with many petticoats underneath, long sleeves and high necks, and often a shawl as well. Their own unique touch is the headdress, which comprises long lengths of fabric rolled into wings resembling the horns of their beloved cattle. Today in the towns older women still dress up in their finery, but more often than not the younger generation wear simple Western clothing. The men once dressed in a variation of the German military uniform of the day, but this practice too has almost died out and is now rarely seen except for the odd old man at an important gathering.

Appearances are obviously important to the Herero, and the story of Ronald bears this out. Ronald is the nanny for the young son of a friend of the manager's. He is an Herero and also a transvestite and he can be found on any one day wearing a stunning Capri outfit or perhaps an understated housedress and necklace, singing the child soft Herero lullabies or pramming him to sleep over the rocks and potholes in the car park. He favours wearing an outfit the colour of the Aeroplane jelly that's being served that day, and it's understood that he has first option on the mother's cast-offs. The parents have total trust in Ronald, who loves the little boy unconditionally. Apparently they are a familiar sight in the street of their town — the mother, father, and Ronald in high heels proudly pushing the pram.

It's time to hit the road and we drive northward on one of only two roads which traverse the land up here. After a couple of hours we start to see Himba by the roadside and in villages, but by the time we get to the small town of Opuwo, the last main centre of the north-west before the Angolan border, we're still not prepared for the sight of them walking down the main street. They're people from a different time, confident, proud, at ease with themselves and their place in the order of things. And what style! Hair, skin and clothing totally covered in a mixture of ochre and butterfat, elaborate headdresses and weighty jewellery. Red-skinned and barely dressed, the women and girls swing their hips so that their hide skirts sway to and fro, while the doe-eyed men rest on one thin long leg and a walking stick, their skirts worn with the pleats at the front. There are also Herero ladies in their head-to-toe yardage, younger men dressed in varying degrees of modernity, and a smattering of tourists trying to look as though they've seen it all before. The street is dusty and full of bars and barbers and, because it's Sunday, both are doing a roaring trade. A Wild West town.

We overnight on the outskirts of Opuwo at the first true hotel we've stayed in. It's surrounded by an electric fence but is still a nice surprise after the rough and tumble of the town. The hotel is new and the décor city-modern, but the food is terrible. Maybe it's the bad dinner or perhaps it's my tender stomach making itself felt, but when we return to our room I'm in a dark mood. I moan that we should have changed rooms to one in the block further away; it's noisy here and the bed is facing in the wrong direction. Neil points out that it's late, there's probably no one at reception, and anyway, we took the last room so there's none left to move to. I'm not that easily placated and continue to pick until Neil has had enough. He's heard it all before he says, there's always a room with a better view or one with a bigger deck. I usually don't even unpack but prowl around a room, opening drawers, flipping on lights, feeling the pillows and counting the number of mini soaps in the bathroom. Then I insist that he phones reception and requests a re-allocation or a second robe. Well he's putting his foot down. With a continent full of new beds in front of us he can see his life as one long line of pandering to my obsessions.

He has a point; I love staying in new places and as a result I sometimes get carried away with it all. But hasn't Neil noticed that so far on this trip I've been so wrapped up in what we are doing and where we are staying that the last thing on my mind has been to make changes? I haven't wanted to change anything. Well, apart from the occasional campsite. To prove a point I declare that this room is growing on me, in fact it's perfect, and we go to bed with African disco music throbbing from the noisy *shebeen* in the valley below us.

We're continuing north, heading for Epupa Falls on the Angolan border. The standard of the road slides as the isolation increases and I can believe what I've read: this is one of the country's last remaining wilderness areas. And that's saying something. All the villages we pass now are Himba, with domed huts made from mud, cow dung and palm leaves. Some look deserted, though all are swept and tidy. Just waiting for the owners to return I suppose. We pick up a half-gentrified Himba, so puffed after running to catch a lift in the only vehicle to pass for hours that he can't talk. It wouldn't matter anyway because we don't understand each other, but I can see that he's embarrassed that he's sweating all over the Troopy's backseat. I give him the only thing I can find to mop his brow, a refresher towel, and when we drop him off he hands it back with two hands, head bowed, the little towel folded into a neat damp square.

How many times since arriving here have we commented that Namibia is all that everyone says it is? It must be at least once a day. It was always hard to believe that a sparsely populated country, with no water and few trees, just grass, desert and mountains, could match the hyperbole it so often attracts. But, quite simply, it takes our breath away. I reckon that one could wake up anywhere here, look around and be struck speechless by the beauty. Yes, it's vast and empty, and just sometimes the ordered straightness of its roads, mountain ranges and dunes become monotonous, but I've never seen colours change like they do here, or valleys stretch so far, or stillness feel so right. Namibia is at once monumental and embracing and there's a sense of place, of belonging, which seems to envelop everyone who breathes her air.

iNTO THE WiLD BLUE YONDER

Epupa Falls is on the Kunene River, which forms the border with Angola in these parts. The sight of the waterfalls as we come over a crest is magical: they're at the centre of a true oasis in the middle of empty, dry desert. There are makalani palms, big old white baobabs, the blue lagoons of the Kunene and water falling over falls everywhere across an area 20 hectares or more. There's Angola on the other side, looking peaceful and unaffected by tourism and over-grazing, and dust and piles of beer bottles all about on our side. We're told that the Himba are a contented bunch who don't steal or take anything that isn't given to them, so there's no need to lock the car or our tents. But who knows what they might get up to after emptying all those bottles so we lock the Troopy nevertheless.

Epupa Camp has an activities manager, Neels, a very affable young South African who takes to calling my Neil, Neily. They get on like a house on fire and are trading practical jokes before the first day's end. Neels takes us for sundowners to view the beautiful falls, and the next day we go white-water rafting, where Neels suddenly becomes very professional and we trust him totally. Although the rapids would be quite minor to the die-hards, they are enough to give us a thrill. Following Neels' directions we all paddle across and disembark on the far bank, Angola, where he proceeds to tell us of the last time he brought his charges here. At just about this spot, armed military (or was it bandits, he couldn't tell) came bursting from the undergrowth, gesticulating wildly and waving AK-47s about. The leader screamed for Neels and his little landing squad to put their hands up, leave their canoes and to walk slowly up the beach. Instead they fled as one, scrambling back into their canoes and paddling away like there was no tomorrow. Neels remembers looking back to see guns trained on them, but he's pretty sure no shots were fired. By the end of this story some of our current team are looking warily into the bushes while edging back down to the water's edge. Neels suddenly shouts and claps his hands, we all jump and make a run for the rafts and are halfway back to Namibia before we've had time to see the big grin on his face.

Every evening Neels takes Neily and me to a different spot by the river for sundowners. On the third night, our last here, the subject turns to children, and Neels asks us what our children are doing. When we reply that there are no children, our choice, he asks if we'd mind telling him what was behind our decision. In the past weeks we've been asked many times about children by both blacks and whites — it's a polite ice-breaker — but the reaction to our answer is markedly different from the two groups. Whites look expectant, waiting for further explanation, and after we say *our choice* they smile knowingly and say *smart move* and everyone chuckles. Blacks, on the other hand, become embarrassed and apologetic that they have asked the question. To them, the only reason for not having children is because you can't, and they ah-ah-ah, touch my hand and click their tongues. To spare them angst, Neil and I have recently decided that in these instances it's better to say that we do have children and we've borrowed the intellectual rights to children of good friends and rattle off their academic achievements and marital status. So whether it's the gin and tonics or the fact that Neels seems to have a motive for asking, Neily and I decide to explain our decision.

It was right at the time — we were in our late twenties in the early years of our marriage, both independent and selfishly maintaining the lifestyle we'd enjoyed while single. On the few occasions that we did talk about it, Neil could see the travel constraints a family would bring, while I could see a lifetime as a mother, not the me Neil married. Who I was would be lost in a talcum mist of midnight demands and constant daily needs. While my friends were desperate for children to make their family whole, I didn't want to share Neil with anyone. It seemed that the maternal instinct had passed me by. But more than this, I understood that this partnership was hard enough as it was and any more than the two of us would topple the balance and make it unworkable.

Neels seems excited by our story then explains that he himself isn't interested in having a family but has trouble articulating his feelings to friends and family, particularly his girlfriend. We try to back-pedal, to qualify our situation by saying *another place another time* — something accepted in Australia in the seventies might not translate to present-day South Africa. But Neels is buoyant and intent on presenting his girlfriend with this new ammunition.

We are taken on a visit to a Himba village by a young educated Himba, complete with wrap-around mirrored sunglasses and gold watch. After he asks and is given permission for us to enter the village, we meet the chief's second wife and her female family. They are very regal and reserved at first, but when I show Mother her photograph on the LCD screen she squeals with delight and shakes her hand saying arh-arh-arh and something else which translates to 'Oh, I am so beautiful!' Our guide explains that the women spend many hours on beauty care and when they're not rubbing their bodies with their ochre moisturiser they're giving themselves herbal steam baths.

We go to a Himba cemetery on the way back and this is also an experience. Many generations are buried here. Hundreds of years ago they were buried upright and to do this their legs and arms had to be broken (after death, that is). The resulting graves are, of course, very small and marked only with a couple of upright stones. Interestingly, the later graves look more conventional to us, but each is marked with sets of bullock horns, the number and size indicative of the wealth of the interred. We're told that there's a big feast of the bullocks' meat after the funeral, and if it's an important person and there are many bullocks, there's meat hanging around for days. Eventually, when it's pretty ripe, it's hung out to dry or thrown into a horrible smelly vat to pickle.

We leave Epupa with Neels in tow. He's quit, and is on his way south to take up a job in South Africa. Even if he gets back-to-back lifts it will take him several days to get there. Our destination tonight is a private concession bordering the world-renowned Etosha National Park. We've turned off onto their road when Neels and Neily both spot lion tracks in the dust and, whoa, we round a corner and there's a lioness ambling down the middle. She looks thin and young, and later we're told that she's a recent mother who's left the pride to give birth and has stashed her cubs up in the rocks while she goes out for food.

Neil and I are still experiencing the effects of the poisoned water, and cramps now accompany the diarrhoea. It has occurred to me that the symptoms are very like giardia and this is confirmed when I read through a dog-eared copy of *Disease and Home Treatment* left in the lodge's bar.

Neels has been able to arrange a lift to the next big town south of here so we have a quick farewell drink with him before he departs, then we settle down to dinner in a courtyard flanked by snakes in tanks. After the meal Neil makes his first Basil Fawlty comment of the trip. A German couple is seated near us, and after we've all eaten, the husband pulls out a pipe and lights up in a cloud of smoke. As his wife tries to wave the smoke away from her Neil calls out, 'You're in a gas chamber!'

There seem to be no hard feelings because next morning they ask us to join them on a drive looking for the lions that we heard during the night. We come across a pride led by two brothers, and the big black-maned one a cranky thing, mock-charging our vehicle and grumbling and growling at the tyres just by our feet. That afternoon we go out again and find the pride munching on a zebra. The big black boy must be full and content because, although he's quite close to our vehicle, all he does is sit under a bush and eye us while he licks zebra gore from his whiskers.

The following day we head for Etosha, but with a stop in Otjiwarongo for a return dental appointment. I've decided to replace my dicky crown and the dentist says he has the equipment to make and fit one in a couple of hours. This is most successful and I leave the surgery in high spirits, particularly after the dentist falls in love with the Troopy and asks if we'll give him first option when we come to selling it. Naturally we say yes.

It's too late to reach Andersson Gate, the nearest entrance to Etosha National Park, before it closes at sunset so we drive on for an hour or so then check into a roadside lodge with relief, both now feeling very fragile from the worst effects of the giardia. We're unable to keep down dinner and after some hefty doses of medicine, which I muster from our first aid kit, we go straight to bed.

The next morning we wake feeling perky and enter Etosha with that fresh and optimistic feeling you have when you know you're on the mend. We check into Okaukuejo Rest Camp and set off in the Troopy for a day of game driving, a leisurely safari on wheels through the bush in search of wild animals and good photographs. The evening is spent with new friends. Alisdair, the archetypal Scotsman, thinks he sees a like spirit in Neil and passes on his treasured copy of *Grumpy Old Men on Holiday*. Germans travelling en masse are his pet hate, followed closely by any number of Italians who might shout to each other across a room or burst into spontaneous laughter at any time.

Sometime during the evening of idle talk and travellers' tales it occurs to me that the tables have turned, and it is now Neil who is interrupting me when I'm halfway through relating an incident. As we walk back to our room I suggest this, that now it is me who is becoming annoyed by the constant interruptions and pirating of a story, but Neil responds that I exaggerate and embellish too much and turn an anecdote into a life story; he's bored and so are the listeners, so he has to speed things up. He's probably right but should have known when he married me that I come from a big family of storytellers who have never let detail beach an amusing tale as it sails towards the finale. Neil and I argue the point about whose stories are (a) more fanciful and (b) more boring until we realise how boring and fanciful we're sounding, so decide to give it a rest.

We have heard many stories about the great waterhole at Okaukuejo, which at any time can have all manner of animals chasing and catching each other. We visit four times and only see zebra once. The other three times there is absolutely nothing. Not even a pigeon. We start to suspect that everyone else is exaggerating or, worse, making up sightings. After one last unproductive waterhole visit we decide to forget it and go out into the park instead. We're about to hop into the Troopy when Neil notices a pair of legs sticking out from under it. A face appears shortly afterwards, a hand shoots out and Tim introduces himself. He's a private guide and was passing through the park with clients when he spotted the Troopy sitting like an apparition in the shadow of a thorny acacia. It's just what he's been looking for, so he's parked his clients in the restaurant and has come back for a closer inspection. He's very impressed and bombards Neil with technical questions before asking shyly if we might be interested in selling. By this stage Neil knows the drill and not only says yes but rattles off without hesitation, '… and we'll give you first option.'

In the morning we drive out in a luminous smoky light, looking for wildlife. The silhouette of a giraffe materialises on the horizon and lopes towards us through the vivid half night and we wait in the Troopy by the side of the road until he crosses in front of us. He's covered 1½ to 2 kilometres in 30 minutes without missing a beat in his graceful, hypnotic progress.

Etosha is vast and it's hard to conceive that it was once four times the current size when it was first gazetted as a national park just over 100 years ago. Then it was the largest game reserve in the world until political pressure in the 1960s reduced it to 22 270 square kilometres. Even so, it's still bigger than some countries and we often feel that we have the park to ourselves. It could just be this tyranny of size, but there seems to be a lack of other tourists. There's also a noticeable lack of lions and rhino and elephants, all of which everyone else claims to have had to elbow their way through. When we move over to the Namutoni area to the east we fare better and see elephants and, on the last evening, two lions waiting patiently by a waterhole for dark to descend. At the end of the day that eerie morning light is noticeable again. Earlier a ranger had explained that it is caused by smoke from the many fires lit by villagers outside the park in winter. It drifts southward and is held in the air over the great expanse of the Etosha Pan, an arid mineral pan at the heart of the park and covering a quarter of its surface. The explanation made it sound like plain old smog, not the Disneyland of glowing half-light that illuminates the landscape around us.

The last two nights we spend camping at Onguma, a private concession just outside the park's eastern gate. These perfect grounds give us renewed confidence for future camping. Here there is just a handful of sites, all well spaced with their own bathrooms, and positioned deep in a quiet and secluded forest. We wake in the mornings to the chattering, hoots and coos of hundreds of birds, and are visited shyly by a little Damara dik-dik, even smaller than the klipspringers we'd seen down south. By default we've discovered what the toggles on the tent pins are for and the tent now stands sturdy and fortress-like, and we've perfected a workable camp layout, something that had eluded us in the past. I suggest to Neil that if all campsites were like this we'd be in seventh heaven, but he's not sold and I fear that for him camping will always be a step short of the Pearly Gates.

On our way north-east we have to pass through Grootfontein and it's the first town we've come across where all the shop-fronts are covered with bars and grilles, and security men hang about like thieves themselves. It's an indication of the increase in population and poverty that we're to find in the relatively fertile north. Along the road, neat organised villages of family homesteads become common and donkey carts are replaced by ox carts. These invariably are wooden sleds loaded with water drums and children and pulled by oxen with beautiful sweeping horns. We pass roadside stalls selling pottery of all sizes and functions, and many ceramic guinea fowls. Further northward the potters give way to carvers and there are giant wooden heads, helicopters, planes and masks for sale on both sides of the road.

Every day we pass things that are amusing, or moving. Two oxen pulling a wooden sled in the typical shape of a boat — but this one has taken the image a bit further and has added two masts with old shirts for sails, and a cane fishing trap dragging from behind. Then outside one village *kraal*, sitting neatly on a stump, is a little tin mug containing corn kernels for sale.

We drive along eating Maynards wine gums and Beacon liquorice allsorts. If the road's not too dusty to play CDs we have Meat Loaf at full blast, Alan Jackson to sing along with, or Ladysmith Black Mambazo if we have a hitchhiker in the belief that they'll feel at home. Our differing tastes in music are obvious as we rotate through the collection of discs that I've put together. Neil has been patient with Queen and grits his teeth through the country and western, but finally puts his foot down when *The Best of ABBA* springs to life with monotonous regularity.

Rundu sits on the southern banks of the Okavango River, which now separates Angola and Namibia. The town is jumping though dusty, and the area looks prosperous and productive. There's large-scale agriculture with irrigation and mechanisation to a degree that we've not seen to date. I convince Neil to go out on an evening river cruise organised by the camp we've booked in to, but instead of seeing hippos and crocs all we spot are illegal Angolan traders, skulking back home across the shallows after a day in Rundu's bustling market.

The Caprivi Strip is one area that both Neil and I had on our want-to-do list. I wanted to see the large herds of game that had been recently reported passing across it from Angola to the Okavango Delta in Botswana, while Neil was fascinated by its history. The Caprivi is an incongruous narrow corridor of Namibia stretching 450 kilometres eastward to Zimbabwe, wedged between Zambia, Angola and Botswana. It was exchanged with the United Kingdom for Zanzibar in 1890 so that Namibia, then German South-West Africa, had access to the Zambezi River and trade routes to Africa's east coast. Because of its position, Caprivi has always been of strategic importance and up until recently it experienced almost continual military and terrorist incursions. It presented big problems to motorists wanting to drive across, not the least being that the road would become impassable every wet season. However the main challenges came from a different source, with landmines, militia and poachers making the area unsafe to travel through. Now, however, the baddies are gone, the road has been paved, and animals migrate freely between the delta in Botswana, Angola and Zambia.

In the centre of the western Caprivi, Popa Falls is more a cascade over a rocky faultline in the Okavango's course than a true waterfall, but it is still impressive and the surrounding bush is lush and pretty. A little downstream we find a lodge stretched comfortably along the banks of the river, owned by an affable and competent Namibian, Horst. The immediate impression is one of confidence and of things being under control, and our little riverside tent is made classy by good linen and an abundance of extras. Unfortunately what is beyond Horst's control is the reserve of the other guests, two young German families. They both have children of about the same age, and bags full of photographic equipment, but that's apparently not enough in common to get them talking together. On the sundowner cruise they are excruciatingly silent and polite, and after a while Neil, Horst and I carry on as though the others aren't there. Pre-dinner drinks are even worse, with them pointedly ignoring each other. What's going on? Do they know each other and are involved in an inter-family feud? Is it because they were never formally introduced? Or are they just not interested in each other? As dessert is served and the parents have a little alcohol they loosen up and begin to discuss photography. But by breakfast the shutters have come down again and it's back to pretending that we're all strangers in a strange land. They are replaced that day by a party of French people: garrulous, urbane and a breath of fresh air. They try to order martinis from the beer- and wine-only bar, and dress in chignons and silk shawls for dinner. They involve us in their conversation and refrain from stating the obvious when Neil asks them if they have a word in French for 'cavalier'.

Horst encourages us to visit Mahango Game Reserve, just down the road. We go in the Troopy somewhat reluctantly, not having read or heard anything about this small park, but it turns out to be a jewel. Here is where all those animals from Angola must be congregating before their assault on the delta. Well, in truth, we don't see huge volumes, but there is such a large variety that we can't keep our list up to date. As we drive out we chance on a show, a private screening that is our first taste of the other side of wildlife watching: being privy to the dramas of everyday lives. Two magnificent handsome black sables, long horns like elegant sabres, engage in battle. They position themselves 100 metres apart, turn, then on dancer's legs take off towards each other at a prancing trot. They stretch out, lower their heads and arch those sleek thick necks, and by the time they connect with the sound of a car crash they are galloping at full speed. They do it time and time again, each joust starting from further apart and with more measured determination. There is a politeness to the confrontation; like chivalrous knights they seem to wait until each is ready before launching into the next attack. Then — did we miss something? — one turns and trots away with a shake of his proud head.

Crossing the Caprivi Strip is a bit of an anti-climax after the build-up we'd given it in our imaginations. Not a landmine or bandit in sight, just a straight, straight road that shows nothing of its past. Although that's been tarred the drive is slow and we get to Bumhill Campsite on the Kwando River, roughly halfway across the corridor, in the late afternoon. After the Spitzkoppe experience of community campsites we approach Bumhill warily, but it's a fine area with a wonderful person in attendance. His shorts are threadbare so Neil gives him a pair to replace them, and he gives Neil a big pile of firewood in return. The campsite, all handcrafted, has an en-suite, and the building and plumbing have been done with thought and care. We have a toilet where the plumbing is encased with hand-woven twine and the toilet-roll holder is a branch with faces carved on it, and there's a tree platform for viewing elephants and hippos which wander past on the riverbank below.

However, we're keen to keep moving as we've decided to visit Zimbabwe and catch up with Neil's cousin, Dave, who'll be in Victoria Falls in a couple of days' time. When we tell the camp attendant that we'll be moving on after one night but will still pay him for the two nights booked, he shakes our hands in appreciation. He disappears, then returns shortly afterwards with another bundle of firewood.

Goodbye Namibia! We cross the border into Botswana with a minimum of fuss, apart from having to run the Troopy and our feet through a dark sticky mixture to kill any foot-and-mouth disease we could be carrying about. We plan to stay overnight in Kasane to re-organise and gather supplies before entering Zimbabwe, where we've heard the lack of just about everything is critical.

Kasane is at the extreme eastern tip of the Caprivi Strip and lies on the banks of the Chobe River. Chobe National Park is right next door and Kasane is the main access point for visitors to the park as well as for those heading to the Okavango Delta and Victoria Falls.

We book into a small lodge on the riverbank, a little out of town and away from the hustle and bustle of en masse tourists that we've become unused to. We walk the lodge's 'nature walk', which mostly follows the banks of the Chobe River, and towards the end we turn a corner and there, right on the path, is a big crocodile, asleep in a patch of late sun. For some pre-historic reason Neil hates crocodiles and he wants to backtrack, and fast. I stay long enough to take a photo, and the resultant shot does nothing for Neil's reputation. In it, the croc is totally ignoring the blur that is Neil running away.

After dinner that night we chat with an American family and the conversation drifts into travellers' talk of places visited and animals sighted. Neil tells them that we've just come from 'Estonia National Park' in Namibia and they don't bat an eyelid. Afterwards when I rib Neil about his slip-of-the-tongue he gives them the benefit of the doubt and suggests that they were stumped by the accent, but from where I sat I could see that they'd never heard of Namibia, let alone one of the most famous game parks in the world.

The next morning we go into Kasane to get diesel, wash the Troopy, send emails and buy malaria detection kits. The town is very busy with tourists as well as locals, and game-viewing and hunting vehicles are everywhere. A safari vehicle pulls up next to us and I look archly at the women sitting in it: strings of whopping great pearls, designer jeans covered in spangles and high-heeled sandals. Are they trying to make it easy for thieves, or blind the wildlife? They've certainly impressed themselves, but look slightly disoriented as they find themselves perched in the back of an open truck in a dusty frontier town.

One petrol station is out of fuel already and it's organised chaos at the remaining one. Zimbabweans queue patiently, the wait for the next delivery nothing compared to the endless wait back in their own country. We leave town much later than we'd hoped, pleased to get away from this taste of a game park hub approaching the height of the season but a little apprehensive of what we're going to find in Zimbabwe.

OH MY ZiMBABWE

Zimbabwean border control is about as bad as expected, the carry-on regarding the Troopy and taxes, fuel and taxes, and road taxes taking time and patience. But eventually we're through, and a few hundred metres down the road we stop for a herd of elephants crossing it. This is an encouraging sign, as I'd been expecting to see poachers rather than animals.

Victoria Falls Safari Lodge is looking spick and spruce and in a condition that belies its age and the state of the country it finds itself in. We're treated like royalty, which we kind of are, Neil's cousin Dave being the owner. The Safari Lodge hugs a ridge on the eastern side of the unfenced Zambezi National Park and overlooks the broad brown Zambezi Valley, which at first glance looks flat and dry. Only after you sit on the deck and watch the goings-on beyond the waterhole below the lodge do you realise that there are dips and rises in the landscape which hide game paths and grassy, shady, resting places for families of animals, perhaps nestling in close to the protective shadow of the lodge in a park rife with poachers.

Dave meets us in the bar and we catch up on family news over dinner in The Boma. This restaurant famously serves farmed game meat of all persuasions, as well as local delicacies such as deep-fried *kapenta*, the little lake fish so loved by Africans, and *mopane* worms in peanut butter. I decide to try the mopane worms mainly because Dave says I'll get a certificate if I can manage to keep one down. As the smiling girl serving the worms is spooning a couple onto my plate I ask her where exactly they come from. I know the good-looking mopane tree, with its soft double leaves that look like dainty butterfly (*mopane*) wings, and I don't like to think that its shady branches could be visited by anything other than harmless creatures. 'From the freezer' comes the cheery reply.

Robert, an old school friend of Neil, flies in from Harare and we spend the next 24 hours with him, he and Neil reminiscing, pulling each other's legs and generally giving each other a hard time. They've seen the famous falls many times when their school train stopped at Victoria Falls, so the normal tourist sights are abandoned for more personal ones. We visit picnic sites eleven and fifteen on the banks of the Zambezi, both places of great peace and beauty, and the final resting homes of Dave's brother-in-law and his father, Neil's uncle. Sitting under the shade of a big wild fig, with the Zambezi wide and ancient at their feet, Neil asks his mate why he stays in Zimbabwe. Why hasn't he called it quits and gone to Australia or Canada or the United Kingdom? Robert replies that maybe he's scared or maybe he's lazy, but mainly, he can't find the heart to leave because Africa has got under his skin.

On Wednesday evening there is to be a cocktail party at the Safari Lodge to farewell Andy, another relative who has worked at the lodge ever since it opened. Dave has very kindly invited us along. I'm a little reluctant and slightly nervous of being the odd people out in a group of workmates but, anyway, we go. Out on the lawn is a huge buffet and waitresses all dressed up in crisp white traditional dresses. Our initial thoughts are that we've gate-crashed a wedding but, no, Andy appears and quickly organises drinks. During the day we'd heard that the hotel had just lost eighteen employees to staff poaching, so this evening we are waited on by the seamstress, the gift shop lady and quite a few from middle management. They all have great fun in their new roles and we do too, particularly when the seamstress responds to a request for one gin and tonic and a double scotch with 'All in one glass?' Two simply dressed guests arrive and for a minute stand awkwardly until someone notices them. In my anxiety to make them feel comfortable I blurt out, 'And where in the hotel do you work?' Well nowhere actually, they are the well-qualified, official representation from the powerful town council, people that Andy has had to deal with over the past years. They are modest and polite, and it must be 50 times harder for them to socialise with all these strangers than it has been for us to wander in.

After the speeches and gift-giving, the hotel's choir sings a couple of *a cappella* songs and then asks Andy to stand with them. With their hands on their hearts they sing *'Nkosi Sikelel' iAfrika'*, 'God Bless Africa', the unofficial anthem of hope for all Africa, and there isn't a dry eye on the lawn.

The main road from Vic Falls to Main Camp in Hwange National Park passes through many villages that would have been neat and prosperous in better days. An article in yesterday's Zambian paper cites 3000 deaths a week from AIDS in Zimbabwe, but it is the neglect and poverty caused by President Mugabe that we're witnessing. The only things looking new and maintained as we drive along are the electric fences of the hunting concessions. We've read that government officials have sold off far too many hunting licences, well over the quota — more licences for lions than there are lions in fact. Corrupt officials might be the cause, but hunters and hunting concessions are complicit. I've even seen in a recent hunting magazine a photo of, among many other incongruous animals, an American bison killed on a hunting lodge north of Harare. How did that get there? I'm torn between outrage and acceptance that these concessions must do what they can to survive in a country gone topsy-turvy.

Even before we get to the park gate we see giraffe, zebra and impala and we feel a pinch of excitement at the prospect that all we've been hearing about Hwange is true.

Apart from a visiting soccer team, Main Camp is quite empty. It is as neat as a pin and the staff spick and span, but there are no tourists. Due to a misunderstanding we've allowed half the time it will actually take to drive in to Ngweshla picnic site where we're to be collected, and the young ranger at the park gate is keen to chat, discuss the lions, even exchange email addresses. Neil patiently ah-ah-ahs and asks about his family, then once we're through and into the park (speed limit 40 kilometres per hour) and out of sight, the Troopy picks up speed and we hurtle past waterholes of buck and *vleis* of wildebeest. I'm certain I see a large cheetah sitting on top of an anthill quite close to the road, but Neil shouts, 'No stopping, it's just a log!' and tears past. We cover the stretch in one hour instead of two and a half and have to apologise to the only other tourists we see for forcing them off the road.

Little Makalolo is an exclusive bush camp of just five tents, very well managed by a young white couple from Harare. One of them, Sasha, is also a guide of some repute and his enthusiasm for the bush and its flora and insects infects everyone. After just a few minutes' game driving with him we forget to look for animals and find ourselves debating the difference between a marula and a mangosteen tree.

The next four days fall into a safari camp's routine of early morning wake-up call and a light breakfast, followed by a morning game drive, brunch, sleep, afternoon tea, afternoon game drive with sundowners, and return drive with spotlighting, drinks, dinner and bed. The nights are particularly cold and we have hot-water bottles and two doonas to keep warm. One morning we wake up to find that the temperature plummeted to −4°C during the night, and everyone emerges with beanies and scarves wrapped around their heads, breath steaming in the cold and hands tucked under armpits. The birdbaths are frozen over, staff are out chipping at the pathway with shovels instead of sweeping it, and Obit, the senior guide and a veteran of many years in the park, insists that his eyelashes have frozen to his head.

Every mealtime Obit entertains us with lectures on life and tall tales. I promise him that I'll record some of his stories as he says that he cannot write. So far I have in my diary:

> *The recipe for cooking mice.*
> *How to treat your first wife.*
> *The time Obit was dragged away by a lion.*
> *The time a leopard was dragged away by him.*
> *Why he doesn't like flying.*
> *Why men have to snore.*
> *How the roster system works when you have more than one wife.*

That's already enough for a bestseller, but I'm told that the best story is yet to come — how to keep warm on a cold night when you have three wives. That one is X-rated.

Godfrey is our guide for most of our stay. The first evening drive is through a deep woodland area, past a grand, dying marula tree ring-barked by elephants. We come upon a waterhole just in time to see a small family of elephants having a mudbath. One adolescent in particular can't get enough of it and he chuckles and swings his trunk about as he slides and splashes. He just can't leave it, even when his mother is clearly trying to move him on and there is another herd in the holding bay waiting to come on down. He tries to walk away; he nearly makes it then turns back with a skip for one more roll.

Godfrey takes us to a place special to him for sundowners. Mbiza Pan is a big wide lovely peaceful spot with palm trees and zebras, and the colours streaking the sky are magical. Godfrey gazes out over the lagoon as though it's the first time he's seen it and his smooth black face glows with pride. He and Neil chat about this beautiful and once bountiful country and to our surprise Godfrey is not critical of its demise; he is a Mugabe supporter. But his arguments are weak and his voice fades as he recites the party rhetoric, and you can only feel sadness for this man who deep down must know that his Utopia is as dead as the great marula tree.

Dinner is served and we've no sooner started on the leek and potato soup than a driver rushes in wide-eyed and babbles that there's a big male leopard crossing the road in front of camp. We all abandon the dinner table and pile into vehicles to go in pursuit. But no luck. We return to the dining tent to find the old waiter solitary at the head of the table, patiently waiting to re-serve the soup. We've just sat back down to resume eating when we freeze at a close-by growl from the leopard, as irritated as us by the constant and monotonous alarm call of a jackal.

It's to be a noisy night. We go to bed but are woken some time later by the munching and rumblings of elephants. They are so close that you can hear their stomachs ruminating through the tent's canvas but they move off, almost soundlessly, when the leopard once again disturbs the stillness with a pussycat call.

In late afternoon light on the last day we drive to a waterhole and down many sundowners while watching elephants lark about on the banks. Then Godfrey draws our attention to a shadowy figure motionless behind tall acacias on the treeline. A huge bull in musth, he lurks still and ominous for at least 45 minutes, his stare fixed on the females. Like a gold-chained barfly propping up the counter and nursing a double scotch, he's checking out the action, biding his time. Finally he makes his move at a slow trot, gold chain swinging. When he reaches the waterhole it's a bit of an anti-climax because try as he might he can't find one female in oestrus. As the sun sets, we watch as he slowly skulks off down the *vlei*, head down, gold chain tucked away.

Mandavu Dam campsite is one of the public campsites in Hwange that is exclusively yours once you've booked it. Visitors can come in during the day to picnic or to sit and observe the animal activity but once the gate is closed in the evening you have it to yourself. The campsite itself is a large landscaped area perched on the edge of a substantial expanse of water with hippos and antelope on the opposite bank and dassies claiming every available rock surface on the shore in front.

Neil has set up a table in the shade of a covered viewing platform so that I can sit at the laptop and catch up on diary entries. As I write I feel a soft nudge at my elbow and look down to find a little dassie sitting there calmly. Next thing, he's up on the ledge and gently moving onto the table, brushing his coat like velvet along my arm and rubbing his nose into my fingers. With a few steps he's moved onto the keyboard. He nestles down, gets comfortable — he intends to settle there for a while. I flatten my hand and he moves onto it, so soft and warm and as light as a leaf. I lift him off the keyboard and back onto the table but he's loath to move, content on the warmth of my hand. Such a gentle companion, not yet learnt to fear the malice of humans.

This camp attendant's name is Richard. He's not been paid for three months and relies on the generosity of others for food. Despite the lack of funds, he keeps the site spotless and manages to always have hot water ready for our showers and a fire blazing for our evening meal. His rifle is with him at all times, even when he goes out in his beaten old canoe to fish. He has one eye and a calmness that belies his troubled and sometimes dangerous life. In the mornings he accepts one cup of coffee and sits with Neil and me and talks. Like the dassies around us, we find patches of sunlight and move from one to another, warming up as the sun strengthens.

Richard tells us of losing his eye when he was a youngster — 'It was nothing, I don't miss it' — and his days as a soldier in the Rhodesian army when he felt invincible, a cowboy shooting at baddies from the exhilaration of helicopters. Then more sinister times, when as a park ranger in the early '80s he experienced firsthand the brutality of Mugabe's Fifth Brigade, as they crushed any resistance to the regime with mass murder and mutilations. Sad, frightening stories of violence and lost friends. It's not surprising that he's unafraid of the dangers that wild animals might present.

Early one morning we decide to drive to Sinamatella camp, just 8 kilometres away but a good hour's drive through game-rich bush on the rough track we intend taking. We ask Richard if he'd like to come along to visit his wife and daughter, staying in quarters there. Rifle by his side, he sits in the backseat of the Troopy, showing the way and pointing out places of interest. As we cruise over a ridge we all suddenly realise that we've driven into a sort of ambush. Four adolescent lions are moving low and cautiously beside the road, completely focused on a warthog making its way across a dry riverbed. Even as the Troopy skids, stops and reverses they don't so much as flick an ear in our direction, so intent are these lions on their prey. We sit for minutes waiting for action, but it becomes apparent that these youngsters aren't the most experienced of hunters. Neil, getting restless, happens to look down at the road beside the Troopy and can't believe at first what he's seeing: a long lean body, looking like a log nestled in the grass against the Troopy's wheels. Totally motionless, here is the mother supervising her offspring. We'd nearly run over her. Richard is very pleased and says that he is proud that his park has given us such a gift. When we drop him off at camp, he thanks us for the morning and for the privilege of riding in 'the Envy of all Africa'.

After lunch on our third day at Mandavu we're lounging around camp, reading, writing up notes and generally taking it easy when three white Zimbabweans arrive. They are resident at the Masuma Dam campsite about 30 minutes' drive east of us and they've come to Mandavu on a game drive. They share their afternoon tea with us, so the next evening we take drinks to them at Masuma to watch the daily display of tens of thousands of *queleas*, a species of finch, as they come swooping and soaring over the water in shadowy 3D clouds. Over sundowners I praise the camp attendants and mention that Richard has been invaluable as well as an engaging companion. The Zimbabwean lady snaps back that he is only looking for a bigger tip then launches into a tirade in which she speaks about blacks, all blacks, with such childish vitriol it's apparent that she's totally lost perspective. Her bitterness and disillusionment is palpable and her husband puts a hand over hers while he explains.

Her parents, intimidated and kicked off their farm by supporters of Mugabe, are now living in a garden shed dependant on handouts. They themselves have lost a catering business — just closed the doors and walked away because most of their customers had either left the country or could no longer afford the luxury of catering. Vulnerable and raw and middle-aged, our companions mourn what they've lost and blame all who are black for their downfall.

WE LAUGHED 'TiL WE CRiED

It's been a long day's drive after leaving first Hwange then Zimbabwe behind. We're making our way through the north-east of Botswana to Nata, en route to Maun, where we're to meet with my sister Viv. There's really only one place to overnight in Nata and that's Nata Lodge, something of an institution where chauffeur-driven businessmen and busloads of tourists are looked after by an efficient team of staff who display that rare skill of coping with herds of tired guests with grace and charm. The cleaning ladies here are even more affable than we've come to expect. Elaborate headscarves, smooth mahogany faces, gossip, laughter and ah-ah-ahs. One sings as they make slow progress, and they stop often to catch their breath or to emphasise a point. Here they come, with their mops and coloured buckets in their hands, ready with a smile and a handful of our favourite teabags. I have to admire the pace at which they move around the lodge — if we walked that slowly we'd fall over.

On the roads around Nata we see cowboys herding their cattle on horses. It all seems so romantic and old-fashioned; their horsemanship is wonderful to watch and the horses themselves are trotting along like prizewinners at the Royal Easter Show. The cattle are in good nick too although they look to be a rangy breed. The beef industry is the third-largest income earner for Botswana and its importance is evident in the network of veterinary fences that crisscrosses the country. The fences are intended to control the spread of cattle diseases, but their placement is becoming increasingly contentious and wildlife experts maintain that the fences prevent the free flow of game. They say that the fencing infrastructure is the main cause of the decline in the country's wildlife, another big income earner, but the beef lobby seems to have the ear of the government and we read in the paper that new fences being erected across a currently cattle-free northern sector will cut off vital wildlife corridors. We hope this doesn't happen in the next couple of weeks.

The group of seven huge trees known as Baines' Baobabs are in the Nxai Pan National Park abutting the main highway between Nata and Maun, and visitors to them are supposed to pay a park entrance fee. But the park gates are further in along the access track, way beyond the turn-off to the baobabs, so, like everyone else, we don't pay and veer off the track to head straight for the baobabs. We've been told that rangers have been known to hide out, ready to nab transgressors, so we agree on an excuse should we be caught red-handed.

The track changes from sand to salt and by the time we see the oasis of tall trees we're driving across a salty crust that cracks and snaps under the weight of the Troopy. It becomes glaringly white and images shift and shimmer on the horizon, but the cluster of baobabs is obvious in this otherwise treeless landscape. Once there, we begin to wish that there was a ranger lurking about because a group of overlanders are happily carving messages and initials in hearts on the trunks of these majestic trees, right by signs banning precisely that.

We call in at the infamous Club Baobab to check it out. On the edge of the Nxai saltpan and shaded only by some baobabs, it offers a variety of accommodation ranging from shabby-chic safari to funny little grass Bushmen's huts containing little more than a couple of cots. The restrooms have bowlfuls of free condoms and there's a funky bar playing groovy music. It's fun and upbeat but has copped a lot of bad press recently for charging for the use of a glass when people order a drink. That might explain why the place is nearly empty but management is sticking to its guns. Maybe it wants to discourage the overlander crowd and encourage a more salubrious, free-spending clientele. Like us. But we decide that it's not our cup of tea and push on, leaving the music blaring into the quiet of the desert.

Lying on the other side of the road to Nxai Pan is the huge Makgadikgadi Pan, also a national park and home to a great wetlands bird sanctuary. It's bordered to the north-west by the Boteti River and we've heard that game congregates here in winter. This time we do pay park fees and the ranger at the gate tells us of a cunning trick the lions have come up with. There is a village on the other side of the river and a veterinary fence has been erected to protect cattle from the wild animals in the park. The fence has a gate in it, positioned in a sort of cul-de-sac on the park side. The lions have worked out that if they chase prey along the fence it will become trapped, herded into the cul-de-sac with no way out except past the incoming lions. As we drive towards the gate there's a strong smell in the air and then we see the evidence of the carnage, with many carcasses and skeletons scattered about.

In the trees above are dozens of vultures, resting or fighting for territory as they wait for the next massacre to be played out on their doorstep.

Email between Viv and me has become more frequent as her arrival date draws nearer. As well as the usual concerns about travel in Africa, she worries that Neil and I might be getting lioned out, that by the time she arrives we could be driving right past wild animals and amazing sights with barely a blink. But the thing is that you never know what's around the corner, the thrill is in the unexpected as much as the discovery. Thinking about it, it's probably the main reason that Neil and I are travelling so well together: we are both constantly excited by what we chance upon, and the anticipation that something new could be just about to reveal itself becomes a carrot which draws us along the road to the next camp, the next national park.

Maun is the epicentre for tourist traffic into the Moremi Game Reserve and the Okavango Delta. The town itself is a dusty mix-and-match of circular one-roomed rondavels and functional modern buildings, while donkeys and goats share the roads with safari vehicles and Zimbabwean traders. The airport, however, is one of the busiest I've seen, with air charter operations providing the only transport into camps in the delta for most of the year.

The town started life in the early 1900s as a trading hub for the hunting and cattle ranching concessions in the area and there's still a frontier feel to it. There's a café just across the road from the airport, the Cafe Bon Arrive, in which every traveller through Maun must have had at least one caffelatte, and it manages to combine a laid-back, cosmopolitan atmosphere with the excitement of discovering the new world.

It's the day Viv flies into town. I wake up early, excited and expectant, and at the airport I can't stand still. When I see her walking across the tarmac I wave and try to attract her attention. Perhaps fearing a scene, Neil wanders off to wait for Viv and me to get our greetings out of the way.

She's here, and we hightail it to Leroo La-Tau Bush Lodge on the opposite bank of the Boteti River to the Makgadikgadi Pans National Park. It's dusk by the time we arrive and just as we walk in the door the call goes up *lion! lion!* and we're waved down to the edge of the garden. In failing light we peer down into the dry riverbed below, just in time to see a sleek golden body fade into the shadows. The frustrated rumble is undoubtedly a lion's, annoyed at having his prey alerted. I couldn't have written the script better for Viv's first bush encounter — she's hooked.

Things don't go as planned after that. At the main lodge to collect the keys for two cabins in the adjoining Xwaraga campsite, we are told that the young manager has double-booked both. There are also no rooms free in the lodge itself. He makes a plan. While we drink free wine and eat a free dinner he arranges for two pup tents to be put up in Xwaraga and later the rheumy old guide shows us the way to them through thick, thorny bush. The tents look pretty good and we settle down for the night in cosy bedrolls with the sounds of the bush around us and a roll of toilet paper strategically positioned between the two tents.

Early next morning we wake to South African accents moving around outside our tents. It's a family of fellow campers, tracking the footprints of a big lion that wandered into the camp during the night and passed right by us. We were too exhausted — or full of free wine — to hear it, but Neil does go quiet when he remembers that he'd gone out at some point in the night for a call of nature of a different sort.

The next day we move to one of the cabins. It's nothing fancy — four beds in a row, dormitory style, with a basic bathroom out the back — but we have a ball. Like many in our family, Viv likes to light fires so while I get dinner organised and Neil polishes the Troopy she sets off to collect firewood and very soon we're sitting around a half-decent campfire. The sun has gone down and we've just topped up our glasses when there's a rumble, then a thundering: the sounds of a big herd galloping our way. I sit contentedly with my glass of red, waiting for some action, but Viv is up and into the cabin in a flash, balancing her glass of wine like the runner-up in an egg-and-spoon race. The herd is now very close to us, just in the bushes beyond the fire, and we're surrounded by their frightened snorts and squeals. The commotion passes us by — just a lion chasing a herd of zebras — but it's an eerie experience, as we can see nothing in the dark of a new moon.

During the night we wake to the sounds of two lions calling to each other across the camp. At times they sound close, but not too close, so we drift off to sleep again. Then I wake again when a person moves around the outside of the cabin and seems to settle down just the other side of the sticks-and-reeds wall at our heads. I'm not too worried, thinking it's probably the guard moving in for shelter from the lions. Next morning when we compare stories it becomes apparent that my man wasn't a guard at all but a big rat that had a nest in the wall just above Viv's bed. She got less sleep than us.

Next stop is Pom Pom Camp in the Okavango Delta and we fly into it in a small six-seater plane. Seen from above, the sprawl of Maun gives way to scattered villages, which change to grassland, then swamp, and in no time we're over large expanses of flooded plains. The pilot points out herds of buck and small families of elephants moving around on the only dry land left, and we can see flocks of large birds sweeping and soaring over the water. As we get deeper into the delta, pockets of high ground form isolated islands and it's hard to see how there's enough room anywhere to accommodate a camp, let alone land a plane.

We have a grand old time at Pom Pom, partly because the other guests are fun but also because the staff is too. The kitchen serves good food, which is just as well because there are Italians and Swiss amongst us. The Italians, two young couples, become great friends with us and we overcome the language problem by drinking wine and laughing. One of the Swiss, a lady who declares that she hates flying and hates jelly, sings us grace one dinnertime so Viv and I reciprocate on her last day by singing 'I Like Aeroplane Jelly' as she drives off for the flight back to Maun. Viv takes over responsibility for the campfire and she can be found in the early evenings fussing with wood and stoking the flames until they blaze like a Cracker Night bonfire.

Each day we are taken on a new adventure. Early one morning we set out in *mokoros*, those slender, slightly unstable dugout canoes that are poled like gondolas through the swamp. We glide without a sound except for the splash-splash of the pole and the huffing and puffing of Neil and me trying to blow life into our frozen hands. Another time we're taken by boat along hippo highways through tall papyrus to a vast waterbird rookery where thousands of herons, pelicans, marabou and yellow-billed storks nest together in noisy alliance.

On our last morning at Pom Pom Neil, Viv and I choose to go out on the water, fishing, while the Italians hold out for finding the leopard that has eluded us all on our previous game drives. In the sparkling, crisp, early morning we've just thrown out the anchor and cast the first line when there's a crackle on the walkie-talkie. The others have found the leopard and if we're quick they'll meet us on land and take us to her. With no consideration for park speed limits or snoozing hippos our boat speeds across the water to the pick-up point, where we pile on top of everyone else in the back of the game-viewing vehicle. The orderly game drive is forgotten as we career through the bush, everyone being thrown on top of the person next to them, and passing branches scratch our hands and foreheads. Someone's beanie flies out the back, forgotten, and cameras are a jumble of lenses and straps bouncing on the metal floor. We're almost on top of the leopard before we see her, so well camouflaged is she in the patchy light. Green eyes, pink nose and beautifully marked coat, she's young and pretty, and preening for us like a catwalk model. No one moves except to press their finger for photos, and there is no sound except for the clicks. Even after the gorgeous girl stretches, sits on a log for a final photo opportunity then pads off into the bushes, we remain dumbstruck by her presence and the honour of her allowing us an audience.

There's a night to be spent in Maun before driving into Moremi Game Reserve. On the outskirts of town, Discovery B&B is a neat compound of colourful rondavels inside a high, secure and private wall. We arrive to find the dinner table set and ready for us in the middle of an open courtyard alongside a well-stoked fire. The manageress apologises for the lack of a local singing and dancing group to entertain us, but with so few guests she thought the troupe would be better off elsewhere. The only other staff members are the cook, an old lady in a brightly coloured sarong called a *kanga*, and a serious young man who waits on us with the studied mannerisms of a trainee. While we're lapping up pre-dinner drinks these two amble over to a couple of rickety stools, hitch up their *kanga* and trousers, put a drum between their knees and beat out a catchy rhythm. To make up for the missing entertainers.

The Moremi Game Reserve might occupy just 20 per cent of the Okavango Delta but it has just about everything you might want to explore. Permanent lagoons, seasonal swamps, dry savannah and dense *mopane* woodlands. It has a reputation for exceptional game viewing and, depending on the time of year, can be explored on land or by boat. The Department of Wildlife and National Parks manages a number of public camping grounds and it is in two of these, Third Bridge and Xakanaxa, that we've booked sites for the next few days.

Third Bridge is in disorder. We drive in to find no camp attendant, a broken-down hot-water donkey and no defined campsites, even though we were allocated one when making the compulsory booking. Elephants have destroyed the water pipes and the bridge on the onward road was washed away last year and no one has got around to replacing it yet. This place is wild. There's a sense of prehistory, of abandonment to the ancient order of things, and we all feel the excitement of knowing that anything could happen. While I set up camp, Viv gets her fire going and Neil has a run-in with the advance party for a mobile safari, or fly-camp, who want to take over our site. We've just avoided the baboons, who are a marauding nightmare at dusk, when a shout from a neighbour alerts us to in-coming hyenas. Viv grabs the spotlight and does a wide sweep of the perimeter of our site. Nothing. Then we see a shadow moving behind the Troopy and the light picks out a form moving low and sly. This hyena is bolder than most and the reason is soon apparent when we see that he has a deep, infected cut around his neck. A loop of wire hanging from the raw wound tells the story: this sorry hyena has been caught in a snare and it's still with him, cutting further and further into his flesh as he grows. He's sick and desperate, and when we report his plight to park staff, who are supposed to call in a vet, they dismiss it with, 'Oh yes, we've known about that one for months.' We go to bed aware that he is hanging around close to our camp, and in the morning we see the imprint of his curled-up body in the dust by the ashes of Viv's campfire.

We're out in the Troopy looking for animals when we're approached by Ralph, an affable guide, who is slightly flamboyant in a sort of old world way, a character from a Hemingway novel, who offers a trade. He's seen that the Troopy is Australian registered so if we give him a case of Fosters he'll tell us where two lovely male lions are sleeping. He settles for the location of a black mamba we've just seen, then, ignoring his clients sitting patiently in his vehicle, he admires the Troopy and falls into deep discussion with Neil about its attributes and features. Ralph asks if we'd give him first option when we come to sell and Neil agrees without hesitation. Months later, reading a magazine article about famous guides of Africa, we discover that Ralph is the son of Jack Bousfield, a renowned Tanzanian hunter turned conservationist. We also read that Ralph owns the famous Jacks Camp in the Makgadikgadi Pans. The Troopy is truly the Envy of all Africa, as Richard had predicted.

The next night is spent in Xakanaxa camp, a slight improvement on Third Bridge. We choose a good site right by the swamp's edge, quite a distance from the nearest neighbours and midway between two ablution blocks. We retire early, Viv to the sleeping capsule and Neil and I to the tent and we're all asleep in no time, despite the bright full moon and the continuous calling of lions a short distance away. At some stage Neil and I are woken by 'Neil, Neil, there's something out there!' coming from Viv in the capsule. He shines a torch in the direction of heavy breathing, and standing 10 metres or so away is a big elephant with broken tusks, waiting patiently for the commotion to die down so he can move on through. Viv decides a toilet stop can wait and we all go back to sleep. A little later, 'Neil, Neil, hyenas everywhere!' and we look out to see Viv, wide-eyed, scurrying back up her ladder while two or three hyenas patrol the perimeter of our site. Just as I'm nodding off again I hear splashing and wading through water and a barely audible 'Oh no, not again' from the capsule, but somehow we all manage to get back to sleep. At sun-up we emerge in time to see the tail-end of a hippo disappear into the rushes and we realise the reason for the midnight visitations, and why no one else was camping in this terrific spot: we're right on a game-worn track leading to and from the lagoon. We just can't understand how we could have missed this yesterday when we set up camp.

It's late in the day when we leave Moremi but we decide to drive back to Maun and take our chances at Discovery B&B. We tear along in the dark and get to town in record time. Just as we turn in to Discovery's entrance there's a loud clunk and a splutter but it's not until we pull up in the yard that we realise that the Troopy has a puncture. Our first. The old nightwatchman comes out and a friendly female appears through the main gate. Discovery is also known as Betty's Guesthouse and this is Betty, the owner, and a more affable and gracious host you couldn't find. She serves Viv and me wine and chats about her village background and family. She asks the nightwatchman, whom she affectionately calls Medula, to help, and he and Neil figure out jacks and nuts and get the tyre changed. It's taken a while and Medula does little more than agree with Neil and ah-ah-ah at the appropriate times, but they've forged a bond. After we eat and Viv and I go off to our respective rondavels, Neil sits up finishing off the wine and chatting with the old man. He warms his spent transistor batteries by the fire in the hope of generating new life in them and tells Neil that he was once sought after by hunters as a tracker. They talk about dreams and hopes and he honours Neil by showing him his bow and arrows, his weapon with which to defend us against trespassers. Neil gives him a shirt and a Fanta and retires, unfortunately to the wrong rondavel. I hear Viv's stage-whispered 'Oh p-leease!' as he tries the door to hers, then we all get the giggles as he stumbles around my rondavel, unable to find the door. Medula, bow and arrow in hand, shows the way.

THREE-RiNG CiRCUS

It's back to Kasane via another overnight stay at Nata Lodge. About three hours out of Maun, on a good straight road with very little other traffic, I'm pulled over by a policeman for speeding. Neil takes over the pleasantries and they have a long polite exchange, man to man, about the flightiness of female drivers. 'It is like this, Sir,' the policeman says as he hands Neil the fine, 'womens are not to be trusted with the steering wheel *and* the accelerator.'

Kasane will be our base while we explore the Chobe National Park, home to large concentrations of game, including the world's biggest elephant population. For our first game, drive we've decided not to take the Troopy in but to book a guided drive. We set out in an open safari vehicle in the chill morning breeze, which is turned into a buffeting wind as we charge helter-skelter down the road to get to the park gates before all the other vehicles.

Luck is with us as our guide is a senior figure in the guiding fraternity here, and he's good. When a carload of 'noisy thugs' attaches themselves to us to benefit from his tracking skills, he purposefully but politely drives through a sand bank where he knows the pests are sure to get stuck. He parks patiently by a tangle of scrubby acacias, waiting for a big herd of buffalo to be ambushed by the pride of lions lurking within. His calmness isn't matched by the excited Italians in front of me, who jump up and exclaim at their first sighting of a baby *leone*. When they are asked to be quiet and to sit still, I have to force the man in front of me down into his seat with a firm hand on his shoulder, and the person beside him good-naturedly clamps a hand over his mouth to quell his exuberance. You have to love their vivacity, their *entusiasmo*.

The park is busy and there are many game-viewing vehicles on every detour we take, particularly if there are lions or a leopard in the vicinity. I can see how visitors new to the safari experience are lulled into a false sense of security: there's a hint of the circus to it all, as though at any minute a ringmaster, *da daaa*, will jump ponies through hoops. Secure in the safety of numbers, there is a reduced sense of danger, of being in the wild, even though it is apparent how excited everyone is by what they're seeing.

An organised boat trip late that day along the banks and into the inlets of the Chobe River is wonderful. It doesn't get much better than this, being right here on the river, part of the passing parade of animals as they make their evening pilgrimage to water. There are hippos fighting for elbowroom, buffalo wallowing in a muddy muddle, and at last we see them after weeks of near-sightings — four African wild dogs padding across a sandy bank.

Each evening we are tired and not too interested in food, so we go to the Old House for dinner. A haunt of the permanent Kasane community, it's comfortable and friendly and one of those places where the quirkiness is endearing, not annoying. We sit outdoors at the same table and order the same thing every night: one Greek salad, one large pizza and a bottle of wine between three. The only thing that changes is the topping on the pizza.

It's an early start for Savute, still in the Chobe National Park but a good eight hours' drive from Kasane on a bad, sandy and lonesome road. We've been travelling for three or four hours when we pass signs saying that it is prohibited to carry uncooked meats further. A roadblock stops us and Neil gets out to deal with officialdom. No, we don't have any uncooked meat on board, and yes, they are welcome to check our cooler. Viv and I wander up the road a bit and see that impounded meat products are being burned in a pit by the verge. These men, in the middle of nowhere and with next to nothing for themselves, are not confiscating food for their own use as we'd supposed, but are carrying out their duty despite their own need and in a place where they're probably never checked. We hear raised voices behind us and turn to see Neil biting big chunks from a salami, all the while protesting that this is 'salami, cooked sausage, see, we eat it because it is cooked'. He chews away, swallows a mouthful then takes another bite and the salami is almost gone before Viv gets through to him that salami is actually uncooked. The officials are unimpressed by Neil's heroic demonstration and they confiscate what's left.

At Savute the Troopy bypasses the public campsite, which looks hot and dry, and, with a mind of its own, drives straight into the Savute Safari Lodge. This is a glamorous joint, with a swimming pool overlooking a waterhole where elephants wander in and out, and individual chalets that come with designer sitting rooms and large open-to-the-view bathrooms. As luck would have it the managers are a young Zimbabwean couple who are caught off-guard by self-driving day-trippers asking for a deal when most of their guests arrive in light aircraft having booked months, even years, in advance. And yes, they just happen to have two chalets free. These are still way over our budget but here is where the three of us want to be and we're soon lazing around the pool as though we're regulars. Other guests, in their swanky designer safari outfits, jokingly give us a hard time, calling us fly-ins and 'the Griswolds'.

That afternoon and the following morning we're taken on game drives. Savute is famous for the number and size of its lion prides and, having tracked one family successfully the day before, the biggest thrill comes early next morning as we're driving out through grassland crisp with frost. Our driver stops when he notices movement up ahead. Minutes pass with nothing doing and his passengers, sitting restless and cold, are itching for action. Then without warning two big male lions appear on the track a hundred metres or so away, walking towards us, single file. They pad along at a leisurely pace, the one in front occasionally stopping in patches of sunlight for his brother to catch up, and when they reach our vehicle the only acknowledgement of our presence is a flick of the ears as they skirt around. They pass so close that you can see grass seeds in their matted manes and hear them huffing in the cold morning air.

It's so good in this camp that we don't want to leave. Unfortunately we can only afford to stay one night but the manager comes up with a cunning plan. We can pitch our tent out the back for a small fee and take ourselves on game drives. This would have been brilliant for us but head office quashes the idea, believing that a family of ne'er-do-wells in the backyard would lower the tone of the place.

After the great experience Neil and I had in Hwange National Park we've decided to alter our itinerary and return to Zimbabwe with Viv. We are keen to show her Mandavu Dam, a special place for us, and for her to meet Richard. We've been telling her stories of our last adventures there with him and of the many animals we saw and heard during our stay.

On the way we stop overnight in Kasane where we fit in one last lazy cruise on the Chobe River and a final pizza at the Old House. We stock up on food, diesel and firewood and Neil buys batteries and big sacks of mielie-meal for Richard. They're all piled in the backseat of the Troopy next to Viv and we head for the Zimbabwean border.

We drive through that part of Hwange where we saw the lions last time — nothing at all there now. Past the little *vlei* where large numbers of elephant and giraffe had always congregated — nothing; and into the campsite to be met by — not Richard, who is off on leave, but Nelson, another old-timer. He has the hot-water fire all stoked up, the toilets and showers are as spotless as they were under Richard's care, and the dassies are out in force, so Mandavu begins to work its charms on Viv regardless of the inflated build-up it's been given. She's a little put out when Nelson proposes that he'll get a campfire going for us but they soon come to an agreement. He'll light it while we're out game driving, but she is responsible for it from then on. I'm beginning to suspect that her preoccupation with having a raging nightly fire has something to do with the belief that it will keep predators at bay.

Nelson, believing that Neil has two wives, is not sure what to call Viv and me. Viv is 'the Sir's Madam', while through seniority I become 'Mummy'. He's also intrigued by our sleeping arrangements and tries not to be caught looking as Viv always climbs up into the sleeping capsule while Neil and I head for the tent.

Neil has given the batteries and mielie-meal he'd bought for Richard to Nelson to pass on, saying that Nelson can have half the mielie-meal if he needs it. Nelson is very appreciative but expresses his unwillingness to take something that belongs to another. Every day he assures us that he has helped himself, thank you very much, and every day when Neil goes up to Nelson's compound the unopened bags of mielie-meal and the batteries sit in a corner waiting for Richard's return.

During dinner lions roar to each other, and with all the water around it's hard to pinpoint their exact location. Just to be sure it isn't really close, Viv does a last check on the perimeter fence with a torch before retiring. Next morning, as we're wandering about camp, drinking coffee, brushing teeth and lingering in the rays of first sunlight, Viv spots the lions drinking at the water's edge just across the bay. Nelson shows me a hippo that has come across to our side of the lake and is lying motionless in the shallow water below our dining area. When I ask Nelson why he thinks the hippo has left the others, he replies pointedly that a young female must have ousted her older rival.

We've left Mandavu and are heading to Makalolo Plains in the south-east of the park. On the way we stop at Masuma Dam campsite for a bit of bird-watching but are distracted when the two young boys in attendance approach and ask if we have any food we could spare. Like Richard and Nelson at Mandavu, they have been stuck here for months and have not been paid in that time, and in this quiet season there aren't enough visitors to give them something to eat. Initially we supply fruit and biscuits, whatever is handy in the front of the Troopy, but these are devoured with such obvious hunger that we empty our cooler as well. One boy asks if we could give him a lift to the next camp 20 kilometres or so further on, where there might be some mielie-meal to spare, so he jumps in the back of the Troopy with me and we set off. He's two-thirds of the way through a packet of Tennis biscuits when he neatly folds up the packet, saving the rest for later. But then he remembers his manners and quietly offers the last of the biscuits to us.

The plight of these boys is just the tip of the iceberg, I know, but our encounter with them is enough to dispirit us and we drive along in silence, each trying to comprehend this wilful starving and displacement of his citizens by Mugabe. Why has it happened, and how has it been allowed to happen? We've heard the rumours: it's ethnic cleansing, corruption, paranoia gone wild, just plain madness. After three months on the road I have grown used to seeing severe poverty, but not in a country that once had plenty, which was the breadbasket of Africa. I can see that Viv is troubled by seeing first-hand a situation which she'd previously only read about, and Neil too is very upset. For once he's speechless and lacks the heart to lecture us or try to explain. We arrive subdued at Ngweshla picnic site where, once again, the Troopy is to be left while we stay at a camp deep within the park, but our spirits lift at the sight of two chubby babies belonging to the attendant here. This family is being looked after by the camp, which supplies food and necessities, just as they keep the pumps at the local waterholes running by donating diesel to the maintenance man.

The big brother to Little Makalolo, Makalolo Plains sits on the treeline of an open grassland a few kilometres away. It is a much larger and more glamorous camp built entirely on a wooden platform, way up off the ground. We're told that this is for Americans, who aren't comfortable down with the wildlife and prefer it to be kept at a distance. The three of us are the only guests in camp for the five days we're there and we do our best to get through the mountains of food that the kitchen sends out. For afternoon tea they prepare at least two cakes and two savoury slices, and one day we are served a huge brunch out by the waterhole under a big shady tree, where the cook fries up a storm on his *braai* and the waiting staff hover, smiling, ready to bat any insects that should fly about and annoy us.

On the second night we're sitting at the dinner table, halfway through a three-course meal when a slurping and a gurgling can be heard coming from the swimming pool at the other end of the deck. Our hostess smiles, puts a finger to her lips and indicates that we should follow her. We all sneak along the deck in the dark and there, at the outside edge of the pool, as if by magic, is a family of elephants, ears back and trunks stretched up to reach the water hovering above them like a lucky dip. All we can see of the youngsters are wayward little trunks reaching up over the lip of the pool, feeling around until they find water. They blow as much water as they suck up, and before long all the others around them are dripping. The older elephants move back once they've had enough to make way for others waiting in the wings and there is no other sound except for water noises. Then two big bulls appear out of the night, foreigners who want a drink too but are wary of their reception. One tries to gatecrash the crush at the trough but is elbowed out, then the other sees an opening at the side and tries the stretched trunk approach. He's politely jostled aside. But after a few more attempts they are tolerated just long enough for them to get a gut full, before the females nudge them out again and they retreat into the night. We've been sitting on the deck not more than 3 metres away and have been completely ignored.

The following afternoon we are taken to a *vlei* that at first glance looks to have a clump of bushes in the middle of the dry winter grasses. As we get nearer we can see that the bushes are in fact lions, a big unruly family of them who at this moment are all stretching and rousing and looking like they might mean business just as soon as they can get their act together. They have heard and smelt what we already know: there's a big herd of buffalo moving through the woodland behind us. The pride is known as the Spice Girls and they have a reputation for being pathetic hunters. But this evening they sense victory and move off in single file down the *vlei*, all fifteen of them, at first nonchalantly then with more stealth as they get closer to the buffalo. Some pause at a waterhole but most are very focused by the time they pass us hiding behind the safari vehicle. They spread out, moving low, and disappear into the woods. It's quiet, too quiet, then all hell breaks loose. There's stampeding, the sound of undergrowth being flattened, the booming roaring call of lions and screams from the buffalo. We can't actually see anything except for the dust and the tops of trees shaking but it sounds like a massacre. Those lions must have finally got this hunting thing licked. Suddenly the buffalo break through the trees in front of us and thunder past the waterhole and over the ridge. There's no sign of the lions. Back at camp we're told by a guide who was on the other side of the woods and saw all the action that the buffalo routed the lions, who once again botched up a sure thing. Their reputation is intact.

We see the Spice Girls one more time before we leave. It's a new moon and inky black as we return from a night drive. The guide suddenly stops, very alert. He motions for us to keep quiet then swings the spotlight in big arcs around our vehicle. We see nothing but can tell by his body language that he's onto something. Then, out of the grasses behind us wanders a lion. Then another. Then there's more to the side and in front of us. We're surrounded, but we're not the object of their attention. The whole pride is focused on something else and we just happen to be in the middle. We watch thrilled and tense as these beautiful girls pad right by the tyres then spread out in formation, now stalking, to melt into the heart of darkness without a sound.

Just outside Hwange is the education centre for the Painted Dog Research Project, where we're told it's possible to observe at close quarters African wild dogs, also known as painted dogs. But we get lost, and after a couple of bad re-directions we decide to go in to Hwange Safari Lodge for help. At the entrance barrier the thin security man marches on the spot and snappily salutes us, military style. We drive in to a hotel time-warped in more pros-perous times. Tidy, manicured, ready and waiting for the tourists who stopped coming years ago. There's not a person in sight except for two Japanese visitors waiting patiently for transport to take them out of there. The hotel is hardly recognisable as the bustling, crowded place Neil and I visited on our first trip together to Africa in the 1980s, where safari vehicles lined up in a long queue to set off on game drives stacked to the roll bars with excited visitors, and the lobby was filled with dozens of people arriving, leaving, complaining, pointing at and shouting about luggage. I find myself wishing that it were still like that, full of the pushy, excited crowds that annoyed me then, because that would mean that Zimbabwe was thriving and vibrant once more, and Mugabe's destruction of this once-bountiful country was over.

NO STOPPiNG FOR TURKEYS

We drive into Zambia and head for Gwabi Lodge on the banks of the Kafue River, close to its confluence with the Lower Zambezi. Here we're to stay the night before spending three days camping and canoeing on the Zambezi, and we think that tonight might be the last good night's sleep we'll have until the paddling is over. The lodge owner's wife takes Viv and me through long grass and under thick foliage in search of the big resident python. We don't find it — *it must be out shopping,* she says — and Viv and I agree to give its empty bed in the rushes a wide berth when we row past the next day. At night, just after we've gone to bed, Neil and I hear movement in Viv's rondavel next door. Her light is on and there are the sounds of furniture being dragged and shutters snapping closed. Neil is concerned but I know what's going on: she's making her room python-proof, and I suspect that she'll get little sleep tonight after all.

The canoe safari is shaping up to be problematic. After all these years Neil still can't resist telling me when to change lanes when I'm driving and when to indicate, so of course I get annoyed and do the opposite. On the water, two to a canoe, it'll be no different. To make things worse, everyone has been telling us stories of couples on these trips constantly bickering, with accusations flying of poor rowing technique and navigational skills — even one notorious time when an engaged couple split up while on the water, the ring hurled into the waiting waters of the Zambezi. I have a quiet word with Viv, suggesting that we all rotate rowing partners on a regular basis.

On the first day we set off with great confidence, Viv with Epsom the guide, Neil with me. For his part, Epsom has assumed that Viv and I are both Neil's wives and that the whispered scheming he's overheard is all just part of the familiar petty jealousies between wives. Not even after he's bold enough to ask and it's explained that Viv and I are sisters does it clarify the matter for him. After all, this is a land where, as a matter of course, wives go to live with their brother-in-law upon the death of their husband.

After one early encounter with the bank and a thorny acacia, Neil and I sail along, the perfect pair. We'd anticipated a leisurely drift with the current, dodging hippos on an obliging river, but the choppy conditions caused by strong headwinds make it a constant battle just to keep moving forward. That evening we beach on a sand island where a forward party has set up a fly-camp. There's dinner cooking on the campfire and pup tents erected with camp stretchers to sleep on. We're tired and sore after our first hard day on the water and sit around the fire drinking Mosi, Zambia's most popular beer, re-living the day, and still no words are exchanged in anger between Neil and me. I can only think that Neil must have overheard my earlier scheming and has resolved to prove me wrong.

We retire early for the night but, whether it's the full moon or our stiffening bodies, none of us sleeps well. At about midnight Neil and I decide to venture out for a toilet stop and just as we emerge from our tent, Viv does from hers. And coming towards us across the sand is a big elephant, who gets as much of a shock as we do. All four of us bellow and beat a retreat. The staff, who are listening from their tent, think this particularly funny but I suspect that this is bravado as the big tusker had been heading in their direction.

The canoeing ends at a river lodge abutting the Lower Zambezi National Park and we stay there for a few days. True to form, Neil befriends the manager, who gives us a discount plus an upgrade, and we spend our last days on the Zambezi in tents that look out over a languid sweep of this generous river. In the mornings we sit on Viv's deck and over coffee watch the water like a blue perfect mirror wake up with the day. We make forays into the park while it's still cool then, after lunch, sit lazy and quiet under the arms of a leadwood tree. Sometimes we raise a casual wave to canoeists drifting past and sometimes we train the binoculars on the Zimbabwean side of the river, looking for poachers. One day a herd of elephants passes through the camp and as we run to hide in the bar the garden boy stands immobile, frozen to his rake. The herd ignores him and heads for the swimming pool, where they reduce the water level by half after just a few minutes' drinking. Due to some dicky drainage, Neil and I have been making a millpond of the bathroom floor every time we shower and this attracts a family of frogs who decide to move in permanently. Relocating them is short-lived so we get used to treading warily when we move around in the darkness of night.

Before we left for Africa I jokingly said to anyone who asked that we'd return home early only if we got sick, or sick of each other. I could say this because I was quite sure that our travelling partnership would fall into place just as it had every other time we'd run away from home over the past 30 years, and that the preoccupations and responsibilities of everyday life would drop away as before. I was confident that, away from our working life, the business of living together would not get in the way of being together. When Viv joined us I was anticipating some changes, a shift in the ballast. Neil must have been too because a few days before she arrived he'd broached the subject, expressing the hope that Viv and I didn't 'carry on and be silly' like we often did at home. This tends to irritate him and make him short-tempered, but we've always suspected that behind his grumpiness is a sense of being left out.

When Viv arrived in Botswana, we were indeed silly, caught up in the excitement of those first few days together, and wrapped up in dodging lions and avoiding stampeding zebras. The dynamics changed and it wasn't long before the effect was felt on Neil and me. One morning we were at a picnic site on the banks of a waterhole, along with a handful of other visitors, when Neil accused me of misplacing his sunglasses and I snapped. Totally and embarrassingly. I can't even remember what I said, but I'm pretty sure the onlookers do. There was silence. Even Neil was struck dumb. But after that I felt good and in a quieter moment I reasoned that I was relieving some subterranean pressure that had built up in our nation of two.

Neil relieved the pressure in his own way. On one long leg I was driving and Viv was co-piloting and we kept slowing down for photo opportunities, or to see what was going on in the markets and up village alleys. I'd also decelerate every time we passed people on the side of the road offering fish, roosters, even a puppy for sale, and Neil was getting grumpier by the minute. 'No stopping!' came from the backseat. Then we drove towards a man holding up something big and strange, a bulky thing with a long neck. I went slower and slower, all the while chattering and guessing with Viv as to what the heck it could be. That was the final straw for Neil. From the backseat came an exasperated 'No stopping for turkeys!'

This wasn't the last time Neil lost patience with our babbling. Viv hadn't seen a rhino during her stay and her last opportunity was as we drove out of Hwange National Park. Everyone said that we were sure to spot one, that there was often one at Kennedy II waterhole, but we cruised past and saw nothing. We had a long drive ahead of us but we paused to photograph a handsome sable. I turned around and there was a whopping big white rhino, grazing near a waterhole behind us. *Rhino, rhino!* Viv and I shouted directions to Neil — *go around there, retrace our steps, not this track it goes nowhere, go off-road, who cares about the rules!* Neil followed instructions up to a point then, after another attack of conflicting instructions, he totally lost patience. We were not going off-road, we couldn't turn around and we could only stay for two minutes. It seemed there was to be no stopping for rhinos, either.

But now, after four weeks together, it's time for Viv to return home. The days have flown by. We've seen so much and had so much fun together; it's been a wonderful time of discovery for all of us. It seems that we've only just adjusted to a happy *tour de trois* and it's going to change again.

We're at Pioneer Camp, Lusaka, on the day she is to fly home. We wake up to a cloudy windy day after a sleepless night. Wedding celebrations in an adjoining village have played loud bad music until 6 a.m. and we are all puffy-eyed and distracted. Viv and I make a silent breakfast and she, through habit, goes out and stokes the hot-water donkey. We sit outside, not talking, and can hear Neil moving about inside, picking things up, putting them down, being busy. He comes out and tries a few jokes, ones we've heard a million times before, but Viv and I laugh anyway because he's trying so hard to lighten things. The drive to the airport is taken up with desultory talk: good weather for flying, have you got money for airport tax, packed your carving? Then it's teary, garbled farewells and promises ... and goodbye. She's gone through security and I try to wave through the gap in the screens.

The next morning it's with me, as I wake, that our nation is back to two again. Viv's not there and it seems incomplete and I miss her. Neil feels it as well and busies himself with making plans for the day. We'll go to an electrician to have a faulty power board repaired, then we'll have lunch in the showground — that'll be an adventure, a distraction to cheer us up. We get through the day and move through the week, but for the first 48 hours the fire has gone out. I'm left with the feeling that one chapter of our journey is over. It was a month of fun and games spent with Viv in places wild and exciting, a holiday within a holiday. Now we have to settle down and make plans for the next few weeks and the campaign to locate Itembwe will soon have to start in earnest.

By the road between Lusaka and Pioneer Camp is a commercial tomato farm, a sea of red and green. Every time we drive past labourers are in long lines, waiting in hope of a day's work or lugging filled-to-the-brim big wooden crates on their head, queuing to get paid. Further on, just around a bend, there is always a handful of people selling ... tomatoes. These are excellent, the best I've had outside Italy, but there's always that niggling feeling that their source isn't exactly legal.

Overall, fresh produce has been of a high quality and what turns up where has sometimes amazed us. A rocket salad in an isolated camp in Hwange National Park, where no gardens or planting are permitted. Salmon in a restaurant in landlocked Lusaka. This was described to us by the young waiter as 'salmon with honeys' so Neil had to have it. No nymphets arrived at the table, but a beautifully honey-cured fillet. We've had some of the best meat pies we've ever eaten from the same shop that sold bright-green slices of sponge cake, and we've bought a really good barbecued chicken that was displayed alongside goat guts and pig's offal. I love *bobotie*, a South African dish of lightly spiced or curried minced meat baked with an egg custard, which I order whenever it's on the menu, and Neil can't go past his mielie-meal porridge, a taste he developed in boarding school. The staple for most Africans in southern and Central Africa, this is a gruel made from maize meal and it's prepared in basically the same way whichever country you're in. It can be cooked with milk and sugar for breakfast, or made thicker, with water, and served with a little meat if available. Known as *mieliepap* in South Africa, *nshima* in Zambia and *sadza* in Zimbabwe, it's at its best when it's cooked by some old camp cook in the bush on a cold winter's morning. When in camp I've taken to asking for a tour of these bush kitchens and I'm always surprised at how the staff manage without much refrigeration and often just a burner or two for cooking. Sometimes the oven is an old wood-burner, shiny black with boot-polish sitting out in the yard, and sometimes the oven is a hole in the ground with a fire over it. The quality of the baking is extraordinary considering these handicaps, and the beautiful breads and cakes produced wouldn't be out of place in a glossy cookbook.

Lusaka, Zambia's capital, takes a bit of getting used to after being in the bush for many weeks. It's big and cosmopolitan, with a lot of Asians and Middle Easterners, and of course there are the street kids. A million in total we've been told, and nearly all a result of being orphaned through AIDS. The boys at intersections are thin and dirty, and they sniff petrol from Coke bottles and beg for food. They are always grateful if you can give them just a piece of fruit or a biscuit, and their hunger is obvious as the food is gobbled immediately. Every morning we drive past the Manda Hill intersection and notice one particular little boy, matchstick thin and soft-eyed, who always sidles up to the female in a car and takes any opportunity to touch her. Just the soft touch of a hand on her arm, barely there, is what he needs, and we are surprised to see that many ladies allow the contact, perhaps because they are mothers themselves.

Neil says a few words to the boys as he's handing over apples. 'Where do you sleep?'

'In the drain, Sir.'

'Ah-ah-ah, that's not good. Who looks after you?'

'Myself.'

'Do you have any family?'

'These are my family,' said with a nod towards the others. These children are ever polite, with a natural courtesy learnt from a mother with dreams for her young son's future.

A sobering drive is along Leopards Hill Road, past the Lusaka cemetery. Beyond the official denominational sections is field after field of neat rows of fresh mounds, most unmarked and so close together that there's barely space to walk between them. We're told that there is a special place for the young homeless, but we don't have the will to visit.

Each new day is so totally absorbing, and there's so much in Africa that is confronting and different. Our preconceptions and beliefs are continually challenged, sometimes on an hourly basis.

We go to bed some nights and find ourselves wide awake, full of what we have seen and the stories that people have told us, wondering where in all of this is justice and hope. At first I was dismissive of what I took to be Neil's cynicism and we would argue the issues for long sleepless hours. Where I saw a lack of infrastructure, he saw mismanagement; when I praised enterprise, he called it corruption; and when I recoiled at the poverty, he said, 'That's life.' But over the weeks I've come to understand his point of view, his frustration with the disparity between what is and what could have been. I've come to question why quality of life for the majority of the population doesn't appear to improve when the rest of the world gives so much, and I am learning that tribal loyalties are paramount and determine career prospects and government decisions. I'm realising that the complexities go far beyond drought, floods and big brown soulful eyes.

THE LiON KiNG

Driving across to the northern Kafue National Park from Lusaka there's a lot of smoke around and the roadside grass on both sides is often burning, even inside the park border. The ranger we've picked up at the main gate recites the official blurb, that this annual burning in the park is to reduce ticks, minimise the risk of uncontrolled forest fires and to provide green grass for the game. Later on another ranger says that it's been done now for so long that the vegetation and wildlife have adapted, and ecologists have advised the practice should be continued. Each national park really is unique and has its own pulse and rhythm, sometimes obvious and sometimes noticeable in more subtle ways. Kafue encompasses woodlands, forests and grasslands, and is home to a unique species of waterbuck, the defassa, which lacks the white 'follow-me' markings on its rump. We're looking forward to discovering what else this park has to offer over the next ten days.

Kafwala Camp — what a beautiful spot, right on the last section of rapids in the Kafue River. Although the surrounding ground is bare, the vegetation around the river is lush and green, with palm trees and vines, and from the river comes the babble of water and the humphing of hippos. We're met by Levus and Bedson who show us, the only guests, to our *banda* by the river. It's large and whitewashed and basic inside, but is one of those places where you feel at home as soon as you walk in the door. The boys look after the camp as though it were their own home (which it is, as they work six months on then take six months off during the wet season), and when they're not sweeping and cleaning they're providing us with a constant supply of hot water for coffee and for showering. The kitchen is wonderful — a separate spotless little building with blackened fuel stove and hanging utensils, but I don't get a chance to work in it as Bedson takes over and prepares all our meals, even though we're supposed to be self-catering.

Day two in the camp, and Levus and Bedson ask us if we'd like to go fishing. We agree so all of us pile into the Troopy and head downstream to a sandy riverbank a few kilometres away and here Neil and I 'go fishing' like never before. The boys sit us on a log in the shade, make sure we're comfortable then go down to the water's edge and cast a line. We watch, shouting encouragement from time to time while keeping our eyes on the crocs on the bank and the hippos in the water. But we soon get bored and the fish aren't biting so we drive back to camp over hardened, cracked earth with the boys singing and clucking along to Ladysmith Black Mambazo. Levus has an engaging lisp and he promises to find us 'rions, repards and harmress snakes' and he keeps us amused with stories of close calls with wild animals he's had throughout his life. There are many 'ah-ah-ahs' and 'sures' and his voice, usually soft and low, gets louder and more precise with the telling. It's a great gift the Africans have that even someone with simple English can relate the emotion and excitement of an event eloquently and be greatly entertaining at the same time. So often the choice of a simple English word conveys much more than a whole sentence would from a European: Bedson hears leopards *singing* at night, and a wobbly table *dances* on uneven legs.

A strange event. I'm standing on a rock by the river, taking last photos before we leave for the next camp in the park, when I'm alerted by a hoot from a hippo and turn around just in time to see him launch himself into a pool at the top of the rapids. I think he'll surface again in the same place, but suddenly his head pops up halfway down, then again at the bottom of the rocks. He's riding the rapids — when all the books say that hippos like to avoid fast-running water. He pulls himself out onto the rocks, waddles upstream and bombs into the water again. Two mates hang around in the top pool, but they're not going anywhere: they've read the textbooks.

Further north, on the banks of the Lufupa River is Lufupa Camp, which lacks the charm of Kafwala but once again the staff are exceptional. Many have been with the camp for twelve or more years and their knowledge of the wildlife is legendary. Barry, for example, takes us on water cruises up the Lufupa, pointing out birds, water monitors and crocs. He's still enthusiastic after eighteen years and his excited 'Look, Madam!' and 'Look there, Mr Neil!' is contagious. We get very involved in following the progress of a little malachite kingfisher along the river for hundreds of metres, then Barry calls up a fish eagle and chucks little fish into the water for it to grab so that we can get good photos.

The first day is very hot, the first truly hot day we've had. Out on a river cruise the boatman comments on the overcast and steamy weather and senses that rain is not far away. At sundown we sit by the river in deckchairs, feeling clammy and drinking Mosi, and watch lightning on the horizon. The crack and splash of an elephant pushing down trees on the far bank float across and lions call to each other from all around the camp. During the night we lie awake listening to the sounds of elephant, hyena and lion as they wander past. A light shower of rain passes through and we feel the accompanying drop in temperature. The wet season has begun. But next morning the place is dry and it's apparent that what we'd thought was the noise of the rain was just wind in the palm trees.

An evening drive turns into a marathon for Neil. We're on the hunt for lion and leopard, and John, a Lufupa old-timer of 24 years, doggedly tracks and stalks for a long time after we should be heading back to camp. It pays off and we find a big old well-fed lion, padding around his dominion. He has many scars, a Mohawk haircut and dribbles a lot but is literally the king of the jungle, having fought off many contenders in the area over recent years to hold on to his kingdom.

Neil, however, has become impatient during this hide and seek ride in the dark, with visibility limited to the sweep of the spotlight and conversation non-existent in our earnestness to sneak up on our prey. He's favouring a bottle of Mosi by the campfire and a conversation over appetisers with other guests, and he can see the probability of this diminishing by the minute. I, on the other hand, could stay out all night. I'm never happier than when on a game drive; it's one of my favourite things. Moving slowly through a land where everything is new and unfamiliar — the terrain, the trees, the light and the scents on the air — each drive is a journey of discovery where I want to absorb every whisper of a breeze and every rustle of the leaves. I can sit for hours with a clear head, nothing else to distract me from where I am and what I'm seeing. And always, the possibility that something exciting is waiting to surprise me. I suspect that Neil finds it harder to tune out, to let himself become completely absorbed by his surroundings. He likes to be on the move and is restless to see what is just over the hill. Our big plans of sitting in the Troopy at a waterhole for hours, waiting for something wonderful to happen, have never eventuated as Neil starts to twitch and shuffle in his seat after five minutes of no activity. At first I would protest and insist on staying put, but the truth is that I don't mind where I am, whether it be waiting by a waterhole or driving over the next rise. Everywhere in this continent is extra-ordinary and every experience one of wonder.

To deal with Neil's impatience I've come up with an idea that has proved to be brilliant — give him responsibility for one of the cameras. He's never been too interested in taking photos on previous travels; once he's seen the spectacular coastline or that herd of zebra he's ready to move on. But now, mulling over lenses and focusing and framing is a distraction that is turning into an obsession, and Neil's shots of birds in flight in particular are proving to be the highlights of our collection.

Bad directions find us taking a wrong turn and driving right up the centre of the Busanga Plains to get to Kapinga Bush Camp. The track is sometimes pitted with cracked, dry earth and other times it's boggy and soft. It is often barely there and it finally peters out in front of some very glamorous tents, the occupants relaxing on their private terraces and trying to take their midday siesta despite the throaty roar of the Troopy's engine. This must be the glamorous Shumba Bush Camp, built high off the ground on wooden platforms like at Makalolo Plains for the wild-animal-wary Americans. A staff member rushes out and quickly despatches us.

Our destination, Kapinga, is on the edge of the plains and looks out over golden grasslands. The day before we arrived a fire came in from the woodland behind and staff were out all day burning a wide fire break around the camp. Our tent is in a great position: isolated, facing the rising sun in the morning and shaded by large fig trees in the heat of the day. It has a sitting room and a large lounge area outside on the deck, which is where we take our wake-up coffee each morning. The only other guests are two Dutch couples and a friend we made back in the managing company's Vic Falls office. We like having other guests around and find they are nearly always friendly and fun to be with.

On each game drive, our guide Solomon takes us to a different part of this huge floodplain. Once it's to the edge of the swamp where lush green papyrus islands hide the elusive sitatunga, a pretty but very shy small buck. Another drive takes us to grasslands so wide that the horizon shimmers with the promise of elephants and buffalo, but they turn out to be just trees when we get closer. It must be a grand sight to see the area during the rains, with just the occasional island of trees poking up from the floodplain. The park has not been conscientiously managed in the past and local fishermen have been allowed to continue damming the deep channels formed in the wet season to catch catfish. Now they can be seen in the evenings riding their pushbikes over impossible terrain, and there they are again in the background of our best hippo-pool photograph.

Another depressing story of poor management in the past concerns the superbly maned dominant lion, who until recently reigned over one corner of the park. He was often seen at night stalking his territory, confident and stately, or in the midday heat sleeping and sidling around the latest of his conquests. Hunting concessions often border national parks under a government's game-management strategy and these, in theory, protect the park from poachers and village encroachment, which in turn allows for the natural balance of animals to be maintained. But in this case it is thought that the temptation of such a trophy just over the imaginary fence was too great and the lion was either baited into the concession or the hunters came into park territory. Whatever the truth, the old warrior disappeared and shortly afterwards a local taxidermist claimed to have mounted the biggest and most magnificent lion's head he'd seen in many years.

On our final day in camp we're joined by a couple of girls, Beauty and Louise, from management's Lusaka office. It's a big laugh to everyone, including themselves, that they're city girls, scared of the bush, and they sleep with their tent lit up like a Christmas tree. They report every noise they hear and are desperate to spot a lion, never having seen one. Solomon takes us on an afternoon drive but, unbeknown to the girls, it's into the area where we might see sitatungas, something Solomon had promised Neil and me for our last drive. It's marshy and treeless, not an area where lions like to linger. After a few false lion sightings, Beauty draws our attention to something small and shiny in the distance, moving low. Both Solomon and Neil are preoccupied with sitatungas and they dismiss it as a guinea fowl, or a duck, or a terrapin for sure. Looking through his binoculars Solomon goes very still then throws the vehicle into gear and takes off at great speed. We barrel towards the little animal, bumping and bouncing and hanging on for dear life, everyone except Solomon shouting still more unlikely guesses at an identification. Beauty hopes it might be a baby lion. But no, we draw up a few metres away to see that it's a pangolin! Not rare, but rare to see one, let alone find one going about its business in daylight. Protected by beautiful shell-like scales, he chugs along on armoured legs, but at our approach he rolls into a tight impenetrable ball. Solomon has been guiding for twelve years and has never seen a pangolin in all that time.

Before leaving Kafue we stay in a lodge on its northernmost border. Built beside the Lunga River, the chalets are more New South

Wales coastal than African bush, but they have wonderful shaded decks over the water. It is here that I see for the first time the fabulous paradise flycatcher in all his finery, a small russet and deep-blue doll of a bird with foot-long elegant tail feathers and a very pretty crested face. He flits and hovers and darts about the branches, busy catching flies I suppose.

Because of its isolation most guests fly into camp and one morning a very shaken English couple and their pilot arrive. Their plane lost its undercarriage on landing but they managed to walk away unharmed, albeit pale and too traumatised to coherently relate the experience. Weeks later we hear that the plane's still there in the middle of the airstrip waiting for aviation authorities to do their inspection. Because no one can fly in or out due to the plane blocking the runway, the officials haven't come.

Most game activities focus on the river and on one cruise a big tusker enters the water quite near us and begins to swim across. Neil and I are busy taking photos when suddenly our guide revs the outboard and heads straight for the elephant. We swerve this way and that in front of the terrified animal until he turns around mid-stream and heads back to where he came from, his eyes red with fear. Neil and I are very angry; it's the first time we've had a guide teasing the animals just so that we can get good photos and when we return to camp Neil voices his displeasure. But what happened is this: the lodge neighbours a hunting concession and although it's out of the hunting season occasional gunshots had been heard over the past weeks. The elephant was heading straight for concession territory and our guide couldn't bear the thought of this beautiful fellow finding himself behind enemy lines so had scared him away, knowing that he was angering us and, worse, breaking park rules that stipulate no interference with the wildlife.

The way north from the Lunga River is better than expected and we're soon off the bush track and onto a half-decent road. We wave to children and smile at mothers who must be happy for a distraction, as the only vehicles to pass this way are the occasional trucks from a nearby mine. We give a lift to a quiet young girl then pick up a boy, probably no more than sixteen or seventeen. He speaks softly to his fellow hitchhiker but to us he uses a booming voice, clearly articulating every sentence. He's all bravado until he tells us that he's going to the next town to collect documents from a sister then take them to Lusaka where his mother is dying. He is soon to be the guardian of his younger brothers and sisters. His voice is strong but in the rear-view mirror Neil can see two big tears, slow and defiant, roll down his proud, young face. He says that he is expecting his journey to take many days, depending on how long he has to wait between lifts. He can't afford fares, and there are no mini-buses out here anyway.

A woman with a plump baby and a plastic handbag flags us down. She has very little English but after a few minutes of silent rehearsal she taps me on the shoulder and says that the baby is sick and she must take him to hospital. This turns out to be a little community clinic in a village about 15 kilometres down the track. She would have walked the whole way if we'd not come along. When we reach the clinic, Neil gives her some coins, knowing that she will have to pay for any medication. She is overwhelmed and kisses my hand. These people have near to nothing, every day must be a struggle for them, and I can only admire their graciousness and humility in the face of misfortune.

iT'S NEVER AS GOOD THE SECOND TiME

We're heading for the Copperbelt, the industrial heartland of Zambia where Neil's family lived for many years. The area is in the middle of the country, right on the border with the Democratic Republic of Congo (DRC), and I'm keen to see it too, not only to drive the streets of Neil's old memories and walk on the rugby field of his past glories, but to get an inkling of what it would have been like to grow up in such a remote but dynamic place. A white family employed there would have enjoyed a life of some privilege, with the mines looking after their every need, from housing to health to entertainment. The lifestyle would have been light years away from what Neil's father could have expected as an electrician back in the Gorbals of Glasgow, or his mother, a nursing sister, would have found in Cape Town's District Six where she grew up with Malay and Cape Coloured neighbours.

General elections will be taking place in two days time and the streets of Kitwe, the Copperbelt's main town, are full of rallies and vehicles driving around with young men hanging out of them, singing, waving and generally attracting attention. A rally rouser goes past our guesthouse at 4.15 a.m., waking everyone up. I would have thought that this wasn't the way to win friends and influence people but these boys, who are trucked in from all over the country, are earning their keep. We are warned that there could be some unrest after the election results are known and that being in the wrong place at the wrong time might be dangerous. Most shops are preparing to lock down for the day, and even brave George at the Acropolis Taverna contemplates closing early but remains open through popular demand. This restaurant is famous all over the country for the atmosphere as much as for the food, and all sorts of debonair and shady characters come and go the night we have dinner there. There in a booth on the side is a Greek family tucking into mezze, while beside us a local man and his four pretty excited daughters are enjoying Fantas all round. A James Brown character in purple velvet suit, stack-heeled boots and gold Stetson moves about importantly, mustering a handful of scantily dressed girls with heavy make-up and high high heels. I can't quite work out what's going on here, but it sure beats a night out at our local taverna back home.

On election eve we drive into town to draw money from an ATM. These all have long queues of people taking out money — another sign that there is fear of trouble after the votes are counted. Sata, leader of the opposition, is in town electioneering and as he drives slowly past in his motley motorcade I wave enthusiastically. I glance back at Neil who is still in the ATM queue, expecting to see him give me a cynical smirk, but I see that he's deep in discussion with the bemused young black man who's next in line, Neil proudly pointing out the finer points of the Troopy.

On the road to Mufulira, Neil's hometown, we stop to pick up an old lady who's waved us down for a lift. When she sees that we're *wazungu*, whites, she comes over all shy and giggly but clambers aboard when local boys egg her on. By the time we drop her off she's composed herself and gives us what Neil recognises as a very gracious thank you speech in Bemba, the local language.

We stop to recalibrate the GPS, then notice a group of women on the opposite side of the road, big smiles, excited, wanting to include us in their happiness. They cross over to show us their treasures: newborn twins, tiny and wrinkly with eyes tight closed, wearing beautifully hand-knitted white bonnets many sizes too big. It is easy to pick the mother, who looks pale and exhausted.

Beside the road, in a field recently green with maize and cassava, are dozens of freshly dug graves. Many don't have markers but most have a memento of some sort: a little bouquet of plastic flowers, a figure woven from twigs, a toy.

The legacy of AIDS is all around. There's old William, night manager of the guesthouse we're staying in, in his seventies and supporting his eleven grandchildren. Their mothers and fathers, every one of William's children, have succumbed to the disease. The lady who comes in to do the books at the guesthouse has taken in her sister's children; both parents are dead. In the streets of Kitwe, Chingola, Mufulira, directionless men wander and beg. Illness, hunger, and the burden of unsecured work in a mining industry once vital and an economy once stable have left these souls displaced and bewildered. Up here the land itself has been ravished, with vast open-cut mines and mountains of slag big enough to cover whole cities threatening to swallow the sky. For me it's a surreal, unnatural place and I can't dislodge the image of men toiling in an underworld of darkness, the spectre of the Grim Reaper hovering, waiting.

Mufulira is, of course, a disappointment to Neil, who remembers a thriving, prosperous main street and paved roads with manicured lawns in the residential areas. The water in the old municipal swimming pool where he once creamed the opposition in gala races is now scummed and green, but the rugby field is looking both used and well kept. And up at the Top Shops there's the old Nigger's Pub, still alive and well, perhaps not yet caught up with the Independence turn of events.

We leave the Copperbelt and head north to Mutinondo Wilderness, a private reserve on a plateau above the Luangwa escarpment. Owned by Lari and Mike, white Zambians with a great love for this part of the world, Mutinondo is an untouched haven of solitude sitting in between giant granite inselbergs. The reserve is famous amongst birders for the variety of birdlife, and as a result of Lari and Mike's dedicated anti-poaching and conservation stance, wildlife is returning through corridors from the North Luangwa National Park nearby. At present, though, it's still safe to discover the land on foot and to wander the dales, which are reminiscent of English country woodlands. If you ignore the snakes, jackals and bush pigs, that is.

Over a welcome drink Mike mentions that they have other Australian guests, just returned to stay again at a bush camp he's set up for them 5 kilometres or so away. They're very interesting, loners, doing research on sitatungas. Would we like to meet them? Curious, we drive over the following day. The camp is on a lovely site on a rise above the river and is quite established; it even has a kitchen. The Australians are welcoming but reserved at first, and clearly only comfortable with their own company. During the conversation they mention that back home they live on a yacht, which they are progressively sailing around Australia. They like the solitude of the sea and can't see themselves living in suburbia, or anywhere where there are other people for that matter. The previous night they'd arrived at Mutinondo too late to push on to this site, and they'd chosen to camp on the airstrip rather than stay in the formal camping area because there was another tent there. They've been in Zambia for long stretches on and off over the last couple of years and we get the impression that it's more for the solitude than for the research. When we get up to leave there's a tangible sense of relief, and when I say politely that we hope to see them again before we leave, a brief look of alarm crosses their faces.

Mike is able to shed new light on a phenomenon uniquely African — the taboo on washing female undies. Way back in 1974 when I first visited Africa with Neil and we'd stayed with his aunt and uncle in Salisbury, his aunt had urged me to give their houseboy all our laundry *except* my undies. She'd looked embarrassed to me. There was something unspoken going on and I imagined Philip rubbing my Cottontails erotically against his cheek.

Many times since when we've been guests in a lodge or camp there's been a discreet note in the compendium about putting out dirty washing to be laundered, but ladies, not your personals. I came to understand that the men doing the laundry were not to be trusted: they either saw a girl's undies as a sex toy, or, to give them the benefit of the doubt, they were too heavy fisted and my knickers would be returned ragged, no longer delicate.

At breakfast on the first morning at Mutinondo Mike suggests that we get our laundry in early, but please, no ladies' knickers. He explains that his staff, all men, find the undies of female guests disgusting and it is only through great loyalty to Mike and Lari that they even touch the offending articles.

Mike and Lari are the first people Neil really talks to about Itembwe and the problems he sees in tracking it down. Up until now he's mentioned it in passing, a feeler put out when asked about our itinerary and where we are heading to next. But now we are getting close, nudging the perimeter, and it's time to seriously start enquiries and follow leads. Although Lari is a Zambian born and bred she's not been in the north long enough to know old history and old-timers, but she's able to confirm that the names on our list are the right ones to pursue, especially Hazel Powell. Hazel has a guesthouse in Kasama, the largest (indeed only) city in the north, and she's reputed to know personally every white Zambian still in those parts and have an idea of how long they've been there and where they farm. Another recommendation is Mark Harvey, a larger than life character who has a bush camp in the North Luangwa Valley and a guesthouse at Kapishya Hot Springs further north again.

Neil and I retire early for the night, keen to get going the next day. But we're unable to sleep and we sit wrapped in blankets in the bay of our open-on-one-side chalet, watching moonlight and shadows move across the valley outside. The landscape is still and everything is peaceful, apart from a bat flapping about the chalet in a holding pattern, waiting for us to move from his exit. Now that the search for Itembwe is imminent it's occurring to both of us that it's not going to be straightforward; it could easily fall in a heap. The reality of no phone lines or mobile phone coverage is sinking in, and Mike has confirmed that even with satellite communication, connections are intermittent at best. Simply contacting people will be a major hurdle. Neil becomes more unsettled as he picks over the negatives that are now piling up in his mind while I try to find the right words to say that it doesn't matter, that he mustn't forget that it was always about the journey.

On our way to Kapishya Hot Springs, where we hope to find Mark Harvey, we can't resist stopping off at Shiwa House, of

The Africa House fame. Kapishya and Shiwa House are part of the vast Shiwa Ng'andu estate established by Mark's grandfather, Sir Stewart Gore-Browne, whose life in Africa forms the basis for the book. The original magnificent manor house was built, despite countless obstacles, by Sir Stewart and is currently being meticulously restored by Mark's brother Charlie, now lord of the manor. Their parents, Gore-Browne's daughter and son-in-law, were strong and influential opponents to poaching and in 1992 they were both murdered, a crime that has never been resolved.

It's a wonderful sight after driving through the dry, sparsely populated bush of northern Zambia to come across this estate of past grandeur and privilege. To help boost the massive restoration costs it has been re-stocked with wild game and guests pay large sums of money to stay and to hunt here.

As we pull up at the main gates in the Troopy, Charlie is there, about to set off on a hunt. In the back of his open vehicle are a very big mastiff, staff in finely pressed khakis and three fat cigar-sucking Americans looking very impressed by themselves. All except the dog carry guns. They move off in a cloud of importance, the big white hunters eyeing the Troopy with something bordering on distaste — or could it be jealousy?

We arrange to have a guided tour of the public rooms of the manor and before long a very affable young man appears and requests that we walk this way. He shows us the chapel and dining room downstairs, which are wonderful, reminders of times more genteel and refined. The library upstairs is even better: a gentleman's retreat of dark timber, Persian carpets and comfy armchairs presided over by rows of faded volumes and magazines. Our guide becomes more enthusiastic as our interest grows and after I've asked to see the kitchens he decides to give us a special treat. We're shown the private guest rooms and I'm sure the Americans weren't counting on outside visitors when they left their clothes in heaps on the floor and underpants hooked over the back of a chair. I'm embarrassed and suggest that perhaps we shouldn't be wandering through their rooms. Remembering the snooty looks the Troopy received, Neil takes his time and checks out the bathrooms and beautiful timber wardrobes as well.

Kapishya is more down-market, a homely comfortable spot on the curve of a little river where hot springs steam and bubble. We arrive to a jumble of guests, some waiting impatiently to be allotted rooms, others just picnicking on the lawns, there for the afternoon. In the midst of the carry-on is Mark, calm, saronged and barefoot, and as entertaining as we'd been told. He does a bit of shuffling with his bookings and manages a chalet for us for the night, and afterwards we sit with him by the river watching a group of white-clad African nuns picnic. They have a little tape deck and they sing and dance along to some very un-churchlike music. They are from a nearby convent and Mark gives them this day in thanks for their ongoing help in looking after orphans, grieving relatives, anyone in need of solace. Mark is intrigued by Neil's mission but is unfamiliar with any long-term farmers still in the area. He suggests that Paul Nielsen, who has a service station in Mpulungu and, of more relevance, a farm in the general area we're talking about, might well be able to help.

Later I join Mark's cook in the kitchen where I knock up dinner for Neil and myself under her doubting eye. While she goes about preparing a three-course meal for eighteen people and I boil pasta, I learn that she has four children, seven counting her three nephews orphaned after her sister and brother-in-law died from 'the disease'. She says without bitterness or anger that she sees her husband infrequently, him being pre-occupied with a new, younger wife.

In the morning she disapproves of the haphazard way I'm boiling eggs and takes over responsibility for our breakfast, sending me out of the kitchen with a warm comforting arm over my shoulder. I promise to try harder so that I might keep my husband from straying.

Before we leave, a Muslim man who has overheard us talking about contacts in the north hands Neil the business card of a friend of his in Mpulungu whom he feels could be of assistance. It seems that everyone wants to help. Neil is buoyed as much by the leads themselves as he is by people's willingness to give their time and knowledge, and it comes back to him that it was always like this here: people, not always whites, volunteering their help and friendship when you were in need.

It's Sunday when we leave, and as soon as we drive out onto the road heading north we see groups of locals all heading in the same direction, all in their best clothes and every adult clutching a worn-looking Bible. One family waves us down and indicates that they'd like a lift to the church a few kilometres further on. I get out and help them into the backseat and off we set. Around the corner another small group waves and points, so we stop and they also squash into the backseat. We are now eight, counting Neil and me, and we're about to take off when a man with two little girls and a Bible comes down the road towards us, indicating that he'd like to be picked up too. Neil is starting to look alarmed but the others in the backseat are already bunching up to make room, so I jump out again to let these ones in, the man into the back and the girls sitting on my knee in the front. This man speaks good English and tells us they are all very late for church. We ask what time the service starts and he says eleven o'clock. Neil looks at his watch; it's already 11.15 and we've still a way to go. 'It'll be over by the time you get there,' he shouts over his shoulder, speeding up.

'That won't happen, Sir, as I am the minister,' comes the reply.

At the church they all tumble out, the ladies straighten their clothes and the girls curtsey to me. One of the last to leave, a roly-poly toddler, stands supported on his father's knees and very formally leans across to shake Neil's hand.

A PARADiSE AND A PiPEDREAM

Once out on The Great North Road, now not so great as time and traffic have left it pock-marked with potholes, progress is uninterrupted though spasmodic. We make it to Kasama by mid-afternoon and find Hazel Powell at the Thorn Tree Guest House. This is the town where Neil worked his first job in the bank, and as it turns out the Thorn Tree is right across the road from where Neil's accommodation was back then. Hazel and Ewert Powell run the guesthouse like a large family home with relatives, friends and guests all mingling throughout the main house and guest wing in a happy muddle. After a late lunch they take up the Itembwe challenge and out come regional guides and several old survey maps. This is the first time that we've seen Itembwe marked on a map, and even though it's only as an altitude reading, Neil knows that the farm has to be nearby, as this high peak overshadowed the farm and gave it its name. He is beginning to get excited but sees the pitfalls immediately — no roads are marked on the map, and even if there were, which one to take when you don't know your destination? It's becoming a rollercoaster of high hopes and low expectations. The Powells not only give us more names, but also try to make contact with several of the people on their satellite phone. Paul Nielsen's name comes up again, and another hopeful suggestion is a white missionary based in Mbala, the closest town to the farm and where Neil went to school for a while. Hazel reasons that the missionary could have picked up relevant knowledge as he did the rounds of his flock in the outlying areas.

The next day we arrive in the sleepy little town of Mbala, known as Abercorn in colonial days. Now there's not a white face in sight and we draw a blank in our search for the missionary even after a very helpful bank manager 'puts his brain on a rack'. Neil explains our mission to him during the long wait for a traveller's cheque to be cashed. He is very interested and regrets sincerely that he does not know where the farm could be. As an alternative, he asks whether Neil would be interested in buying some fine farming land?

We've just one name left, Paul Nielsen, so it's down into the heat of the rift valley to Mpulungu, 40 kilometres away. This town, on the southern tip of Lake Tanganyika, is Zambia's largest port and the place is bustling with locals, refugees and visitors from other ports in other countries around the lake. We see baskets of fish for sale all along the road and also carried around on the heads of brightly dressed ladies. Accompanying the oppressive heat is the oppressive smell of drying fish, the *kapenta* that are harvested from Africa's inland lakes.

We easily locate the Nielsen's service station but there's bad news: the African staff inform us that Paul has just left and his wife won't be in until the following day at ten o'clock. The Nielsens live on a farm back up the escarpment an hour or so away, and there's no way of contacting them.

We find a decent but neglected 'resort' on the shores of the lake. It's built on a beach made up entirely of smooth rocks and small boulders, and it looks deserted until a couple of pretty sisters appear and rent us a chalet. There are no other guests and there is no food in the restaurant, but in the morning we are woken by a rooster crowing and chooks clucking, and two freshly boiled eggs appear shortly afterwards.

We return to the service station after ten to find that Mrs Nielsen has not turned up, so on the off chance we go down to the lakeside to track down the name on the business card Neil had been given. This man, who owns a *kapenta*-processing factory, is also a Muslim and he appears annoyingly fresh and cool in his long white tunic. He's friendly, interested in our story, but ultimately unable to assist.

Back at the service station, still no Mrs Nielsen. We sit in the car park in the Troopy, with the windows up and the air-con blasting to keep out the heat, petrol fumes and *kapenta* funk while we reassess the situation. The only way forward I can see is if one of the Nielsens turns up in the next couple of days and has some information. Neil has been losing heart with each visit to the service station, and now he voices his concerns. He's frustrated with all the dead ends, he's worried that I am getting bored with the process, it isn't fair to me to be interrupting our journey with this thing that was all about him. But I know him better than that. He's itching to be doing something, going somewhere, anywhere; it's just not in his nature to be hanging around. Every dead end has been bringing us one step closer to the inevitable: we decide to call the search off, with some relief on both sides.

We're on the road back up the escarpment to Mbala when we pass a slightly worn, very old Mercedes coming in the opposite direction, driven by a white woman. This has to be Mrs Nielsen, so we turn around and arrive back at the service station just as she's putting the kettle on. Greetings all round and over a biscuit and a cup of coffee Neil tells Mrs Nielsen, Beryl, of his plight. She is eager to be of assistance and her response to the photos is a positive one. She thinks that her husband might know the whereabouts of Itembwe, so why don't we go up to their farm and ask him? When we express doubts about finding their place she volunteers a staff member to show the way. So it's back up the escarpment, turn right onto the main road, left at the second dirt road and drop off the employee at the corner to catch a bus back down. We drive along a deeply channelled road until we get to the Nielsens' track. Ten minutes later we see the farm and there's a man working on machinery in the barn: Paul Nielsen. Neil produces the photos and Paul, still with a hint of Danish heritage in his speech, says, 'Yes, I know where that place is.'

And he knows this because some years ago he helped a neighbour to salvage the verandah columns from the falling-down Itembwe farmhouse and they used them to build a rather grand carport at the neighbour's homestead. Paul downs tools, produces coffee and maps, then declares that he will show us the way. But there's no hurry, he says. 'Come and look around my farm first.' The tour ends at a chicken coop in which a couple of surprisingly calm chickens share space with a beautifully marked, very fat Gaboon viper. Paul gazes at him proudly and it's pretty obvious that this was all Paul wanted us to see in the first place.

We drive along overgrown tracks for an hour, then two, past abandoned broad-acre fields and through *mopane* woodlands brilliant in russet and bronze. The elephant grass gets higher and bare rock faces loom on both sides, overshadowing the Troopy's path. Neil is sceptical; he can't get his bearings until we come to a natural spring feeding a ribbon of dense green undergrowth, and a large cave up in the cliffs to our right. We are now very close, as this is the spring that supplied Itembwe with water, and Neil is fingering a blurred photo of the family sitting in the mouth of the cave. Now we get out of the Troopy and proceed on foot, and Paul is as excited as Neil is when we eventually elbow through tall grasses to stand on the overgrown remains of a house. Brick buttresses stand like sentries guarding the gaping cellar where sunflower seeds were once stored, but apart from them everything else has been swallowed by vines and bush. All that is left of the garage is the grease pit; the maize fields have long ago reverted to bushland; and someone since has planted an avenue of tall eucalypts along the original driveway — but this is undoubtedly Itembwe. Neil wanders about, kicking through rubble, trying to trace the outline of foundations and looking for anything recognisable wrapped in the undergrowth. I can see that he isn't sad but very pleased, and content too. The excitement of finally finding the place, this phantom from his childhood, is proving far greater than any nostalgia for a lost past. We wander down to the old orchard where apple and almond trees are even now flowering white and pink, and look back up the quiet African valley. It got the better of the Glynn family and has proved to be too much for everyone ever since.

On the way out Paul fills Neil in on the more recent history of the area and the irony of the tale makes Neil laugh. After Independence all the farmland up here was progressively taken over by blacks. The whites had proved that cattle ranching wasn't viable so the government hatched a bold plan to clear thousands of acres for broad-acre agriculture which would supply the whole central

African region with wheat. One fellow in particular, a government minister, had knowledge of this, so through manipulation and trickery he acquired huge tracts of land, Itembwe included. Unfortunately for him he was assassinated by someone even more corrupt. His wife inherited the land and it had lain forgotten and neglected ever since, slowly reverting to the original bush. She's had it on the market for some years, and it is this that the bank manager in Mbala had innocently offered to sell to Neil.

Paul takes us on a detour to an abandoned homestead where the only construction to survive the ravages of neglect and pilfering is a stone carport, handsomely supported by six white columns standing straight and true — and they look just as smart as they did in the photos of the old Itembwe house. When we return Paul to his Gaboon viper and say our goodbyes it's like leaving an old friend. His generosity has made the mission possible, but most of all he has shared in the dream. Neil will be forever grateful to him and feel a little guilty as well, because Paul had smashed a new pair of reading glasses in his eagerness to unfold maps for our search.

I'm not surprised when Neil suggests that we head for Tanzania the next day. He has put his memories to rest, achieved his intent, and as usual he's greedy for new places, new horizons. He drives back to Mbala full of tales from Itembwe days, but by the time we get there he is making plans for the weeks to come.

The accommodation options in Mbala are limited and it is getting very late, so we decide to return to Mpulungu for the night. By now the road down is familiar, and the entertaining conversation of an old *medula* who hitches a lift makes the ride seem shorter than it is. When we'd been speaking to him, the *kapenta* factory owner had recommended a hotel by the lake and now we drive in with high expectations. The black manager and her young son look after us well, but the executive *banda* we're allotted, not quite completed, is more like a prison cell, with bare cement walls and bars on the windows. Just as well we're still in good spirits after the success of our day. We're told that there is a little cottage made out of beer bottles we can move to, but apparently that is hotter and darker, the builders not yet having figured out how to construct decent windows without the bottles crashing down. In the evening the kitchen ladies cook us a good dinner but the next morning, after a troublesome night's sleep in the cell, Neil is grumpy and takes exception to the leather-hard fried eggs Evangelica serves up. He says they are terrible. She says they are well cooked. He says that even he could do better. She says that she'd like to see him try. They are both having a wonderful time, then Evangelica challenges Neil to a competition, a fry-off with me as judge as long as I don't let my faithfulness to my husband cause the clouds to fall on my choice. To this end Evangelica stipulates that they will send out the eggs anonymously, and soon after Neil and she have disappeared into the kitchen two plates of fried eggs arrive in front of me. One looks like a greasy car crash, no different to Evangelica's first offering, while the second has two perfectly fried soft yolks smiling up from just-set whites. I declare it a tie.

NGORONGORO WiTHOUT THE CRATER

The border crossing into Tanzania at Kasesya presents a problem. This is not really a town at all, more an outpost where chickens scratch around a few simple dwellings and the inhabitants are all immigration or customs officials. They would only see ten to twelve tourists a week, and in the wet season none at all because the through-road becomes impassable. When we arrive the immigration officer who should have been manning his post has headed off to Mbala, many kilometres away, and has taken his entry and exit stamps with him. He could be back tomorrow. Or Sunday. Why don't we go to Mbala, find him and bring him and his stamp back in our LandCruiser, the customs official asks. Even he can see the pitfalls in that idea, so very agreeably takes us through the big gate to the Tanzanian side, where he explains our situation to the officials manning the post there. On his way back through the gate the Zambian asks us shyly if we could spare a book or a magazine. He has a hunger for reading and in this remote part of the world the only book available to him has been a Bible, which he's read over and over again. I give him some novels and a map, and he's over the moon. At least he'll be able to find his way out of there should the isolation become too much to bear.

Now on the Tanzanian side, we respectfully listen to a little lecture from the immigration officer on the problems of leaving a country unofficially, as opposed to illegally. The subtlety is beyond me but we thank him profusely when he at last stamps our passports.

I feel buoyant, raring to go, and Neil is whistling a little tune as he recalibrates the GPS with one hand and tries to keep the Troopy on the road with the other. Itembwe has been found and left behind and now we have before us new adventures in unfamiliar places. Neil had only been north of Zambia once, and that was the time 30 years ago when the two of us travelled south from Nairobi. Already the potholed roads, the denuded landscape, even the dwellings in the villages are different to anything we've come across so far on this trip, and soon we'll be meeting Africans of different ethnicity to those encountered already. We're anticipating a language problem too, as Swahili is the official and also most widely spoken language in Tanzania and Kenya, and although we remember that it was easy to learn, general conversation in the places we will be passing through could well be reduced to monosyllables. Now we can't wait to be a part of it, and head northward with that old sense of excitement bubbling around us and making us impatient to reach Sumbawanga, a regional centre where we hope to find accommodation for the night.

Well the road, a major route linking the south and north of western Tanzania, is one of the worst we've travelled on. It's so washed away in parts and the corrugations so deep that we progress in fits and starts. The only other vehicles we come across are the occasional local mini buses, with people hanging out the windows and bikes and chickens and relatives tied on the top. They wave and give the Troopy the thumbs-up, and we wave and smile proudly. The road passes through small, neat villages but mostly we are alone in this forgotten corner of the world.

At the reception desk of the Moravian Conference Centre in Sumbawanga we're told that all hotel rooms are taken, something that we should have worked out for ourselves when we saw the large number of new white church-insigniaed Land Rovers crammed into the car park. The only other choice in town is the Mbizi Forest Hotel, a hotel for locals located in a back street, and said to be quiet by African standards. Having two whites turn up in a big expensive vehicle sends the staff into a dither and we're treated with great respect. This must be how Stanley felt when he landed at Ujiji. Our incredibly cheap spotless room has an en-suite and a TV, and the bright face of a giant panda smiling up at us from a garish red and yellow blanket. There is also a sign behind the door saying that two adult males are not permitted to sleep in one single bed, which creates some disquiet in Neil.

The next morning we drive on into Katavi National Park with no bookings and no clear directions. The rangers at the park gate tell us we'll find a couple of lodges if we drive past the river full of hippos, turn next right then next right again, and 'Oh yes, keep your windows up — tsetse flies.' We'd passed many dark blue and black flags strung out beside the road on the way in and the rangers inform us that these are tsetse fly traps. Sprayed with something fatally attractive to the flies they're very successful as long as they remain seductively open and the rangers remember to keep up the spraying.

We brazenly drive right into Foxes Katavi Wilderness Camp and ask for a bed. They just happen to have four of their five tents unoccupied so we're in, and by the time Manie, the manager, returns from a game drive Neil and I have unpacked, had lunch and are sitting in big comfy armchairs with a glass of chilled white wine. We've also become acquainted with Freddy, a lone adolescent elephant with an identity crisis who wanders into camp at the same time every afternoon and hides motionless behind the tents if anyone inadvertently comes too close.

The camp is positioned on the edge of the woodland, looking out over a broad yellow grass plain. Just a kilometre or so away is a dry riverbed with five springs spread along its course, and it's here that the animals come in the dry season to drink. In the mornings we set off in the safari vehicle with Manie, drive by long migrating herds of buffalo and zebra on the plain, then along the riverbed past loping families of giraffe, hippos by the hundreds, topi with babies, crocodiles in caves and lions on heat. It is the Serengeti without the crowds, Ngorongoro without the crater. This is what people were talking about when they spoke in hushed awe of Katavi. Because of its isolation no one we'd spoken to had actually visited the park themselves, but everyone seemed to know its reputation and what it was capable of delivering to anyone determined enough to get there.

I love staying in national parks and in tented camps in particular. You can lie in bed with all the sounds of the bush around you, and go on game drives where you never know what's around the corner. Like on the first morning out with Manie, we did just drive around a corner and there was a hippo walking towards us on the track, almost totally covered with oxpeckers. He looked like one of those little porcupine cakes from childhood birthday parties.

So much is different here in Africa; sometimes I can't believe what we accept as normal now compared with life back home. Bad instant coffee, mozzie bites all over us, and Nivea cream instead of Dior. We're still living in the same changes of clothes that we've been carrying in a tote bag since Botswana, and we've been brushing our teeth without toothpaste for more than a week. Neil says the real test will be when I can go for a week without washing my hair — little does he know.

We find the road north from Katavi even worse than the one out of Sumbawanga and it takes us more than eight hours to travel the 300 kilometres or so to Kigoma. This is a prosperous-looking town with an interesting history. For centuries it was the main port for shipping salt from the nearby salt mines to the Congo and further inland. Then, during the slave trade, it was a stopping-off centre on the route eastward to the coast. In the early 1990s the immediate area was inundated by 500 000 Rwandan refugees, and following that, populated by almost as many United Nations officials, personnel from NGOs and associated agencies, and various hangers-on.

The Troopy is lost on the streets amid a convention of white Toyota LandCruisers bearing aid insignia and driven by earnest Europeans. It's surprising that more English isn't spoken. As it is we're struggling to be understood. Earlier when English failed, Neil could get by with the little Bemba he could remember from his youth, but here we are both often at a loss. There's an elaborately courteous procedure when you first greet someone, even if it's just asking directions or sitting down in a restaurant.

'Good morning.'
'Good morning.'
'How are you?'
'Thank you. I'm well. And you?'

'I'm well thank you.'

'How was your journey?'

'Good. Thank you.'

'*Karibu*. Welcome.'

'Thank you. *Karibu*.'

Neil can never quite master the pace or the formality. 'Hey, is this the road to Kigoma?'

Pause.

'KIGOMA!'

Exasperated pause.

'K-I-G-O-M-A. Kigoma. Yes, yes, I'm well. Good morning and thank you. Now which way is Kigoma?'

Yesterday we accidentally tore the solar panel off the roof of the Troopy. We were heading down a steep drive into the grounds of a restaurant someone had recommended when there was a crash, a crunch, and we were jammed underneath the covered portico. Neil reversed out but that was our undoing. The solar panel suddenly flew off and landed in the grass beside us, the glass completely shattered. We chucked it out but kept the roof racks thinking that we might be able to exchange them for favours somewhere along the track.

Inside the rather grand building we were shown to the restaurant, no more than a café really, with formica tables and plastic ornaments from China. The staff seemed a bit nervous and we couldn't work out if it was because we were whites or because of the other guests, a government official and a high-ranking army officer with their gun-carrying bodyguards. The menu was a mixed bag and I ordered spring rolls, and Neil a chicken curry. My chair faced the kitchen and through a hatch I watched impressed while the cook methodically made paper-fine spring-roll pastry from scratch. Neil's choice may have been a mistake. First, a kitchenhand walked past holding a live chicken by the legs, there was a dull thud, a quickly terminated squawk, then the kitchenhand sat on a stone and expertly plucked off the feathers. We waited over an hour for the meal to be served but it was worth it, particularly when the waiter asked Neil how the chicken was and he replied, 'Frightened.' Even the general laughed.

We've chosen to stay at the Hilltop Hotel, which is perched on a cliff a couple of kilometres out of Kigoma. The owners also have a tented camp in Gombe Stream National Park to the north of the town, and another one in Mahale Mountains National Park about 150 kilometres to the south, both on the shores of Lake Tanganyika. Gombe Stream is the chimpanzee sanctuary made famous by Jane Goodall, while Mahale is reputed to be one of the most beautiful national parks in Africa, as well as being home to eight species of primate, including a large number of habituated chimps who have been gradually exposed to humans over a number of years, so that they become accustomed to us and tolerate our presence. Neil and I want to visit Mahale and the plan is to travel there on the MV *Liemba*, a steamer that plies the eastern shore of Lake Tanganyika between Kigoma and Mpulungu in Zambia. This voyage is one that Neil has always dreamed of doing. Thirty years ago when we were in Tanzania we were told that the *Liemba* was unavailable as it was being used to train insurgents for water-based combat, but Neil suspected that the real story was that they'd just run out of spare parts. Either way, the ferry wasn't running and we couldn't get a seat on the train to Kigoma from Dar es Salaam anyway, so the plan was shelved. Now we're hitting more obstacles, as the *Liemba*'s once-a-week schedule means that the voyage to Mahale is not practical. This is probably why most park visitors fly in. We ask about charter flights.

'Yes certainly, Sir, that'll be US$1200 each.'

'Okay, how about the private launch you advertise?'

'Of course, Sir. That'll be US$800 each, each way.'

These figures seem to be plucked out of the air and vary depending on who we speak to or the time of day. We're also hampered by the fact that it's Ramadan and the hotel owners are Muslim. Management appears only intermittently, the travel office is closed and we have to rely on reception staff receiving direction from a higher power in Arusha. After two or three days of investigating different alternatives and being stonkered at every turn, Neil is happy to forget Mahale and move on; there'll be other opportunities to observe chimps and other national parks of spectacular soaring scenery.

But before we leave town there are two things that we want to do: visit the spot at Ujiji where Stanley came ashore to greet Livingstone, and go down to the port to at least look at the *Liemba*, the apple of Neil's childhood eye.

Historically, Ujiji was Tanzania's key port before Kigoma eclipsed it early in the twentieth century, when the Germans made it an administrative centre for the region. It's only 6 kilometres away but the step back in time is a giant one. A colourful, languid sort of place now, it doesn't seem to feel the need for signage and it takes us some time to find the turn-off down to the Livingstone museum. The Troopy has a job to negotiate the narrow laneways, dodging chickens, children and deep rain-gorged ruts, but we're eventually directed to a neat museum complex standing near the water's edge. An immaculately dressed caretaker presents himself and proceeds to show us around the museum, with its gorgeously garish papier-mâché Livingstone and Stanley, larger than life-size. Then he takes us to the monument erected under the same mango tree which shaded the famous 'Dr Livingstone, I presume?' scene.

Our guide's spiel about this famous exchange is delivered with enthusiasm, and we find it both informative and interesting — and certainly undeserving of the mocking description in the guidebook we carry, even though our guide does seem to get personally involved in the saga as it enfolds.

Back at the wharf, Neil chats up the Port Authority official, telling him how happy he, Neil, would be if he could get a good look at the grand old lady of the lake.

'Come with me, Sir, and we'll see.'

We're ushered through old tin gates and cargo yards, and suddenly there in front of our eyes is this wonderful, rusty and listing vessel, straining under the weight of hundreds of tonnes of mielie-meal and great lengths of timber and steel. The mielie-meal explains the odd get-up of the piece workers bowed low under the bags of flour — they are wearing ladies' skirts and blouses, which must protect them from the flour that coats their shoulders and legs. Some of these labourers are mere boys and some are wiry old-timers, and they're all glistening from the exertion and the heat. More are hanging about in the background, clutching blouses, hopeful of getting a little work in a gang. The captain appears, a straight-backed man with skin the colour and sheen of melted couverture chocolate, and after formal introductions he invites us aboard. Neil is looking like a boy in a toy shop. To get aboard we must walk on a narrow plank, literally the gangplank, which the labourers are jogging across with tremendous balance considering the weight on their shoulders. The captain is proud of his charge and shows us everything, from the little first-class cabin on the upper deck to the dark, airless and sweltering hold of third class, with its crude wooden benches and even cruder toilet facilities. I don't say it, but I'm glad that we're not travelling on her, as the crush of passengers and cargo when fully loaded must be oppressive.

At four o'clock, the official departure time, we settle onto the Hilltop's terrace with a supply of newspapers and magazines and wait for the *Liemba* to sail out of the harbour. We've almost given up when, just before eight, she appears low in the water around the point and makes her slow, glorious way across the bay. As a breeze picks up and the evening settles, she sails off into the dark red sunset.

Meals at the Hilltop are always interesting. Most of the guests appear to be civil servants and aid officials who walk importantly about, attend meetings and sit down to government-sponsored buffets in the colonial-style restaurant. These are sober affairs though, as the hotel is teetotal due to the religion of the owners. A few other tourists pass through and sometimes we sit talking with them over coffee. One young Belgian couple is overlanding like us, but in the opposite direction. When Neil asks about the condition of the roads in Uganda the girl pales and whispers something to her partner, who has better English.

'Oh,' he says, 'the roads are drivable, but my girlfriend is still shaken by what we came upon on the road which passes by a corner of the Queen Elizabeth National Park.' It appears there was a tumult of people blocking the way, noticeably distressed but strangely quiet. As he edged his vehicle past slowly they could see on the road blood, torn clothing, a leg with a shoe still on it. A policeman waved them on but not before explaining that a labourer, a member of a work team that was repairing the road, had been taken by a lone male lion some hours before. The other men had run away in fear, and the lion had dragged the bulk of his meal off into the undergrowth but had then left it there for reasons unknown and disappeared into the bush as silently as he'd arrived.

It's six days since we first checked in and the Hilltop Hotel can't believe that we're finally leaving. They haven't made out our bill just in case we tell them, as we have every day since arriving, that we want to stay one more day. But here we are packed up and ready to go. The staff have washed the Troopy and filled it with diesel, and we're handed a boxed lunch as a goodbye gesture. Then, as we're about to drive off, they warn us one last time of the dangers we can expect when travelling in Rwanda.

We had thought hard and long about visiting Rwanda. We'd read as much as we could find on its current status and our first inclination had been to leave it off the itinerary. Apart from the safety issue, there wasn't anything or any place that we really wanted to see there, or not enough to put ourselves at risk for anyway. We had no real desire to witness the misery left by the genocide in 1994, and we knew that roaming bands of displaced militia ambushed tourists from time to time and still carried out acts of great cruelty against innocent villagers in outlying areas. Perhaps we were lulled into a false sense of security by the success of our progress to date, but as we drew closer and saw on the map that there is a great shortcut to Uganda's south-west through Rwanda we began to think 'What the heck, let's take that route. We'll stick to the main road and see a little of the country as well as saving a day or two's driving.' By the time we got to Kigoma the decision had been made and we were now looking forward to seeing a little of this troubled country.

A WiNG AND A PRAYER

Despite the terrible road we make good time. There aren't so many villages now but we pass a number of huge, sterile refugee camps behind razor-wire fences. We pull over for lunch in a forest and are immediately overcome by flies. Not tsetses but some other sort of insistent gadfly with sticky inclinations and designs on our chicken sandwiches. Although we haven't seen another vehicle for hours, now a mini bus comes bumping past and the occupants wave and laugh among themselves at these crazy *wazungus* trying to eat lunch under a blanket of dust and flies.

Buoyed by our progress to this point we decide to push on into Rwanda and aim for Kigali, the capital. Thirty kilometres or so before the border we pick up a hitchhiker, Gerry, an African American who's been travelling around Central and East Africa for over a year. He's tall and thin and dressed like a local, and I think he might be a fugitive from justice back home. Neil thinks that he's probably just a fugitive from his mother, a gospel-singing missionary. Softly spoken at first, Gerry's accent becomes more hokey as he gets more deeply involved in discussions with Neil about George Bush, Iraq, the Rwandan genocide and how being black in a black country has its disadvantages. Still on the Tanzanian side we are stopped at a roadblock and approached by police. They suggest that we might like an armed escort to the border as bandits have been active on the next section of road, but Gerry whispers *no, not any more*. We decline the offer and drive off, Neil muttering that the only bandits around here are the police who are less concerned for our safety than making a buck in their self-appointed role as security escorts.

The border post straddles the Kagera River at Rusumo Falls. These impressive falls plunge down a steep, deep ravine and carry a huge volume of water even at this dry time of year, and I want to get a better look. So while Gerry chats to acquaintances at immigration and Neil goes over the Troopy's *carnet* with the Rwandan authorities, I walk back to the bridge, guidebook in hand. This bridge reads prominently in recent history as it was across its uneven planks that hundreds of thousands of refugees fled from the Rwandan genocide. In one 24-hour period alone it's estimated that 250 000 people crossed while below them massacred bodies tossed and tumbled over the falls.

Before we drop Gerry off at a cheap doss house on the outskirts of Kigali he gives us tips about the city, which is just as well because it's night-time and we're driving with no maps, no street lights and no idea where we're going. We're also driving on the right-hand side of the road but our headlights are positioned for left-hand driving, so we blind on-coming traffic and they beep and flash their lights constantly. We don't know where we are or where we want to be and we're regretting our earlier decision to push on to Kigali. Just as we were warned, the city is very hilly and the roads winding; none of them seems to go in a straight line so we end up going through the same roundabout several times, in different directions. The GPS has thrown its hands in the air and Neil and I are both privately starting to worry whether we'll ever find our way out of the roundabout, let alone locate a hotel. Optimistically we stop at an ATM to withdraw cash and a young man there whom Neil gets talking to kindly drives to a hotel with us following in the Troopy. The feeling of relief when we turn a corner and see the grand entrance gates to the Hôtel des Mille Collines is great. I would have checked in even if it was the most expensive place in Africa, and Neil says afterwards that he was prepared to take the presidential suite if that was the only room available. The hotel doesn't quite match up to its entrance but it serves us well. We have dinner by the pool, jostling for elbowroom with NGO personnel, journalists and well-dressed, important-looking Africans. It is only weeks later that we're told that the Mille Collines is *the* Hotel Rwanda.

The next day we head for the Ugandan border, and the countryside surrounding the road is breathtaking: steep green hills and narrow fertile valleys, both totally covered by a network of farmed terraces and fields. In the muddy riverbeds we see men, covered in mud themselves, panning for gold, and we remember that Gerry had told us this was becoming a huge environmental and health problem in Rwanda as the gold-diggers use mercury and arsenic in the processing. There are bananas and cabbages, rice fields and tea plantations, and everywhere people look to be doing something. Everyone waves and when we stop to take photos I'm surrounded by hopeful subjects in no time, young boys with slow smiles. I can sense a prevailing feeling of incomprehension but there is no sign of the troubled young souls who apparently wandered the streets just a few years ago, lost and afraid in a world they no longer understood. It's impossible for us to comprehend the horror that many of these people must have lived through, the fear and loss, then disbelief at surviving a world gone mad. From what I can see now, driving along this main road, there's a sense of purpose, of moving on. People are picking tea, hoeing terraces and planting vegetables, and we pass through a big market town which is jumping with activity. I see optimism, but an underlying sadness in many eyes as well. There's evidence of international aid wherever we look; every project we pass is proudly signed as aid-funded and any other vehicle on the road not carrying tourists belongs to an overseas aid agency. The rest of the world has picked up the pieces, but the Rwandans are slowly putting them together again.

In contrast, Uganda feels relaxed and comfortable, and the pace is slower. Perhaps it's the proliferation of gum trees, a legacy of some well-meaning agencies in the past who thought that eucalypts would quickly cover the hills stripped bare for firewood. Or it could be that we're driving on the left-hand side again and signs are in English. Whatever it is, we immediately feel that we're in familiar territory.

Our first stop, Kabale, proves to be more than just another scruffy African town and it gives us our first taste of Ugandan hospitality. The lovely smiling gentleman behind the counter at the Uganda Wildlife Authority office takes many minutes to explain directions and road conditions to our next destination, and comes outside to wave us goodbye when we leave him. But that's nothing compared with the proprietor of a bookshop who, unable to supply us with a map, takes us under his wing. He leaves his store unattended and leads us around all the other shops in

Kabale where we might be able to purchase one. He's very disappointed when no one can provide the map we need and apologises profusely.

We drive on to Lake Bunyonyi and choose a place on the shore to stay until our first bookings in Bwindi Impenetrable Forest start in three days' time. The lake is very beautiful, surrounded by terraced green hills and dotted with green islands. These have also been planted with eucalypts, and one particular island has Australian wattles, melaleucas and Norfolk pines as well.

The first afternoon there are a few big drops of rain, nothing more than a sun-shower. The temperature drops but we put this down to the altitude. The second afternoon brings our first true afternoon downpour. Lasting for fifteen minutes or so, it greys out the sky and silences the birds. Then it stops as quickly as it began and the goats start to bleat, the birds resume chirping and the lake's surface settles to mirror a blue sky once again.

There's a small village, a homestead really, on the hill behind us which is populated only by women — who have been abandoned by their husbands or run away from dreadful marriages — and their children. These women built and decorated all the houses themselves and reputedly allow just one man in, someone they've employed to do any heavy labour. Every morning the ladies can be seen bent over the gardens, weeding and gossiping, and every afternoon disjointed rehearsals of 'Don't Cry for Me, Argentina' drift down from their church.

It's Sunday and we sit on the terrace with other travellers discussing what we've seen and what we've heard. Stories of overcrowded orphanages in Rwanda, murdered national park rangers in the Congo and bodies by the road in Uganda. From the ladies in the church drifts their slow sad song and when they reach the line 'So I chose freedom' all of us on the terrace, even the staff, stop and fall silent, so moving is this simple reminder of hope and injustice and the ongoing menaces of the region.

Neil and I have long discussions about the position that the average black African finds himself in, and more specifically, how we feel about their situation. I'm acutely aware of the disparity as we drive along in our fancy car jammed full of clothes and food and consumer goods, dispensing waves like royalty and leaving a dust trail so thick that pedestrians are forced off the road. I'm embarrassed when we pass people in the rain, moving through life soaked to the skin, while we debate whether we want to give a lift to someone who might leave a puddle on the floor. But I drive right past all the time back home; I don't feel responsible for anyone there. I have no problem being called *ma'am* in a shop in Sydney, but feel uncomfortable with being addressed as *mummy* here. Both are terms of respect, so am I being over sensitive? I say no, because at home if I met another person in the street, I wouldn't expect to be called *ma'am*.

Neil looks at it with an academic eye. Realistically, he says he sees no reason for whites now to feel guilt for the sins of their forefathers or angst for anyone who might be living in circumstances different to their own. He's right of course, but not all of us have the advantage of experience here. His argument is one borne of an acceptance of the situation, for as a young boy he would have been desensitised by the attitudes of the adults at that time. There's also a degree of anger in his assessment, a feeling of opportunity lost. He only ever lived in a white British Africa and it's obvious to him that now in those countries the fundamentals of roads, education and health are in poor shape. He's had a glimpse of what could have been, and is disappointed and blameful because it's been lost. We find it hard to reach common ground and argue this topic endlessly.

We've sat at dinner and had to listen to a middle-aged white male talk loudly about 'these bastards running the country' and 'the lazy nig-nogs' on his farm; presumably the waiter who has just carried out an intelligent conversation with him is not only invisible but also deaf. However, it seems to me that this type of racism is dying out and the children of those who practised it in the past come from an altogether different place. I can't think of a single young white African we've come across on this trip who's spoken disparagingly to or about black Africans, and at last there seems to be an acceptance that the biggest difference between black and white is a cultural one. Neil suggests that this attitude occurs only because young whites have learnt to be politically correct, but I'm convinced it's more than that. The ones who have chosen to stay in Zambia, Zimbabwe or South Africa are living in a different world, certainly an imperfect one, where cronyism and corruption live alongside another kind of racism, but it's their world. As one young white girl in South Africa said to us, 'Sure we have big problems, but we're all part of the solution.'

We set out on a minor route that passes through the eastern sector of Bwindi Impenetrable Forest. What a name! It conjures up failed expeditions and dark forbidden secrets, and throws down a challenge to those brave enough to breach its boundary. The road is narrow and winding, and the scenery spectacular. We stop to take photos of the border line between cleared, terraced farm lands and the dense green rainforest of the national park; a more obvious sign of human needs fighting against human ideals would be hard to find. First a family of olive baboons, the alpha male with a long, flowing coat and all of them huge and skittish, crosses the road, then later a troupe of blue monkeys follows suit. Neil has to stop the car to let a beautiful giant green chameleon with pointed horns and the most dramatic, curled tail creep cautiously across.

A short, sharp downpour in the afternoon causes us to pull over and sit it out, and we have to concede that from now on these rains will be a daily occurrence and camping is out. A relieved smile crosses Neil's face.

THE PLEASURE OF THEiR COMPANY

Bwindi Impenetrable National Park is home to half the world's population of mountain gorillas, and three habituated families can be visited from Buhoma, a small settlement straddling the park border. We have booked three days' accommodation in town, hoping that we'll be able to pick up gorilla tracking permits at short notice for one of the days.

We arrive at Buhoma late in the day. The village has a number of gorilla curio shops, gorilla rest houses and even a gorilla orphan centre for human orphans, but it still manages to present a laid-back face, unaffected by tourism. The next morning we front up to the Uganda Wildlife Authority's office early and yes, there are two cancellations for the day's gorilla tracking. And even better, the vacancies are for the R group, the gorilla family that usually hangs out closest to the town and which will require much less strenuous trekking.

We have our packed lunch, binoculars and bottled water in backpacks but these are carried for us by porters. There are also trained guides and armed rangers in our little platoon, as we are dangerously close to the Congo border where poachers and rebels have been known to murder the innocent. We set off up a vehicle track into the forest, everyone excited and chattering about fitness levels and camera settings. Neil and I wave to the staff as we pass our guesthouse and they call out, 'Good luck, good luck, Mr Neil!'

At first it's not quite the slipping and sliding that we'd anticipated but it's not long before we veer off into the forest and start climbing. In single file now and with the rangers protecting our rear we follow a rough track of damp leaves and not much sunlight. It becomes very steep and one girl loses a zip-on leg of her trousers while another lifts her T-shirt to fight off red ants. Talking has stopped. I have a strong young porter who takes my hand and pulls me up the slippery muddy bits. The head guide is in radio contact with the trackers who have gone out at first light, and after 45 minutes he turns to inform us matter-of-factly that the gorillas have been located and they're just ahead. We take a last drink of water, disentangle our cameras and leave everything else behind with the porters. We climb up one last rise and there in front of us are two fluffy little black balls wrestling and squealing and rolling all over the others. Over there is a mother gently cradling her baby, gazing into its eyes, and with infinite care picking a twig from its scrunched-up little face. To the left, sitting happily against a tree is the silverback. We're all momentarily taken aback by the ordinariness of it all. A family in their leafy living room, having a nibble, scratching bellies, farting occasionally. They've allowed us to share their morning, and it's only later that we understand what a great privilege that is.

Getting to Ishasha Gate in the south-west of Queen Elizabeth National Park from Buhoma should be straightforward but we misinterpret directions, head back towards Kabale, have a fight about it, and then finally find ourselves on the right track.

Lush low forest lines the road as we near the park and baboons lounge about on the road and all over the verges. As soon as we turn into Ishasha Gate we see that here is something different to any park we've experienced so far. Big herds of antelope, such as Ugandan kob and topi, and buffalo and zebra are all grazing on green rolling hills that are more Switzerland in summer than winter in Africa. It looks so domesticated that we have to remind ourselves that we've come here to see tree-climbing lions.

The camp we've booked into is on the banks of a small river and we arrive to the busy sound of water flowing quickly around bends and over rocks. We're greeted by Nathan, who is tall and has a gentle smile. He shows us around and we discover that some of the water music is coming from a tree overhanging the river. It's heavy with hundreds of weavers' nests, the busy buttercup birds noisy with importance as they fuss with home renovations.

Nathan is easy company and he laughs when he hears that on our way in we've driven right under the lions' preferred tree for resting in. His colleague had just radioed in to say that two lionesses had been spotted heading for the tree about 40 minutes ago. We would have seen them, if only we'd looked up.

We settle into camp routine quickly and decide that here is where we want to stay for a few days. The road network throughout the reserve is extensive, and unlike those in some parks we've been to, it covers the best parts. After an initial recce with a park ranger we take off early each day in the Troopy, searching high and low for those lions. Some drives take us through green grassy fields of wildflowers and once we come out on the banks of the Ishasha

River, the border with the Congo. We watch dismayed as two beautiful big tuskers pad across the river towards an uncertain future, as gunshots are often heard coming from the bush on the other side.

Every afternoon at siesta time the sky clouds over, a strong wind whooshes through and then heavy rain pelts down, so much of it that trying to focus on the next tent is like looking at it in a shower-fogged mirror. It's exciting yet also peaceful to sit in our tent and watch all that commotion outside, knowing that in a few minutes it'll be over, calm will return and the weavers will be singing again.

It is here at Ishasha that we meet David, who is to become the guiding light for the Kenyan leg of our journey. He is a senior guide with Abercrombie & Kent in Nairobi and we very soon get the feeling that he loves safariing and the African landscape as much as we do, and that his special places would be ours. I give him a few guidelines and before we've left Uganda David has put together an itinerary that we would never have thought to follow if left to our own devices.

We leave for the Mweya Peninsula, the hub of tourism for the park's north, on a road that bisects the national park. No one has mentioned the road much except to say that it is used by large trucks transporting goods between Uganda and the Congo, and that after rain it can sometimes be tricky. A mild warning compared with those given about most other roads, and besides, we've already driven on part of it when we visited a fishing village days earlier. Initially it's okay, the main obstacle being large families of baboons using it as a private sitting room. The afternoon rainstorms seem not to have affected it much, we mention in passing to each other as we tootle along. Two-thirds of the way into the trip ruts start to appear in the road, and the black cotton soil it's composed of looks more and more like wet and shiny playdough. The ruts inevitably get deeper, we get slower, and the treads of our tyres fill with the dense squelchy cotton soil, making them no better than bald. Then in slow motion we slide off towards the bank, tipped precariously at 45 degrees. Luckily, the bank is high and we come to rest against it before we can topple over onto our side. Through some pretty crafty driving on Neil's part we manage to reverse out and crab along for a bit in the right direction. Bang, we slide and drop into the ruts almost up to the dif, but the Troopy is still moving in a forward direction and we progress along these upside-down railway tracks until we reach dryer ground. A convoy of trucks approaches from the other direction and it's just good fortune that we didn't meet them earlier on. Neil is decidedly calm and from this moment on he and the Troopy can do no wrong, such a good team are they.

Every second person who's been to Uganda has spoken to us of Ndali Lodge with great fondness. It sits high and precarious on the lip of a deep lake in an extinct volcanic crater, and its rose- and lavender-filled cottage gardens mirror the comfy ambience inside. A slightly crazy place in an oddball English sort of way, with chipped, mismatched crockery and house dogs sleeping under coffee tables. Our cottage porch looks out on a peaceful, dreamy landscape over more volcanic lakes to the cloud-covered Ruwenzori Mountains, the Mountains of the Moon. The latches on the doors in our room are handmade, carved in the shape of wild animals, and the beds are canopied with bright Moroccan blankets.

There's an interesting group staying at the lodge: a South African travel agent and his charges, an elderly couple whose eccentricities are right at home in Ndali, and a retired doctor and his mates. At dinner the conversation turns to malaria and the pros and cons of taking anti-malarials, and the others are interested in what Neil and I have decided on in light of our travelling for such a long time. We'd been loath to cart around a year's supply of tablets — for two of us they would have occupied a drawful of precious space, and the cost would have been exorbitant. However, before we'd left home we'd heard from contacts in Zambia that there is a very effective and cheap treatment available in southern Africa, but in case we couldn't source this miracle cure when we needed it we carried a good supply of Lariam, which can be used as a cure as well as a preventative. We're pleased to hear that our dinner companion, the doctor, agrees with this decision. But he adds, looking pointedly at my bare arms and Neil's shorts, that prevention is the thing. So long as we're diligent with applying a strong mozzie repellent and covering up before the sun goes down we should be fine.

Dinner is over and we're saying our goodnights when the travel agent sidles up to Neil. He's *very* interested in the Troopy, he says. He'd been looking it over earlier on and wonders if we'd ever consider selling when we finish with it. Yes? He slips a card into Neil's hand, leans in close and whispers out of the side of his mouth that he'd appreciate first option.

To access Kibale National Park, where we hope to track chimpanzees, we've booked into a tented camp nearby. It's situated on the edge of a forest and the access road passes right by a village school. The track's surface is so muddy and slippery that the Troopy slides out alarmingly at 90 degrees, first missing a parent unlucky enough to have just walked out the gate, then a tree, then a fence post — all to the glee of the pupils craning out of the glassless windows. For the next two days, every time we drive past the school we run the gauntlet of this tricky track and the kids laugh and wave every time, those in the yard running over to the fence when they hear us approaching, and stray dogs, keen to join this carnivalé, running along beside us and yelping and nipping at the Troopy's wheels.

We've been forewarned about the rather poor state of the accommodation at the camp. It is under-funded and neglected by the owners we've heard, the tents small, too close to the ground and too dark, and nearly always wet. Well, the tents are a bit mouldy and the bedding damp, and the lack of running water means that the staff have to carry over buckets of hot and cold water for washing, but their warmth and friendliness is genuine and the cook's efforts to feed us big, filling meals with limited ingredients are heroic, and when the dramatically coated black-and-white colobus monkeys move into the canopy above the camp, the waiters fetch us from our tent to watch — 'Quickly mummy, they are here!' — and at dusk the garden boy continually re-positions our deck chairs so that we can follow the path of the rising moon.

After the ease with which we got to see the gorillas we anticipate a similar smooth run when booking for the chimpanzees in Kibale. We drive straight in to park headquarters, confident that we'll be able to go chimp tracking the next morning. So we're a little put out when the ranger informs us that the morning is already fully booked. He's sympathetic and radios the head ranger but, no, they have a big group from Norway booked in and Norwegians always turn up. We reluctantly book for the afternoon group but, everyone knows that chimps, even habituated ones, are more active in the morning and easier for the rangers to locate. The head ranger gives us permission to be there in the morning anyway, on the unlikely off-chance that the Norwegians let themselves down.

We wake up late to a wet morning but the staff bustle about to get us to the park in time. They're as excited about our chimping expedition as we are, and they've prepared a hearty breakfast and send us off with a packed lunch. But as we get closer to park headquarters the rain gets heavier and by the time we arrive we've decided that it's too miserable to be trekking through the forest. Instead we go on a long drive, mainly to fill in time until our afternoon booking but also to eat the packed lunch so that we don't disappoint the kitchen.

After a couple of hours it's stopped raining and the sun has come out. At the agreed time we roll up to the assembly point in the heart of the forest to register and meet our guide. This is Gerard, a slight, wiry man who looks to be in his thirties but turns out to be as old as me. He has bright eyes and an efficient manner and is at first reserved and untalkative. The reason for this emerges when we are told that we're the only people booked in — good news for us but it means meagre tips for Gerard.

We set off at a pace through thick bush, with Gerard stopping only to tell us the dos and don'ts of tracking. It's very muddy underfoot but not steep, and it's oddly quiet. Every now and then we stop to listen and then from deep in the forest comes a haunting hooting call, followed by the frenzied drumbeat of hands against a hollow buttress. Now we move even more quickly; the lone calls are sounding louder and closer and Gerard shows us knuckle prints in the mud. He signals for Neil and me to stay put, then he disappears into thick bush for a minute before coming out with a finger to his lips. We follow gingerly, trying not to make a noise but desperate to keep up. He turns around and points to a tree just ahead: a largish male chimp sits propped against its base, watching us. Then bedlam. It's like we've walked into a battlefield, with deafening screams and hoots all around us, while the trees shake and leaves and urine rain down. Gerard is calm and smiling, pointing up into the trees. Look there, and up there, and just right here. There are at least 30 of them: testosterone-fuelled males chasing accommodating females; bulky chesty youths lobbing sticks at each other; and adolescents stretched out along branches, yawning and scratching. A youngster swings down on a liana, curious to get a better look at us. It's such a thrill to be here, just the three of us with this big happy family. Neil and I take photos of each other with smiles from ear to ear. Gerard lets us stay for well over the allotted time and we only head back once the troupe starts to move off themselves, the boom boom booming of the buttress drums becoming fainter and fainter.

Gerard is much chattier on the return and he points out delicate luminous flowers like shiny silver cachous, and fungi with lacy cream caps. He shows us fresh footprints of the elusive forest elephants and for a while we track them, but have to turn back when the ground becomes too boggy and the forest too thick for the inappropriately dressed Glynns. As we walk along Neil talks to Gerard, and once he's learnt that we aren't wealthy American doctors with a big house and many cars he relaxes and they establish a cautious rapport. We learn that his wife and family live in a village in the south of the country and he finds this separation very stressful. He longs for the day when he can work close to his family but is torn by the need to earn enough money to support them. When Neil tells him that that is a universal problem, that many husbands in other countries are taken away from their family by their work and find it difficult, Gerard is sceptical. I start to tell him about the time that Neil worked in another city during the week and I would only see him on Saturday and Sunday, but it becomes too involved in the telling. We get back to base and when we say our goodbyes Neil gives Gerard a hefty tip, but he's embarrassed by it and goes quiet. I whisper to Neil that maybe it isn't enough, but no, Gerard indicates that he is grateful. Not for the first time we've not appreciated the difference between a working relationship and friendship, and while a tip is expected in the first instance, it is insulting in the second.

On the drive back to camp Neil asks me what I was getting at when I referred to his working stint in Melbourne. We've never discussed it, not the impact of it, except early on when we agreed that it was necessary, good for his career. I was happy for him because he was happy, and there was a tacit understanding that there was also an ego thing happening. To ride a taxi to the airport every Monday morning and breakfast in the Qantas Lounge with all the executives in their power ties before jetting off to hotels where they greeted you by name and boardrooms where what you said counted. So we talk about it now. I remember Friday nights when Neil arrived home grumpy and too tired to listen to anything other than the TV. He remembers coming home to me chattering on about insignificant events and people he didn't remember. I felt that he wasn't interested in my week, and he felt that I didn't understand his. Social life was reduced to Saturday night and the rest of the weekend was filled with Neil sleeping and me doing a week's worth of washing. On both sides was a feeling of detachment, that the weekend would be over and on Monday morning we could each get back to our week. The fact that friends were doing the same thing seemed to validate it for a time, but we couldn't or wouldn't acknowledge the truth that the partnership was operating as two sole traders. Then one fine day it was taken out of our hands when Neil's presence in Melbourne was no longer needed and he could work out of Sydney again. We went on holidays, came back and, without us knowing it, life returned to normal.

Back in camp we continue to click with the staff and by now we're being treated like part of their close family. I get lost in the intricacies of making bread-and-butter pudding with the lovely old cook, while Neil has long complicated conversations with the young night guard about their hopes and fears for Uganda's future. When Neil suggests to him that it is up to everybody, but particularly people like him, to make their homeland great once more, he replies softly that not everyone has the wings to fly.

The morning we leave camp it's overcast and drizzly, but the entire staff put on sparkling white uniforms and line up to shake our hands and wish us a safe journey. We're very moved and I'm close to tears as we take off, the old chef crouching down low so that we can see him in the side mirrors as we drive away, waving madly and blowing kisses.

THE GOOD OLD DAYS

We need to visit Uganda's capital, Kampala, to have the Troopy serviced and to pay for the next leg of our trip. Those in the know have warned us about the unruly population and the congestion on the streets so we've decided to arrive on a Sunday when the crowds will be less. This would have to be one of our biggest mistakes. How were we to know that Sunday is the day to stock up on provisions, visit relatives, take the donkey cart out for a spin? We have a map but this is useless when streets aren't marked and they're blocked to view anyway by the sheer mass of humanity. We head in the general direction of the city centre, but progress is thwarted by pedestrians on the road and broken-down buses. For minutes at a time we don't move at all, then inch forward only to realise that we've just passed a possible route of escape. Three hours after hitting the outskirts of town we emerge on the other side and vote unanimously that this is our least favourite city of the trip.

Thirty-five kilometres away on the shores of Lake Victoria is Entebbe, an altogether different place. Although the capital's airport is here, the town is much smaller than Kampala and quite intimate in comparison. It has few crowds and big, well-tended houses surround the town. This is where diplomats and the wealthy reside, and a number of international-standard hotels dot the lake's shoreline. We choose one of these and it's not long before we're out by the pool with a tall drink, observing the spoilt carryings-on of expat children. The hotel's fine but the staff are unsmiling and surly, the first time we've come across this in Africa. It's either the result of pandering to all those loud and demanding Europeans or, more likely, they're left over from a time when Ugandan hotels were government run.

Refreshed and refuelled, we're on the road north to the famous Murchison Falls National Park. It's Uganda's largest protected area and in the '60s it was crammed to overflowing with huge herds of game. Then came Idi Amin, and his ban on tourists combined with uncontrolled poaching started the decimation of the wildlife. After he was ousted things got worse, and the animals in the park were killed for rations by first the military then bands of guerrillas. There was little left. But political stability brought a change in the park's fortunes and since the early '90s animal populations have been steadily building. We've been told that the journey is worth it for the falls and the Victoria Nile alone, so even the presence of the murderous Joseph Kony and his Lord's Resistance Army to the north of the park is not going to put us off.

We stop for lunch in Masindi, a market town en route to the national park, and as we're getting back into the Troopy we see a funny thing: maybe twenty or thirty well-dressed men, marching in a group down the main street. They all seem quite happy and acknowledge us with a smile, and I'm sure they would wave too if only they weren't linked together with shiny steel handcuffs and surrounded by armed guards.

We have booked to stay in a hotel that borders Murchison Falls National Park and sits on the banks of the Victoria section of the White Nile — the far bank. This presents a problem as the ferry that connects the park to the rest of the world is out of action: both engines are kaput, having had no care or maintenance. There is another way to get our vehicle into the park, tantalisingly just a few hundred metres across the water, but that's to drive right out and around and enter from the north, a half-day's drive through land held by the Lord's Resistance Army. We choose to cross the river in a little barge and rather churlishly decline a hotel game drive because the price, instead of being reduced to accommodate hapless tourists like us, has been put up to take advantage of a captive market.

Instead we take a boat upstream to the base of the Murchison Falls themselves. Although the falls have been renamed and are officially the Kabalega Falls now, everyone, including the locals, can't seem to lose the more history-laden name and our boat captain continually refers to them as 'the Murchisonis'. They're spectacular: the water explodes through a narrow cutting in the rocks above into a swirling dangerous basin below, and I've read that in his heyday Amin threw his enemies from the top into this deadly whirlpool. Now, the boat manoeuvres up close to the bank where many very large crocodiles are asleep on the sand, dreaming of the good old Amin days.

The next day we move to a more atmospheric lodge back on the southern side of the river. We have a little isolated chalet built over the water and it has a deck and a good amount of wildlife of its own. Only once before have I seen so many geckos under one roof and that was during a plague of flying ants. Bats fly in at night if we leave the front flap open and bright orange-and-blue *agama* lizards hide in our towels and under the mat. Out on the deck we sit and watch clumps of water hyacinth float past while hippos snuffle around in the long grass on the far bank like giant shiny slugs. Droppings from one of the geckos in the eaves above land on my shoulder, and Neil juggles a little handful of stones to pelt at the monkeys when they get too close to our drying laundry.

It's very humid here but luckily storms pass through daily, giving us a brief reprieve. One night a ferocious wind comes up, along with great flares of lightning and rolling, rumbling thunder. The wind blows furniture off the deck, collapses our mosquito net inside, and causes waves to break on the Nile in front of our chalet. It stops as quickly as it started, leaving behind a dead calm, and torches go on in neighbouring chalets as everyone is up with the wonder of it all. Then the wind is heard rushing our way again bringing with it a short sharp downpour of rain before it's finally gone for good, and we all go back to sleep.

Another guest, a Belgian, invites us to join him on a mini safari and early one morning we set off in a dinghy to look for a shoebill in the papyrus islands, but it's to no avail. This large stork-like bird is not so much shy as hard to find in the tall reedy swamplands they inhabit in Zambia, Uganda and Sudan. These swamps are, by their very nature, largely inaccessible, but we thought we were in with a chance here on the Nile, poking around the shirt-tails of papyrus reached easily by boat. Photos in the lodge prove that shoebills are out there somewhere and show just how strange and unique these birds are. The body is impressive, with artistically arranged grey feathers that become darker and larger towards the upper back, but the head is what makes this one of the most sought-after birds in Africa: a stumpy topknot of feathers on a sleek neck, and a heavy bulky bill, broader than the head itself. The *sabotier* the Belgian calls it, 'the clog wearer'.

Next is a game drive in the national park, but this gets off to a bad start when the driver dropping us at the barrage, where we're to catch a boat across the river, locks his keys in the car. He finds a short length of wire and tries to open a window — no luck. Our host puts his weight into breaking a seal — still nothing doing. Another driver sidles over and tries his luck, then someone wanders down from the sidelines with suggestions. Neil gives it a try and someone else offers advice, and before long there's a clutch of earnest faces all hovering about the vehicle, giving their opinion, trying to pop the lock. I step back to take a photo and have to laugh at this scene of twelve wise men, well intentioned but, unfortunately for us, all bloody useless.

We eventually get the door open so feel free to leave the driver with his charge and cross the river to the park. Our little safari collects a ranger and a guide and sets out, but very soon it's stopped by a large herd of elephants blocking the road. We pull up and the tourists among us take many photos of the family grazing, a big bull calling the shots. Then suddenly the Belgian drops his camera bag and it hits the decks with a loud crack. The elephants freeze, the bull bellows and they all turn and run away in panic. They're trampling over bushes and fallen logs, mothers are covering younger ones who squeal and bump into each other, and the patriarch, still bellowing, herds his family into the safety of the trees before they can be shot. The guide with us is very distressed and explains that this terrified reaction is still instinctive for some animals in the park, many decades after the wholesale slaughter of wildlife has stopped.

All in all Uganda has been a surprise, as my idea of Africa is still brown dry plains with the occasional waterhole and concentrations of plains animals always dusty and thirsty. Here it is green, green, green with lush vegetation and planted fields everywhere. And it's always mountainous, or at least hilly. Just as everyone told us, we've found Ugandans to be friendly and smiling (Entebbe hotel staff aside); even women wave as we drive past. If we stop to ask directions the Troopy is engulfed in willing guides and there's usually one who offers to come with us to show the way.

Lake Albert lies to the west of Murchison Falls National Park, where it forms part of the border with the DRC. We're told that the road running alongside it is particularly scenic so we decide to return to Entebbe via the lake, just an extra three hours or so added to the trip. The road from the park to the lake's shore is okay and passes through rich agricultural plots with strip villages and muddy, closed shopfronts. The surface is unpaved of course, but we've come to prefer this to a tarmac road booby-trapped with potholes and warped bitumen. We come upon a large herd of thin, lacklustre cattle lying on the road. Neil slows the Troopy to a crawl and, as he's previously done when confronted with similar bovine roadblocks, rolls slowly towards them, expecting them to stand and wander off the road. But these ones are slow to move; they don't seem to register that a large heavy vehicle is edging to within an ear's flick of them, and the nearest one soon disappears from view below the sight-line of the Troopy's bonnet. 'They'll move in a sec,' I confidently predict, as Neil keeps the Troopy rolling forward and revs the engine. It isn't until we feel resistance, then a definite 'bump bump' the size of a skinny leg, that we understand that these cows, either through disease or pig-headedness, are not going to budge. Neil admits defeat and skirts around them through a field of dry, dying maize.

The old port of Butiaba is pretty and flat and its roadsides are covered in flowering wild impatiens. This was once an important trade centre but its fame now comes from the fact that it's the place where Ernest Hemingway crashed in a light aircraft for a second time in this part of Uganda, suffering injuries from which he never fully recovered. Neil and I wander over to the wreck of an old cargo vessel, stranded on a shore of pink and white impatiens and abandoned machinery, then we come upon a sandy beach covered in mauve and lilac mother-of-pearl shells. My friend Elaine would have a field day here — and I am momentarily homesick for the days when she and I would potter along beaches in search of the perfect shell.

Heading towards Masindi the road passes through a beautiful forest, and as we drive slowly through it with the windows down, listening for monkeys and birdlife, an odd thing occurs. A guy on a motorbike comes carefully toward us, balancing on the pillion seat a wrapped-up parcel that is clearly a body. It has a blanket tied around it, and its bindings keep it in a semi-seated position. It's strapped on tight but still rolls from side to side in a parody of the bogeyman at the Luna Park ghost train.

There are much more pleasing sights awaiting us on this road. We first caught a glimpse of a great blue turaco when we were in Bwindi Impenetrable Forest and it immediately went on our list of must-see birds. An elegant and slightly exotic bird with rich blue-green plumage and a crest like a legionnaire's helmet, it's let down only by its uninspiring call. Everywhere we've gone subsequently has promised plenty of turacos, but they've always seemed to elude us ... until now. On Masindi road a great blue turaco flies matter-of-factly across our path, so low and slow that we think the Troopy could hit it, and so close that we can see the red tip on its bill. That is rewarding enough, but shortly afterwards the crimson crest and wings of the darker, more glamorous Ross's turaco drift towards our windscreen like a re-run in slow motion. Neil brakes and swerves, and it flies on past without altering its flight pattern by so much as a centimetre.

We're back in Entebbe and although the planned sightseeing has been curtailed by the need to finalise forward bookings and have the Troopy serviced, we take the time to visit the Uganda Wildlife Education Centre, formerly Entebbe Zoo. This is primarily to see shoebills, as we've realised that the chances of seeing them in the wild are becoming slimmer by the minute. We arrive at the centre just as a group of very cute young school children are leaving. One little girl, about five or six and all togged out in a uniform of blue pleated skirt, white Bermuda socks and blouse with an attached pretend blue tie, leaves the others. She has a big smile on her face and many beads in her hair and she walks straight up to Neil and softly rubs his forearm up and down. A teacher calls her away and she moves off, still smiling, and we can only think that she was intrigued by the golden hairs on Neil's arms.

We feel more comfortable being in Entebbe this time. Not only did we take the drive back through Kampala traffic in our stride, but subsequent shopping trips into the city centre mean that we are now comfortable on the roads and can negotiate them like residents. We've chosen to stay in a different hotel, this one with friendly, helpful staff and tortoises in the courtyard. A general air of progress prevails even though it's in the midst of major renovations. Some locals tell the story of one party of guests finding themselves roomless because the builders, in an uncharacteristic fervour of activity, had demolished eight rooms more than they should have.

In the evening a young boy from housekeeping and a supervisor knock on the door and ask if we'd like turn-down service and the room sprayed against insects. I say yes and the obliging young man sprays Doom in all the corners, turns down the bed and fixes a faulty lamp as well. No more than five minutes later there's another knock on the door and the same team from housekeeping ask if I'd like the room sprayed and turn-down service. I laugh but they're straight faced so I can only assume that I've sadly reached the age where all white females look the same.

Jinja is to be our next port of call, a stopover on the drive to Sipi Falls over by the Kenyan border. Driving out on the Entebbe–Kampala road — now so familiar that we notice what's going on around us — we're struck by the great number of aid projects. Roads, schools, children's homes, craft centres and agricultural ventures: every second sign seems to be announcing the financial support of one overseas agency or another. We become so engrossed in these signs — how many there are, how much money is being spent and which countries are most involved–that we're on the outskirts of Jinja, 80 kilometres away, before we know it.

GOODBYE AND WELCOME

Jinja is a great little town, dilapidated and poorly maintained as most Ugandan towns are, but with wide streets of solid colonial buildings and well-kept double-storeyed houses. The long main street is lined with old verandahed shops reminiscent of a colonial country town in Australia, and this impression is further enforced by a small community of Australian expats. The guesthouse we stay in overnight is owned by Australians, and Ozzie's Café in town is run by a wily old bird from New South Wales. She has been in Uganda for twenty years and, in her words, is carrying on a love/hate relationship with the country she's wound up in. Underneath her tough façade lies a generous heart, as she's fostered many orphaned children and hopes to take her adopted daughter, now a teenager, to Australia for 'a trial run' as soon as she can muster up the dough.

Jinja lies on the northern shoreline of Lake Victoria at the mouth of the Victoria Nile, and here can be found the official source of the Nile, or more specifically, the source of the White Nile. The natural landmark of the Rippon Falls is now underwater, owing to the construction of a dam upriver in the early 1950s, but the site is marked and has a lovely park on the east bank where local sweethearts wander secretly arm-in-arm and souvenir sellers mope hopefully about. Even though I realise that this one spot can't possibly be the sole source of the famous river, it is still a thrill to be looking out over water that will eventually flow into the Mediterranean Sea, more than 6000 kilometres away.

Roadside signs heading out of Jinja suggest that the number of aid agencies could be eclipsed by the number of churches. These, spun from more local roots, come with inspirational names: there's the Hell Fire Gospel Church, God's Herbal and AIDS Ministry, and the one I'd like to belong to, the True Vine Church. Passenger coaches are also christened with imaginative names that are emblazoned in big bright printing across their brows. Most — like 'Victory is Mine', 'Red Eagle First Class' and 'Linear Express' — are designed to engender confidence in the brave souls who venture on board, so we have to look twice when 'White Cock' comes hurtling towards us. I suggest that it could be named after the owner's pride and joy, the king of his henhouse, but Neil thinks it could be a racist slur.

At Sipi Falls Rest Camp we're introduced to Nelly, a local girl who takes us on walks around the many waterfalls and through the town. She is earning money to complete secondary school, and then she hopes to win a scholarship to go to university. In her opinion the people who earn the most money are lawyers, doctors and those who work for the Revenue Department, and one of these careers is her goal. She greets many town folk along the way and we're struck by the courteous manner in which she speaks to everyone, whether they are wearing neat Western attire or dressed literally in rags. Some encounters are polite and brief, others are more lengthy, flirtatious, but all involve a handshake, an arm around a waist or just a light linking of fingers. Neil is surprised that, while growing up in Africa, he never noticed how tactile African society is and this leads him to realise that there is most certainly a lot more that he just didn't see. It makes him uncomfortable to think that he lived his young life disinterested in another society that was trying to survive alongside his relatively privileged one.

The only other guest at the camp is a woman from the German Consulate who is involved in the design and implementation of aid programs financed from Germany. She has a positive outlook for Uganda's future, seeing a curb on corruption as overseas loan bodies insist on transparent auditing. But it's got a way to go yet, judging by the unfortunate situation she's found herself in.

Her job requires her to work side by side with local authorities in distributing aid money and overseeing projects, and she believed that the German government had finally established a situation in Uganda where funds it provided were being effectively funnelled to their intended cause. Her thirtieth birthday was looming, and family and friends back home had been asking her what she would like as a present. She suggested that a small donation from each of them would finance a new school building and they happily agreed, so she confidently collected their money and got the school project underway. She used the now-established line of command and worked with trusted officials, doing everything just the same as if she were operating in an official capacity. But the money went missing. No one seemed to know where it was or who had it when, and she was too embarrassed to tell the folk back home that she had lost the loot.

We leave Uganda with mixed feelings. Neil loves the place, its greenness, its generosity and its history. I find that I'm looking forward to crossing into Kenya and can only put this down to wanting to get back to the dry brown landscapes of my mind's Africa. It isn't that I don't like Uganda — who couldn't, with its beautiful scenery and wonderful people? — it's more a pull to move on.

At the quiet Malaba border post the chief immigration officer invites us into his neat but shabby office and asks us if we've found Uganda to our liking. Thinking that this is some sort of test we have to pass before he'll stamp our passports, we voice all the right praise and nod enthusiastically. He shakes his head sadly and begins to tell us of the problems he sees facing his country. Neil is the first to twig that this is not an official interrogation but a social visit, and before long the two of them are discussing the present and future state of the nation. The chief gets around to mentioning that he wants to develop a resort at Sipi Falls, would we be interested in investing in it? 'No? Just thought I'd ask.' Some time later we get up to leave and our new friend farewells us as if Neil were his brother going off to war. He shakes our hands more than once and we drive off past him standing in his doorway, waving. *Bye bye wuzungus! Kwaheri, kwaheri karibu.* Goodbye, goodbye and welcome.

Our first stop in Kenya is in the lush Kakamega Forest, where we stay at Rondo Retreat, a calming and peaceful place of green lawns, cream cottages and towering trees. It is run by the Trinity Fellowship, a Christian society committed to conservation, and has a very English feel. There are wide verandahs with chintz furnishings, and landscaped gardens, and the overall effect is one of understated civility. It is a birders Mecca and visitors are here either for the birdlife or on retreat, as the name suggests. The forest is incorporated in a national reserve and has an enviable diversity of flora and fauna, as well as its important bird population. The figures are amazing for such a relatively small tract of land: there are 400 different butterflies, seven primate species and 27 species of snake. We stay for two days and luckily encounter none of the latter on our long walks through the forest, but do notch up 32 types of butterfly.

Then it's on to Ruma National Park, in the far south-western corner of Kenya, which has been recently re-established to protect the only population of roan antelope in the country. Financed by overseas loans, the park is surrounded by a fancy new fence and has modern offices and very keen staff. It's a pity that the funding didn't extend to improving the gravel approach road, which is so potholed that we move at a crawl, but the internal tracks are good and well maintained. We've heard rumours that the park has a problem with poachers as it is surrounded on all sides by villages, and there's an incongruous bicycle track running inside one border which locals use as a short-cut to get from place to place.

We're directed to Oribi Guesthouse, a park rest house that has had a facelift too thanks to the influx of funds. It's bright but basic and perched on a ridge overlooking the Lambwe Valley in which the park sits. The view is wonderful and the cottage attendant welcoming, and we've just unpacked when there's a knock on the door and two friendly faces peer in. Here are the park warden and a minister from the local church, and they've popped around to say hello. We sit in the lounge room exchanging pleasantries, admiring the view, praising the virtues of the new park. Neil is sending me eye messages — what are they doing here? Do they want a donation? — but after a polite period of time they leave with a friendly cheery-bye and the attendant informs us shyly that perhaps they just wanted a cup of tea.

At dusk we sit on the terrace and watch the sun go down behind the last of the afternoon's storm clouds, and in the failing light try hard to spot the handsomely horned roan antelope on the valley floor below. We eat and read by lamplight and go to bed early. We're both fast asleep but wake with a start when car doors slam, followed by agitated voices just outside our cottage. Neil peers out through the curtains and sees lights shining on shadowy figures down in the garden. It's got to be poachers caught red-handed so he throws on some clothes, grabs a torch and bursts out of our front door to join the action. I stay in bed under the protection of the mosquito net. In no time things go quiet and the vehicles drive off, and Neil returns with the news that it was just the warden and staff with a visiting expert inspecting the outflow from our troubled septic tank.

Game drives in the Troopy over the next two days reveal plenty of giraffe, waterbuck and locals on bikes, and of course there's the protected roan antelope, looking content and unconcerned about their uniqueness. With big ears, strong horns and short, stiff manes running down their solid necks, their most distinguishing feature is a startling bandit-mask face of black and white. The warden had told us of the paradox which confronts park management: to attract more visitors it should have large predators like lions, but with these the roan population would quickly diminish, negating the reason for the park in the first place. As it is, it's an attractive and well-stocked park, but 24 hours is enough to see everything it currently has to offer.

The drive from the border through the far north-west of Tanzania is breathtakingly spectacular and it makes us wonder why this part of the world is ignored in travel itineraries and guidebooks. The road is excellent by African standards and not very busy, and when we cross the Mara River we know we're within braying distance of the Serengeti. This is confirmed when quite bizarrely we see zebras and wildebeest grazing to our left, while goats and cattle wander around on the other side of the road. The number of dead dogs left on the road is a little disconcerting, but more worrying is the unconscious body of a young man lying with his bloodied head and upper body in the way of oncoming traffic and surrounded by others who are pointedly ignoring him. Why hasn't someone dragged him off into the gutter for safety? Has he been left there as a sort of punishment because he was drunk, or a thief? We don't find out the answer to his predicament but we do learn the reason for the preponderance of dogs — the locals like to keep them to protect their stock from hyenas.

We spend a couple of nights in Speke Bay Lodge on the banks of Lake Victoria. If we were to swim 250 kilometres due west across the lake from here, we'd land very close to the hotel we stayed at in Entebbe. Instead we take a boat trip to the nearest village and under a blue, blue sky three young men, boys really, row and sing as they knock their oars on the side of the boat in a slow, hypnotic drumbeat. At the village a little girl latches onto my finger with a tight lobster grip and proudly leads me around the compound, showing me off to her friends. They gather around to have their photos taken and out from a *banda* trots a little chubby toddler to join them, round happy face covered with the remains of a mielie-meal lunch. The other kids join Neil and me as we have a good laugh at his appearance and an older boy tells him good-naturedly to go home and wash his face if he wants to have his photo taken. He's reluctant to leave but, intimidated by our amusement and the older boy's authority, he walks off, stiff with embarrassment, chin on his chest and bandy legs dragging in the dust. He doesn't appear again until we're being rowed away, then we see him on the shore with his face slightly cleaner than before, now with the telltale smears of mielie-meal all over the tails of his tatty T-shirt. He has tried his best, but by now our cameras are packed away.

THE CiRCLE OF LiFE

With English silver on the table and wood panelling in the tents, Kirawira Tented Camp in the Western Serengeti gives us the impression that we're on safari with the Prince of Wales. The pre–World War I one. The staff seem a little bewildered that we've turned up in the Troopy but I suppose that most of their guests arrive by private plane. However, they put a brave face on it and give us a prime tent perched on a rocky outcrop looking out over forest and plain, and northward as far as the Grumeti River. At dawn I'm up just in time to watch a family of elephants trudge single file back into the trees through a dreamlike misty rain. It's a quiet and peaceful place, but this could be because we are the only guests.

A ranger is organised to guide us on an afternoon game drive, and we've been out for only 30 minutes or so when the light drizzle turns into a solid downpour. Thinking of the Troopy, Neil wants to turn back. I want to continue so that I can see what animals do when it's raining, and the ranger wants a drive in a big powerful vehicle so we press on. With no English, just hand signals to direct us, the ranger takes us down gullies of wet black cotton soil and up steep slippery banks, past giraffe standing stoically and bedraggled, baboons looking miserable. At one point he opens the door, jumps out and disappears from view, and we can't see what's going on through the fogged windows and beating windscreen wipers. Then he returns with a prize: a large leopard tortoise for me to photograph.

Driving eastward from Kirawira through the Serengeti's western corridor we see some wonderful sights. Two giraffes gracefully, hypnotically entwine legs and necks in a courting ritual so erotically choreographed that I believe I can hear Ravel's *Bolero* playing in the background. Then minutes later more courting: a male secretary bird up in the sky weaves around his mate, then dives straight down to earth, pulling up only at the last minute. The sky-larking Lothario does this again and again in a display of reckless bravado that must surely sweep her off her feet. We drive to the Grumeti River to see for ourselves the monster crocs that gorge themselves on hapless wildebeest and zebra crossing the river during the migration. But this time of year the river is running at a trickle, and although there are many large crocs, the only monster we see is a huge hippo, the biggest we've ever seen, lurking solitary in a shallow slimy pool.

All the guidebooks we've read show the great migration moving in a big clockwise circle, heading northward in winter to Kenya's Masai Mara through the western side of the Serengeti, staying in the Mara during the spring months, then moving back down into Tanzania to the vast grasslands of the south-eastern Serengeti, brought to life by spring rains. With this in mind we've estimated that we'll intercept the migration in the Lobo area of the north-eastern Serengeti and have booked camps accordingly.

Still driving through the western corridor, we stop for a large herd of wildebeest crossing the road and take a couple of photos to pass the time. Ten minutes later it happens again, this time a few dozen more wildebeest passing in columns from north to south, and we joke that we are witnessing a mini migration, not for a minute believing this to be true. Just 5 kilometres further along and we are forced to stop again, not so much by the road blockage but by the spectacle of what's happening. There are many hundreds of wildebeest coming in on our left in long ordered queues, heads down, grumbling and snorting to each other, kicking up dust. As far as we can see they come, and the sound and the sight of it takes our breath away. Then we see that huge herds have stopped and are congregating in clearings to the right of the road, standing silent and still in the shade. We have to admit that we are, in fact, in the middle of the migration.

The manager at the next camp we stay at, up near Lobo in the north-east, is a friendly chap who is bemused by what he sees as our free and easy travel ethos. He spends time with us every day and lets us wander around the lodge as though we own it. He can't believe that we want to stay there for more than a couple of days and sends a ranger with us in the Troopy on game drives. This isn't the gift it should be, as the ranger doesn't speak English and is after all a ranger, not a guide, so he relies on pointing at animals we've already seen and mumbling their species in Swahili. When we tell the manager, tactfully we hope, over an evening drink, *thank you, but we don't need the ranger anymore*, he is disappointed. Rangers are stationed at private lodges and camps as much to keep an eye on the adherence to park rules as they are to advise and give guidance, and this particular ranger's officious poking about

THE CiRCLE OF LiFE **187**

in camp had been getting on everyone's nerves. The manager must have thought he'd found an excellent solution to the problem when we came along.

Ndutu Safari Lodge is in the Ngorongoro Conservation Area, just outside the Serengeti National Park's unmarked boundary. We drive in over the endless plain that is the eastern Serengeti, no animals except for a few scattered gazelles and no vegetation except for tinder-dry stumpy grass. In front of us mirages hover while Ngorongoro looks down from the sideline. As we approach the lodge the scrubby bush gets browner and more desolate looking, even though boggy sections of road are proof of recent showers. We are shown to a small neat room with one small bed, right by the kitchen. Oh dear. Neil's only comment is, 'And we're booked in here for *three* nights?' While he's back at the office asking to change rooms I look out towards Lake Ndutu and see a family of elephants making their way across the front of the lodge. Oh yes. By afternoon teatime we're ensconced in the honeymoon suite positioned way off at the perimeter of the lodge and it doesn't matter that when we sit on the king-sized bed it sounds like the shunting yard of Central Station.

Hamisi is to guide us on game drives and when he tells us that we're likely to see big cats both Neil and I are secretly sceptical. Big cats here? But Hamisi has become friendly with the local crew of a Dutch filmmaker who's here to make a documentary on cheetahs for the Discovery Channel, and they go out each day for many hours, tracking and filming. The filmmaker, a true gentleman, allows us to tag along once his prey has been spotted. We go out through the forest and into the trees, then come to a river gully, a green shock after all the brown. Before we know it we're following three cheetahs, brothers, walking with intent, and then Hamisi shows us a leopard with his kill locked in the crook of an acacia tree. The leopard gazes down on us with lazy gold eyes and the most he can do is flick his tail and occasionally stretch his long lean body.

From then on its cheetahs, leopards and lions, and we can't wait to see what the next day brings. We go out morning and evening and start to feel ownership of the first leopard, magnanimously allowing other guests to follow us to his tree.

One morning the rain buckets down and the staff are all sunshine and smiles. It's the first true drenching of the season and it heralds the new season of plenty. Plenty of grass, plenty of wildebeest — and plenty of free time, as the waterlogged roads make it difficult for tourists to get through.

Our last afternoon drive promises to be a good one with a revisit to a lion kill, but it nearly gets us kicked out of the Ngorongoro Conservation Area. We're sitting watching happy lions half-heartedly keeping vultures from their buffalo carcass — well, in truth the Troopy was surrounded by lions — when a vehicle full of official-looking people pulls up beside us. The passenger seat holds a woman with a black beanie on her head and a rifle between her legs. The head ranger. In a tirade of Swahili that becomes more and more shrill she berates Hamisi and us for driving off-road and for disturbing the lions at their kill. We have flattened vegetation and flouted the rules. She demands our permit and threatens a big fine. Hamisi is stunned. We fear eviction. Then light dawns as Neil recognises her vehicle as a private one belonging to a neighbouring fly-camp. It's payback time, as that camp of rival National Geographic photographers had recently received a fine after a complaint about bad park conduct from our friend the filmmaker. Their revenge has been swift.

It's wonderful to see this land, as baked and as brown as crispbread when we arrived, come to life after the rains. The landscape of just three days ago is now a shock of green stubble, and waterholes that were hard-cracked have birds dipping and weaving above them. Hamisi tells us that the cheetahs are moving out onto the plains in anticipation of the coming of the wildebeest and, true enough, on our last drive through the grasslands the first of the wildebeest come snuffling over the horizon in a haphazard column, escorted by zebra and followed by a lone jackal. In the lush grasslands that this will soon become, they will graze and give birth and linger until the time comes to continue their journey. The clichéd circle of life — but there's no finer description.

Leaving the lodge we drive past a huge herd of cattle attended by young Maasai boys. Such a strange sight in a game reserve, but what is more unsettling is the obvious poverty of the boys. They're dressed in red and blue rags and have none of the noble bearing of the Maasai of my imagination. Even in their poverty, however, they're adorned with beads and bracelets and stand straight and proud. One has bone plugs through the lobes of his ears, while another has a stone glued with a floury paste into a lobe already stretched and elongated from the weight. They all carry a stick and a spear, and a dirty plastic water bottle containing the dregs of milk, curdled. They ask for fresh water and accept it with dignity, allowing me to take their photograph in return.

THE GREATEST SHOW ON EARTH

After considerable discussion we decide that we can't pass the Ngorongoro Crater without visiting it. We've been to the crater once before and now we worry that we'll find it a crowded cartoon of what it was 30 years ago. In addition, we are now in the early days of the wet season and, although we've been assured that that means fewer people, it also makes the park roads boggy and impassable. In truth there's no avoiding Ngorongoro, as the road we must take to Arusha from Ndutu and the Serengeti climbs the south-western slopes of the crater then runs around the southern rim for a distance. Whenever the road passes close to the crater's ridge, visitors are able to snatch a tantalising preview of what lies below: a crater floor measuring 20 kilometres across, the world's largest intact, unflooded caldera. Even from up on the rim the large herds of animals it supports can be seen spread across its 200 square kilometres.

To take advantage of a little-used access road into the crater we book into the Sopa Lodge on the eastern side. This is perched on the ridge opposite most other hotels and we are hoping that it'll be a little less crowded over here. When we arrive we find busloads of package tourists, and at dinnertime the dining room is packed and noisy. I surprise myself by snapping at the man behind me in the buffet queue, and when we are charged US$25 for a lunch pack of little more than crackers and a boiled egg Neil is mightily annoyed and argues with staff, then management, to have this absurd charge reversed. After months of having to share our lives with no more than a handful of others we're finding this environment of big business and herded crowds hard to take.

In the morning the car park is packed with safari vehicles; it's a sardine tin of cameras, baseball caps and windcheaters. A sympathetic guide clears a way through for the Troopy and we escape, off down the escarpment. It's still early and there's hardly anyone about when we get to the crater floor, and the air is crisp and still. First off we spot one of the remaining big Ngorongoro tuskers mucking about in a secluded forest by himself, then a few zebras wander out of a gully. We see gazelles, hyenas and wildebeest and it's not long before the track in front of us is clogged with animals and we're forced to stop. By the riverbed a lion pride ambles from one sleeping spot to another and everywhere we see baby zebras, still wobbly on fluffy uncertain legs. Families of hyenas lie about in puddles, kori bustards strut their stuff, and a yellow-billed kite swoops down from the sky and takes Neil's sandwich out of his hand. It may be crowded and it may be trite, but it's still one of the greatest shows on earth.

En route to Nairobi we spend a night in Arusha. The town is bustling with importance since the UN's International Criminal Tribunal for Rwanda set up shop in her centre, but where we stay, on a coffee plantation a little out of town, is peaceful and quiet. Very quiet, as their generator has broken down and no one seems to know how to fix it. In the dark we sit on the porch of our little chalet surrounded by a true English cottage garden, and later we dine by candlelight on the porch of the lodge's restaurant. It's dark and drizzling and not as romantic as it sounds.

David, our friend from Abercrombie & Kent, has booked us a room in his club for our time in Nairobi. It registers as we drive in to the pampered pink estate that this is Muthaiga Country Club, the home away from home for Karen Blixen, Denys Finch Hatton and a bookful of white Kenyans and associated hangers-on since it opened in the early 1900s. It was infamous as the playground of the Happy Valley set between the wars, and famous as the city bolthole of the Earl of Erroll, before he was shot dead by a jealous husband. It's a comfortable place of regulations and common values, where friendships are forged and reputations sometimes lost, and people know a good kedgeree when they see one. I study the goings-on at the bar, alert for secret liaisons and indiscreet behaviour, but there is no sign of mischief.

We're under David's generous wing and as well as showing us the sights of the city he fills us in on the gossip and intrigue of the white Kenyan population. It's a change to hear of accidental shootings, incompetent aristocrats and fallings out over polo ponies instead of political woes and the predicament of the black man in the street. We're getting an insight into another Africa, one a half step removed from poverty and corruption, and we're able to forget those for a few sunny days of scandal.

Roughly 150 kilometres north-west of Nairobi lies Lake Nakuru in the Great Rift Valley. The road to Lake Nakuru National Park passes along the escarpment of the valley, and judging by the wooden lookout points we see set up by the roadside stallholders, the views must be fantastic. But today there's a heavy mist blanketing everything and for much of the drive it's hard to see the road in front of us, let alone the valley below. Lake Nakuru itself is a Rift Valley soda lake and the algae it generates attract thousands of flamingos — we've been told 'millions' — when the conditions are right. These, plus a healthy rhino population, are what we're hoping to see.

Naishi House is a stone English country cottage located in a shaded acacia woodland in the heart of the park. It belongs to the Kenya Wildlife Service and is usually booked out months in advance, but David has pulled a few strings. It has lawn-like grass and ivy on the walls, and smoke from the hot-water heater makes it look warm and inviting. This feeling is confirmed when Irene the caretaker comes out to welcome us. She is gracious and fun and between bouts of laughter she arranges for a ranger to guide us the following day.

Stanley the ranger comes out to find rhino and lions for us. He is a Methodist and engages Neil in a theological discussion about science versus Creation, whether Muslims believe in heaven and where our souls go when we sleep. I am on his side until he passes on the news that the place of a wife is to cook and clean and cut grass for her husband's cattle.

It's been a lionless morning when I see the telltale ears and twitching tail of a reclining pride. Stanley is excited and relieved and congratulates himself on bringing us to them, when Neil points out that they are in fact warthog. Stanley is not embarrassed but is blameful of Neil — 'There is one in this car who is not a believer.' I agree. If Neil had really wanted them to be lions, as Stanley and I did, they would have been lions. Stanley has enjoyed himself very much and reluctantly gets out of the Troopy with a promise to pray for Neil, that he may come to his senses and give up the idea of becoming a Muslim.

In the park there are lots of white rhino, magnificent and huge and apparently happy to share their home with ogling tourists. One youngster who is barely a half-metre tall seems to have mistaken the Troopy for an admirably proportioned relative because he comes galloping towards us at full speed, a little grey barrel with a smile on his face. When his mother takes off after him Neil throws the Troopy in reverse and we beat a hasty retreat, forgetting for the minute that white rhinos rarely charge. We stop, they stop, then on they come again, and it finally occurs to us that the mother is just playing chasings, urging the little guy on to stretch his legs.

David has arranged for us to stay next with friends of his at their lovely old farmhouse on Lord Delamere's ranch, further up the Rift Valley. A succession of Lord Delameres has farmed in the valley for just over 100 years and at the estate's peak it covered 300 000 acres and employed hundreds of the local Mau. Currently held by the fifth Lord Delamere, it's still a formidable holding and the Delamere name continues to be prominent in the agricultural history of the country.

Neil and I arrive rather late in the day to be greeted by YoYo and Grahame, a bottle of rosé on ice by their side. Also there to meet us are several geese, five Jack Russells and Wellington the Rhodesian ridgeback. Wellie is still bearing scars from the night he was dragged off the front verandah by a leopard. The leopard was scared off by staff but they couldn't find Wellie, who had run away in panic. Hours later he was discovered a few kilometres away, weak and bleeding, and unable to breathe properly as the leopard had torn his throat. He was waiting at the end of the airstrip for his master to fly back to his side.

We spend the first evening with our hosts walking the fences and confiscating snares. Poaching for bushmeat is a huge problem, and the next morning we come across the filleted carcass of a gazelle quite near the house. We later dismantle more than a dozen snares in the space of an hour or two.

After a late lunch and a number of chilled rosé wines we decide to go for a spin in Grahame's plane. At the airstrip he is just starting on his pre-flight check when he jumps back from the plane in alarm, an arm over his face. Then we hear it, a low drone coming from the cockpit — it's as though the plane has started itself without us — and when Grahame shouts 'Bees!' the situation becomes clear. Sometime during the night a swarm of bees snuck into the plane and they're now having a fine old time, buzzing about and wedging their way into any available space they can find. They form a solid block in the cockpit and are emerging by the dozens from the engine and the wingflaps. It sounds and looks as if the plane is about to lift off. Grahame has already phoned to the house for cans of Doom and we proceed to spray every accessible nook and cranny until we're confident not one bee remains buzzing. The bodies are swept out, Grahame completes his check and soon we're in the air, soaring above the lakes and old volcanic craters of the Rift Valley accompanied by the lone drone of a concealed survivor. When we reach Lake Nakuru Grahame dips and banks over Naishi House to attract Irene's attention, and I wave like mad.

We are still in bed when Grahame flies off to work early the next morning and, just as the sun comes up, he dips down low and loud over the house in farewell to YoYo. It's a sweeping, soaring goodbye, somehow personal even though the roar must be heard for miles around, and I can understand how Denys Finch Hatton captured Karen Blixen's heart.

It's a long drive today to reach our home for the next few days, a Maasai concession bordering Amboseli National Park. The only road we can take is back through the centre of Nairobi, and as we pass the university we get a flat tyre at the same time that we notice there's a graduation day celebration in progress. The highway is a busy one and Neil pulls onto the verge as best he can. Two young men immediately approach with offers to assist and they help me position the safety triangles so that oncoming vehicles don't ram into the back of us or, worse, run over Neil's legs as he's stretched out under the Troopy. Another man motions from the bus stop that he's available if needed, but there's really nothing anyone else can do so Neil declines all help. I stand at the back, waving off any cars that seem to be approaching too fast or too closely, and I notice other cars pulled over, all with flat tyres. There are four of us in total, but the Troopy appears to be the only one carrying a spare. The other drivers all stand about on the highway guarding their rear tails and making calls on dodgy mobiles for someone to come and get them out of there.

Thirty minutes later and we're back on the road. At the next intersection there are dozens of street vendors moving along the median strip and between vehicles, selling anything from jump leads to soccer jerseys. We stop for the lights and one ambitious chap with a broad smile has several types of hats for sale, all piled on top of each other on his head. Neil has a brilliant idea and we quickly agree to give the vendor the electric jug and hair dryer sitting in our glove box, still unused and still impractical. He could surely make a few bob on those. But he understands little English and appears confused by our gesture; he seems to think that we want to exchange these for a couple of hats. Or does he know that they are pretty useless items to the bulk of the population who have no need for a hair dryer? Other sellers have gathered around, curious to see what is going on, but they show great restraint and don't interfere. The traffic lights turn green and the cars in front are moving off. At the last minute our friend spots the cigarette lighter lead dangling from each appliance and their potential dawns on him. He accepts them with a big smile as we start to pull out, and we can see him in the side mirrors waving and calling out, 'Asante! Asante sana mzuri rafiki!', 'Thank you, good friend', and he waves so vigorously that his hats topple off his head while his friends laugh and laugh.

RiNGS ON THEiR FiNGERS AND BELLS ON THEiR TOES

We arrive late in the afternoon at Porini Camp, located deep in the Selenkay Conservation Area bordering Amboseli National Park. This huge private reserve is owned by the Kisonko clan of the Maasai people and it is reputed to shelter a great diversity of wildlife. Amboseli is known for its elephant herds as well as its great views of Mount Kilimanjaro, just over the border in Tanzania, but there are plans afoot to downgrade it from a national park to a reserve, which will allow for limited use by humans. In effect this new arrangement means that the Maasai will be permitted to seasonally graze their cattle within the boundaries, something which is, in fact, already happening.

The Maasai we'd previously come across were children herding cattle and old ladies on the side of the road, so driving into camp to be met by a half-dozen Maasai warriors wearing *shukas* and jewellery, and leaning on tall thin spears is awesome, in the true sense of the word. Their welcome is formal but friendly and there's a definite sense that we are invited guests in their domain.

I drag Neil along to anywhere I can ogle the warriors. Smooth-skinned and as lean as a bullrush, they are truly vain and exotic creatures. The spotter on an evening game drive spends most of the time looking at himself in the rear-view mirror and he isn't at all embarrassed to be seen doing so. Sexy too: a soft red *shuka* draped over the shoulders to expose a V of bare smooth back; a beaded bracelet slid over the wrist with fingers as slender and as fine as an artist's; a direct gaze with watchful eyes. They consider themselves to be the only true men on earth and I believe them, travelling companion excepted.

I'm keen to visit the Maasai's *enkang*, their homestead, a few kilometres from camp and Neil reluctantly agrees to come too. A handful of warriors are our escorts, and one who speaks a little English answers questions with reserve. I ask him why he doesn't have stretched earfuls of bright beaded jewellery and he responds snootily that he is educated. I'm beginning to see the dilemma for these proud young men: they are keen to embrace the modern world of wealth and opportunity, but are still deeply rooted in the conviction that they are a race apart and that their culture is vastly superior. In Arusha we came across an example of this split personality. We'd been directed to a carwash attached to a large modern hotel/casino complex and noticed that the Maasai watchmen there were much older and fatter than those normally employed as security guards. Oh no, we were told, these are the wealthy owners, and they sit around their city property every day in their red *shukas* and sandals just as they would sit around their homestead in the bush, watching for anything suspicious.

We arrive at the *enkang* and are greeted formally by the chief, a surprisingly small man compared with the others. He has a charismatic demeanour and magnetic eyes, and I'm sure he's flirting with me. We're relieved when he tells us that they will not try to sell us jewellery and trinkets, and that he will let us know when it's unacceptable to take photos. We're introduced to many women and more warriors, and all the while children in a mix of ragged traditional and Western clothes follow our progress shyly. Flies hang around their eyes and mouths but they seem not to notice. One little girl finally musters enough courage to touch Neil's hand and then sticks by him like a prize for the rest of our visit. There is evidence of cattle and their by-products everywhere: in the walls of the houses, in the calabashes of curdled milk, in the dung which we step in more than once. The whole place smells like a cross between a barnyard and an old yoghurt carton but it's homey, not unpleasant. Without understanding each other's language I learn from a mother who looks old but is probably in her late twenties that she is treating her sick baby with a herbal mixture, and so that I can appreciate it she rubs a little onto my arm with the same tenderness that she administers to her little boy. We leave with a farewell from the ladies, a half-hummed, half-sung chant that wafts and weaves in my mind and is still there when I wake late in the night.

We're slowly making our way to the resort town of Malindi on the east coast so we leave Porini and move on to Tsavo West National Park, further east and nudging the border with Tanzania. It too has good views of Kilimanjaro and is reputed to have prolific birdlife, but we've heard that game is sometimes hard to find in its vast acreage. The road in to Finch Hattons, our home for the next three days, deteriorates the closer we get and just a few kilometres out the track disappears under lakes of recent rain. The Troopy forges through and doesn't miss a beat, although my heart does once or twice. We finally arrive at the lodge's gate to hear the news that all day other four-wheel drivers have had to be pulled out of the mud. What a trusty warrior the Troopy is, and what exemplary driving on Neil's part.

There are hippos in the waterhole below our platformed tent at Finch Hattons. Most nights at sundown a mother pushes her baby under the platform to protect him from harm while she goes inland to graze. You can see him in the beam of the *askari's* torch, bewildered by the light but only slightly alarmed by the intrusion into his special place. He has scratches on his face and an open wound in his side so his mother is wise to shield him from attack by an aggressive male, or perhaps a hungry croc. During the night we can hear him grazing and more than once we wake when he knocks against our floor as he moves about.

After two game drives we discover that game in the park is, as predicted, thin on the ground and we take to sitting on our deck watching the goings-on in the waterhole below. One day when the hippos are being particularly photogenic I suggest to Neil that he goes over to the other side of the waterhole to take a photo looking back at the hippos, with me posing on the deck of our tent in the background.

Off he goes, then soon appears on the opposite bank. But in the time it has taken him to get over there a big croc has decided on a sun-baking session and has beached itself at the water's edge, out of sight to Neil. I wave and point; Neil waves back and moves towards where I'm indicating. The more I gesticulate, the further down the bank he goes, following what he thinks are my instructions. Only when he realises that I am looking more fraught than fashion model does he stop and cautiously look over the bank. My hero, he takes the photo anyway although the hippos aren't there anymore, having been scared away by the ruckus on the deck.

The road that we were recommended to take to Malindi is supposed to be good, a highway in fact, but it's busy and a long way round so we decide to take a shortcut through Tsavo East National Park. This goes well, but once we exit the park on the other side the road deteriorates to such an extent that progress is in fits and starts, over dips so deep that we don't see an excursion of small children crossing in the pit of one until we drive into it, and the motorbike in front of us disappears completely from view before zooming up and out the far side. Although the drive is slow and a little nerve-wracking for Neil, it's never tedious and we put this down to the fact that we've grown to be so relaxed, so free of outside concerns that we can find pleasure in the smallest things, and continually discovering what's just over the hill or behind that bush has become a sort of addiction. By now we have total faith in the Troopy and have no fear of breaking down or not getting through. Months ago we lost the feeling of having to get to a place by a certain time; we know we are self-sufficient and we've accepted the quirks of the satellite phone and GPS. We carry plenty of fuel, food and water, Neil can change a tyre in 30 minutes and a bed is a ladder away. We also know that we have enough money to get us out of anything and enough time to stay wherever our hearts desire. We can afford to live for the moment and have learnt to savour every one of them.

David has rented a house for us at Malindi to be used as a base and to garage the Troopy while we spend five days on the island of Lamu. The cottage is just like a comfy beach getaway anywhere in the world, but here we have the added benefit of staff to cook for us, to turn the fans on and close the windows when the heat descends, and to sweep the yard of leaves and to guard us from intruders. It's a novelty for us and I'm all at sea when it comes to telling Shadrack what we'd like to eat and when we'd like a cup of tea. Neil is more used to this and chats away, interspersing food preferences and timeframes with queries about Shadrack's life and family. Before long Shadrack has confided that his family is coming from their village to stay with him in his quarters for a few days of school holidays, without the knowledge of the owners — would we mind? One afternoon we return from an outing and as we drive through the gates there's Shadrack lying in the grass in the shade of a mango tree, wife leaning against his bent knees, two little ones sitting on his chest while another two hunt for beetles in the grass. As we roll past they all wave and laugh and Neil calls to Shadrack to stay there, we'll get our own tea. With just enough money for the fares to get here, their days are spent down on the beach or in the cool of the garden, and one day we come home to find little wet footprints leading from our pool to Shadrack's rooms in the garden.

Malindi itself is different to all expectations. I was anticipating a cosmopolitan, glamorous place something like Tangiers, while Neil thought we'd find beautiful sandy beaches and good restaurants. We should have learnt by now that no place in Africa is totally exotic nor wholly idyllic. What we find is a large, closed community of resident Italians, dirty beaches with flat surf, and many young Maasai men hawking their wares and their bodies. We are excited to find a cluster of *salumeria* and *panetteria*, but that elusive great seafood restaurant on the beach is nowhere to be found.

From Malindi we fly to Lamu, having left the Troopy under the watchful eye of Shadrack. Here too David has rented us a house, and it comes with a housekeeper and a cook, so 'self-catering' takes on a whole new meaning. The house is in the little village of Shela Beach, about 3 kilometres from Lamu Town, and suits us well. It's very hot here, and the air is heavy with humidity and frangipani. Lamu Town is a World Heritage Site and the whole island is Swahili, very much like Zanzibar used to be, with narrow lanes, Arabic architecture and women in black. There are no vehicles on the island so donkeys are used for everything — apparently there are over 4000 here — and they appear to be treated well enough. We have a mosque next door and are woken at 5 a.m. by the morning call to prayers through a loudspeaker, and there's a stable below where donkeys bray to each other throughout the night. One night dogs and chickens join in as well. During the day our neighbours play some sort of frantic Arab music and the din from generators used by private homes during power failures is all around, but somehow it's still peaceful.

The main topic of conversation among locals is the blackouts, the frequency and length, and the inconvenience suffered. On the edge of Lamu Town we pass the source of the island's electricity, a mini power plant with a bank of four generators attended by many personnel. But at any given time three of the generators seem to be broken, in need of maintenance or new parts, and the fourth is left to run on a meagre supply of diesel because most of the supply is sold by staff on the black market as soon as it's delivered.

How many times have we witnessed the Africans' love of rhythm and dancing? It must sit in their souls and come as naturally as breathing. Walking through the narrow back streets of Lamu Town we hear drumming not too far off and getting closer. Around the corner come two young girls, happy and laughing, beating a basic rhythm on drums almost as big as themselves. A little fellow of three or four has attached himself to them and he follows on behind, hips grooving and plump little legs making the moves. A conga line of one.

At The Boma restaurant in Vic Falls we'd watched as a family completely forgot themselves and took over the celebrations of the table next to them. The group of business colleagues on that table had asked the band to play 'Happy Birthday' and before the third line was sung the family was up, dancing and swinging, singing happy birthday to themselves, congratulating each other as well as the true birthday boy on the next table and enjoying the occasion so unselfconsciously that the whole restaurant followed suit, shouting requests to the band, while the business group tried valiantly to sing louder than the family and dance more wildly.

On the waterfront below our house is a hotel called Peponi's and its public bar is where everyone who lives in Shela congregates for sundowners. Believing ourselves to be eligible we ingratiate ourselves into this group, even though we can only speak one language and the conversations jump from Italian to French to Swahili. The regulars seem to be an eccentric lot. One glamorous and slightly grand British lady tells us she is a doctor and responsible for health matters in the village. She is due in Malindi shortly to perform an intricate operation on a sick child. We're later told that this is all in her head, she's just an expat running out of money. We share a table with the grand-daughter of Jomo Kenyatta, Kenya's founding father, and an Irish writer — a drunk — whose name I should remember but whose books neither Neil nor I have read. Princess Caroline of Monaco has a wonderful house around the corner and there's a beautiful French lady in a wheelchair who stays at a reserved distance from the clique. Made a paraplegic after a bad road accident in Paris twenty years ago, she has a contingent of young men to help her around and is rumoured to have a Maasai lover.

In Lamu Town we meet some more odd birds. There's the Australian–Englishman we have coffee with every morning who is always on the verge of leaving, but who in the meantime cadges beds from sympathetic expats. Then there's the Swahili guide who keeps popping up all over the place and hectoring Neil after we refused his offer to show us around town. But when it's time for us to leave, he's there at the jetty to wave us farewell and to wish us *salama sana*, 'much peace'.

Towards the end of our stay on Lamu I finally have a meal that's good enough to write home about when our major–domo, Kombe, serves chilli crab. His meals have always been good, prepared with care and a subtle touch, but this night is different. The stars have come out and angels sit on his shoulder. It's a feast, a feeding frenzy, with blood-red sauce on our hands and broken shell and body parts discarded over starched white linen. I haven't enjoyed a meal this much since the time in 2002 when I left a trattoria in Milan to a standing ovation. That night, at a table by the kitchen door, I had rabbit stew with polenta and it was so good, so perfectly cooked and so subtly flavoured, that I couldn't stop eating. I didn't want it to ever end. The waiter brought me a second helping, then a little more, and when Neil and I finally got up to leave the kitchen staff came out and farewelled me like the celebrity I'd proved myself to be. *Bravo signora! Arrivederci! Buone notte e bravo signora!*

On our last evening in Lamu we sit on the public terrace of Peponi's, looking out over the dhows in the channel. The bar is surprisingly deserted and the waiters bring us our usual without being asked. The light is mirror-sharp and the air is still. The water is so clear that the boats' rudders are visible and they make barely a wake as they slide past.

On the boat that takes us to the airport we fall into conversation with a young couple returning to Tanzania after a week's R&R on the island. They've loved it here and I have too, so I'm confused and disappointed when Neil says that he's glad to be leaving. He explains that he found the heat and humidity debilitating and the noise, closeness of the houses and narrowness of the laneways claustrophobic. I'd never suspected that he wasn't totally comfortable here or any less enthusiastic than me, as I'd come to believe that we were now so finely attuned that my likes were his likes, and his mine. I didn't even think to ask if he was loving the place as much as I was, and he'd been far too good-hearted to tell me.

From now on we're going to be anti beachside cottages that come with staff. Initially Malindi was fine and Lamu was paradise, but down the coast at the town of Watamu we find ourselves in a neglected, musty cottage that neither of us likes. It's an old lady's holiday home, with an ageing houseman who can't cook and a proprietary Burmese cat that swipes at my ankles when I walk past. Spiders nest in the sagging shelves where sun-bleached books gather dust, and hornets drone around faded curtains. There's an open verandah across the front of the house, but no fly-screens and no through-breezes to ease the stifling air. One room has been locked off — Neil thinks to hide a skeleton, but more likely just the detritus of an old lady's life.

On our first night Neil spends a long time rigging up power boards with extension leads so that our internal bedroom is surrounded by oscillating fans. He puts mosquito coils under my bed and pegs the mozzie net in place after it billows all over the room with the force of the fans. Before he climbs under the net he Dooms the moths, cockroaches and strange scaraby things that creep around the floor. After 30 years of marriage he is still my protector, my knight in shining armour.

WHiTE FLOWERiNG BAOBABS

The drive down the coast is long, with the border crossing back into Tanzania tiresome and slow. The weather is very steamy and the road gets progressively worse the further south we travel. In the absence of liquorice allsorts and wine gums we've taken to eating Cadbury Eclairs while on the road. These we buy in 1-kilogram bags and a handful each makes a good lunch. From time to time we pass roadside signs for shops and institutions with names to rival the best Uganda had to offer. We've seen the Mamma Mercy's Home of Little Childrens and then, showing more confusion than originality, Them Bulls Pork Butchery.

Neil and the Troopy have forged a bond made in heaven. After initially sharing the driving equally, we reached a happy compromise way back in Zambia: Neil drives and I navigate. I drive too fast for Neil and when I'm behind the wheel he's constantly checking the speedo and telling me the speed at which

I should overtake. He's so nervous that he forgets to look at the map, and when he does he's forgotten the name of our destination. On the other hand, I'm an excellent navigator and only when the sea is to the west of me do I get confused. As we progressed northward and the state of the roads deteriorated I was intimidated by their condition and would tackle them at speed, whereas Neil learnt early on to read their trickery and deceptions and how to coax the Troopy through them.

Roughly 80 kilometres down the coast from the Kenyan border we find Capricorn Beach Cottages reclining on a stretch of quiet, palm-fringed beach between the towns of Tongoni and Pangani. We fall in love with the place as soon as we drive in. Sitting on a grassy slope beneath flowering baobabs and strangely scented frangipani, the little estate of just three cottages and a residence is the extended home of the owners. Apart from a wave and a *jambo* in greeting, everyone keeps to themselves. Ladies deliver freshly baked baguettes and homemade yoghurt in the mornings and saunter across to clean the cottage later in the day, but otherwise we're left in peace. This is more like self-catering as we know it. There is a small, low-key lodge to the north, and a fishing village on the southern side. In the evening, the fishermen go out to sea in boats crammed with crew, maybe a dozen in one vessel, and when it gets dark their lanterns settle on the horizon like fairy lights on a Christmas verandah. Then just on dawn a flotilla of small dhows heads out to the day's fishing, their sails elegant and angled into the wind. Men with dilly-bags wade out through the low tide to hunt for octopus, while on the beach, garden boys with slow, distracted strokes rake up seaweed brought in by the tide during the night.

Without the restrictions imposed by set mealtimes and socialising it's easy to fall into the rhythms of the sea. At low tide we gravitate to the beach, the only place where there's a wisp of a breeze to relieve the heat and humidity. It's also the best time to look for shells and to watch the daily life of the villagers, who use the exposed beach as a walkway and the outgoing sandy water to scour their pots and pans. As the tide comes in a cooling breeze comes too so we lounge about on our terrace, reading and writing and talking about nothing much. Shooting the breeze. The freedom is wonderful without houseboys and neighbours to consider. We get dressed when we feel like it, take cold showers whenever we get too hot and sometimes I only get around to combing my hair in the afternoon. The only sour note comes at breakfast one morning when we have to acknowledge that the jar of Vegemite is finally running out. Like life here, I'd hoped it would never end.

Despite this comfortable beach-combing existence I determine that we should go on a little outing, so one day we set off in the Troopy to explore Pangani town and Ushongo, a beach resort 20 kilometres or so further down the coast. There's a ferry crossing to negotiate at Pangani and this turns out to be the funniest car ferry I've ever been on.

With a maximum vehicular capacity of two, it's compact and a jaunty red and it looks seaworthy enough. We follow a pick-up down the alarmingly steep concrete ramp but, just as we're about to embark, the ferry drifts out so that its boarding ramp is hovering 15 to 20 centimetres above the shore. *Hakuna matata*, no problem: two men jump up and down on it until it's low enough for us to mount. We quickly do so and it's just as well because the ferry has now drifted to an angle at odds with the shore and it's only some fancy driving on Neil's part that gets us safely on board without one or more wheels dropping off the edge. We nestle in behind the pick-up; a few pedestrians come aboard then we're off —

straight into a 180-degree turn, so that the ferry crosses the river backwards. At the other side we have to egress in reverse, off and up another steep concrete ramp that is accommodatingly wide. Our return crossing is more exciting still, as we do a 180-degree turn on the entry side of the river and then again on the opposite side, so this time we can drive off pointing in the right direction having enjoyed a panoramic 360-degree view of the entire river in the meantime.

Since our first day on the coast in Kenya Neil has forbidden me to pick up large shells or buy any shells at all from the guys on the beach too old to go out fishing. Firstly, it is illegal; secondly we have no space to be carrying them around; and thirdly, they're fragile and wouldn't make the journey home in one piece. However, at Ushongo we have coffee at a deserted resort on an isolated stretch of beach, and seeing no opportunity for the waiter to make a living from tips, Neil relents and allows me to purchase shells from him. While the waiter and I laugh and ah-ah-ah at his daring, Neil climbs up the branches of the most majestic of baobab trees, the crowning glory of the resort, to pick the perfect flower. I come away with a bag of big and fragile seashells, surely illegal, and a beautiful dusky baobab blossom that has discoloured and withered by the time we're back at the cottages.

Christmas is a week off and we are forced to move on after five days because all the cottages have been booked for the festive season months in advance. Our plan had always been to find a quiet place which we could settle into over Christmas and now, disappointed that it can't be Capricorn, we'll have to find someplace else. There looks to be quite a selection of seaside towns further south, closer to Dar es Salaam, so we set off optimistically.

First stop is Bagamoyo, a place written about in glowing colours and spoken of enthusiastically by other travellers. They must have been here in their hippie days because all we find is a jetsammed beach crowded with rowdy students and abutted by rundown 'resorts'. We choose an upmarket-looking place but looks can be deceiving. The picture on their brochure of an elephant in the savannah should have alerted us to the confused persona of this beachside establishment. We're in a brand new wing, the room large and light-filled and adorned with expensive European fittings, but this place has been built by non-builders. Windows, way too small for their opening, are kept in place with thick globs of plaster. Cut, sharp-edged tiles protrude at corners and the bathroom floor drains away from the plughole. Then the children on the beach could have come up with a more professional construction. But the odd thing is that the owner, a tall, dignified Ethiopian, loves the place and is as proud as Punch of it. Can't he see that he'll soon be sued by a guest with a great gash in their leg? We get talking to his son, who is home for Christmas from studying law overseas, so perhaps it has crossed his mind.

Christmas in the Hotel Sea Cliff, Dar es Salaam. If you ignore the Maasai doormen and the cheery black housekeeping staff, this hotel could be in a capital city anywhere in the Western world. There are classy rooms with up-to-the-minute décor, restaurants with international menus, and efficient front-of-house staff, and the clientele covers everyone from tourists, expats and country residents in town for the festive season to diplomats and wealthy locals from the surrounding suburbs. It's a convivial, cosmopolitan place that we can see, after a few days of exploring, mirrors the city's personality.

I'm up early on Christmas morning to phone home but only get to say a few quick words before the satellite connection drops out. Lunch for us is to be low-key, so we opt for a sandwich on the terrace rather than the gala Christmas buffet. The tables around us fill up with locals in their Sunday best. Families, sweethearts and couples — they have all made an effort. The women are beautifully groomed, some wearing hats, and the little girls are in their special dresses, new for Christmas. Most sit at their table with a bottle of Sprite or Fanta, sipping slowly to prolong the occasion, and the hotel staff treat each with the respect due a big spender. A group of Taiwanese men sit at a table close to us and all four light up cigarettes while they drink and talk loudly. Neil is getting tetchy but reaches breaking point when cigarette smoke hovers over our food like nuclear fallout. He leans toward them: 'No smoking!' They apologise and stub out their butts. I whisper to Neil that this is a smoking area as it's outside, but he's unrepentant. 'It's no smoking *around me*!'

SMART PEOPLE iN FLASH CARS

Neil has been fascinated by Tanzania's Selous Game Reserve for years, and the more he's read about it the more interested he's become. It's a place of superlatives: the largest single game reserve in Africa; the heart of a huge ecosystem of uninhabited woodlands, the largest on the continent; considered to be the greatest surviving wilderness in Africa; home to the largest populations of large mammals but also a sanctuary for endangered ones, in particular the African wild dog. Add to this the fact that the southern sector, 90 per cent of the reserve, is all hunting concessions with just half the remaining land given to photographic tourism, and you have a pretty remarkable place. At first glance the number of private hunting concessions is alarming, but Neil has read that their introduction has been a successful experiment in game management, as their anti-poaching ethos has allowed decimated animal populations to regenerate. He has to see this place.

The reserve is hard to access at the best of times, so we've been advised to fly in now that the rainy season has covered roads and flooded rivers. We leave the Troopy surrounded by admiring workers at the offices of the company managing the Sand Rivers Selous. This lodge, the most isolated of any in the photographic sector of Selous, is where we're to stay for the next four days before flying directly on to Zanzibar to see in the New Year. The flight is great fun. The New Zealand pilot dips over herds of elephant and buzzes giraffe off the airstrip before we land. We're met by Goodluck, who remains with us as our personal guide throughout our stay. He's charming and keen, and has a good knowledge of the local flora as well as the fauna. We're lucky to have been allotted him. Sand Rivers Selous is situated on a bend in the Rufiji River, which at this time of year is overflowing and swift moving. Because of all the recent rain it's even more bloated — a 2-kilometre-wide infinity swimming pool reaching right up to the lodge and lapping at the open sitting room.

Game drives with Goodluck are stymied at every turn by flooded and boggy roads, so he takes us on a trip upriver to cruise through Stiegler's Gorge, a narrow neck in the river where the water flows swiftly between boulders and overhanging branches. But the strengthening current is too much for the motor on our little boat and it struggles to make headway. Just a few hundred metres from our goal we're forced to admit defeat and turn the struggling boat around. With the motor turned off the boat planes on the current at breakneck speed back the way we came, bouncing over rapids and whizzing past sun-baking crocs. A startled hippo lunges at us, giving Neil a fright and making both Goodluck and me laugh, and the turbulence caused by swirling water and loose sand creates Rotarua-like boiling and bubbling all around our little vessel.

Also staying at the lodge are a Dutch family and a Scottish family, both good company and lots of fun, and an elderly Belgian couple who spent many years in the Congo and who have been on 26 safaris subsequently — or so they inform everybody. They see themselves as experts on all things African and quickly dismiss the adventures of others. In no time they have alienated themselves from the staff as well as the other guests and by their last meal at the lodge they sit alone, impressing only each other with their vast knowledge.

The canvas and stone chalets are open-fronted and a beacon to every mosquito in the Selous. The Dutch suffer badly from night attacks, but the Scots don't seem to mind the minefield of bites on their ankles and legs. Neil and I have stuck to our anti-malarial plan of protection rather than taking a prophylactic medication, and although it's now more a philosophy than a regime, we've suffered only a few bites. After Goodluck takes us to the lonely grave of an English researcher who recently died from malaria, we have a flurry of slapping on repellent and wearing long sleeves and trousers at night, but that only lasts a few days.

The Scottish family is on the same flight out as us and we share a few anxious moments when we arrive at the airstrip to find it wet and sodden, and with an alarming patch of boggy black cotton soil right in the middle. The jolly pilot is unperturbed by this — after all, he says, he just landed here — and he taxis at full throttle down the strip then at the last moment veers off the runway, around the cotton soil and over tussocks and holes, and back onto the strip before lifting off at an acute angle. We're all a bit dishevelled from the bumpy detour but when the Scots father has gathered his wits he announces that he is 'right pleased', having had to pay no extra for a ride more exciting than the dodgem cars at a theme park.

Our next port of call is Zanzibar, and we are interested to see how much it's changed since we were here 30 years ago. Stone Town is the same but different. The same narrow alleys and crumbling buildings, but now crowded with European tourists, curio shops and touts, and reckless drivers behind the wheels of cars going too fast.

We stay in a small hotel just out of town, and once we get used to the room facing a rubbish-strewn tidal channel, we settle in well. I eat tiger prawns or lobster for every meal and Neil convinces the staff to chill his beers in the freezer every evening. Not everything falls into place, however. I go into town on a shopping expedition for cheap clothes and in search of Freddy Mercury's real home, which I am desperate to have my photo taken in front of. Both ventures draw a blank.

A dhow trip over to Prison Island on our last full day in Zanzibar seems like a good idea, so early in the morning we head into town to organise a boat. At the little cove where the dhow touts hang out, we do a deal but so involved are we in the negotiations that we don't notice we're the only tourists there. Around at the boat harbour, the fact that all the dhows are anchored offshore should have said something as well. There's a shouted Swahili exchange and the first two boats approached decline to take us out, but then an old sailor in an even older dhow agrees. It's tricky getting the old boat close enough to the beach for us to clamber aboard, but we manage it and set out through a big swell.

What a perfect day — romantic, exotic, sailing in a dhow to places unknown! After a couple of minutes it registers that we're the only boat out and that the swell is very big, with white caps breaking all around. The boat is heavy and has only a small engine, and the spark plugs appear to be becoming affected by water because the motor periodically splutters and conks out, leaving us to drift at an alarming angle to the swell. We slide down into troughs, the skyline disappearing, then zoom up to hover momentarily on the peaks, just long enough to show us how far away from the island we still are. We pass battened-down container vessels and ocean-going ships, feeling dwarfed and vulnerable, and the crossing that would normally take 30 minutes stretches to an hour, then an hour and a quarter. Closer to the island we notice way over to our right that there are in fact a few other fearless day-trippers heading across, their boats bobbing, disappearing from view, but they all seem to be making better time than us and by the time we're near the island there are a number of others already there. Some have dropped off their passengers and are anchored, bailing out water, trying to keep upright and head-on to the wind. Others are hovering, waiting for the right moment to surf in close enough to the beach for their nervous cargo to disembark and wade ashore. On the third try our crew manages to manoeuvre close enough to shore for Neil and me to jump out the back between waves and we make the beach with soaked shorts but dry cameras.

The island is a bit of an anti-climax after the crossing, and even the sight of dozens of giant turtles can't distract us from the thought that we're going to have to do it all again on the return leg. The time arrives and our crew bring in their boat. It's tricky and wet but we get back on board. There's some initial difficulty in getting out into deep water, but once there we ride on the swell and the crest of the waves all the way back. At the landing beach we're greeted by a posse of tourists who, less brave than us to face the sea, clap and whistle as the old boat surfs ashore.

We fly back to Dar es Salaam and the Hotel Sea Cliff to make plans for the next week or two. Neil has a little crash in the Troopy when he reverses out of a carwash into a fancy sedan occupied by two smart young black women. After a few hysterics and shouted advice from onlookers, the girls agree not to call the police if Neil agrees to pay for the smash repairs. All three go in the Troopy in search of a panel beater and an ATM, and it's not long before they've got a quote and the cash, and Neil has learnt a lot about the girls' aspirations and dreams for a good education and a wealthy husband.

In the morning's paper there's a report of a fatal light-aircraft crash in the Selous. Five days after we flew out from a waterlogged airstrip, a chartered flight has crashed on landing and, according to the report, one passenger 'succumbed to death'. It's a different airstrip and a different airline company to the one we flew with, but the story is a sobering reminder of our joy flight out of the park.

We've been looking forward to getting back to the bush, and Mikumi National Park is conveniently a half day's drive out of Dar on the TANZAM Highway, the main artery linking the port of Dar es Salaam with land-locked Zambia to the south-west. On arriving at Foxes Safari Camp we find that the manager is an Australian, a lady in love with Africa, and Tanzania in particular, and desperate to earn enough cash to be able to afford her own little piece of paradise. We are the only guests, and rather than the manager taking us on a game drive, we take her out in the Troopy. The tsetse flies here are ferocious and she'd not have been able to stop for any length of time in her open safari vehicle without being set upon, so to be able to sit and observe the parks goings-on from the Troopy, windows up and air-con flowing, is a treat.

There are lots of elephants in the park, and most mornings they're on the road leading out of camp — probably because it's the only dry land around. One bull has charged us two days running and this time, after another such challenge, Neil thinks he'll do what people have been suggesting and charge the Troopy right back at him. Well, that big boy isn't fazed and just keeps on coming until he reaches the front bumper, where he pulls up just in time. He flaps his ears like a demented butterfly, tosses his massive head from side to side, and with one big front foot kicks dust over the bonnet of the Troopy. Pleased with himself, he moves off the road and lurks behind a bush, so Neil puts his foot down and we edge past. Out he surges onto the road again, bellowing, and chases us off. As we look back from the safety of distance he doesn't look so big or so fearsome, just a young bull throwing his weight around.

The day we leave the park we do a final drive past those waterholes and grasslands where we've had good sightings before. Park rangers have been excited by the first wildebeest calf of the season and when we come to a herd quite close to the road we can see wobbly little baby feet through the legs of a protective ring of females. Then we're told that a giant black python is out sunning himself so we make a beeline for his haunt by the hippo pool. No luck, we've missed him again.

We continue along the TANZAM Highway and make an overnight stop in Iringa, an important administrative centre for the region to locals, and for tourists it's a place to stop over on their way down the highway or into the Ruaha National Park, 100 kilometres to the west. The MR Hotel is in a back street, close to the bus terminal and opposite a shop selling music tapes and CDs, which are played at full blast. Although there are Muslims to be seen in the street, the town turns out to be predominantly Christian, and teetotal. When we ask where we can get a drink the hotel manager looks askance and in a low voice suggests a local bar over by the market. He is worried not, I suspect, because he thinks that it's too seedy for us but because he fears we'll return to our room drunk and disorderly.

We're in the petrol station the next morning, filling up on diesel, when a big fancy LandCruiser nudges past with a cheery face behind the wheel. *Our-oo! New South Wales! New South Wales Australia?* He scans the Troopy admiringly, slaps the side of his door. *Our-oo!* We wave and drive off, Grace Kelly and Cary Grant in their convertible on the roads of Monte Carlo.

One thing Neil always does is talk to people. The waiter in a café, the maid cleaning our bathroom and the man filling the Troopy with diesel, Neil chats to them all. He starts with general pleasantries, moves on to enquiries about family and children, then more personal exchanges. He learns many things, but the main thing is this: whether they be in a village in Tanzania or our own street back home, people all desire the same things — food on the table, the opportunity to work for a fair wage, and access to a good education for their children. After just a few minutes Neil usually comes away with the number of children in order of age and who they are living with and why, whether the husband has many girlfriends (he always does), and always, always, which parent, brother or sister is dead. AIDS is sometimes mentioned but never straight away, and we've come to understand that this is not always through embarrassment or shame, but simply through incomprehension.

On the way to Ruaha National Park we pass through some unexpectedly beautiful scenery. At one point it could be mistaken for forested green English countryside, and further along an avenue of overhanging trees on the Never-ending Road (its real name) leads to a couple of little red bridges crossing a babbling stream.

What's even more surprising is the presence of people who look very like Maasai. There was no sign of them in or around Iringa but out this way you can't miss that there's quite a settled community of them. They seem to have diversified into farming, just a little, and we even see one out in a field hoeing. It doesn't look right. Herding cattle, loping across grasslands or just leaning one-legged on a spear we're used to seeing, but bent over a hoe, *shuka* and jewellery swinging, is a first.

The Foxes Ruaha River Lodge is right on the Ruaha River and we arrive to find the family and staff standing on the bank deciding whether to abandon camp and move to higher ground. Although it's not raining here the river is brown and swollen, fed from the catchment valleys further upstream. The river rushes past the dining room and laps at the steps of the chalets, covering grass and foundations. We all stay put as the height of the water drops in a matter of hours, and over the next few days we witness this constantly, the rising and ebbing of the river, unrelated to any rains we're receiving at the camp.

That first day brings other excitements. We park in front of reception while we check in. A staff member is hovering outside and when we've finished our business he informs us that a snake has just slithered down the passenger's side of the Troopy from the sleeping capsule and dropped to the ground. 'But don't worry, it is heading towards the water and it is only this big,' he adds, opening his arms as wide as they can go.

Ruaha is the country's second-largest national park and it has a reputation for being remote, wild and bursting with a great diversity of both flora and fauna, particularly predators. We're keen to go out exploring, but the land is sodden and we're advised that we'll be limited to areas of high ground where game will be difficult to find. That doesn't bother us, so a young guide comes along to escort us around flooded roads and overflowing rivers. Instead of searching for wildlife we drive around at will on the slippery tracks, admiring the view from these elevated positions and chatting to the guide about his life and ours. The Troopy crawls up over a rise and there reclining in front of us is a handsome young leopard, trying to dry out in a sunny patch on the road. For a second or two he continues to lick the water off his sleek flanks then suddenly there's a flash and he's gone like a puff of smoke, and we're left asking ourselves if he really was there.

As predicted the more remote corners of the park are inaccessible but we've seen enough to make us want to come back in a more accommodating time of year. We'll soon have no use for our copy of a guidebook to birds of Central and East Africa, so the day we leave we donate it to the young enthusiastic guide to whom we've become attached. He is overcome with gratitude and tells us softly, tearily, that he would never have been able to afford such a book. He asks us to write in it that it is now his, so that others won't steal it and management won't accuse him of theft.

Kisolanza Farm sits by the TANZAM Highway in the south-west of Tanzania. This region is called the Southern Highlands of Tanzania and we comment several times on how similar it is to the Southern Highlands south of Sydney. There are eucalypt and pine plantations, and European-looking farms scattered about over rolling green hills. Kisolanza itself covers a large tract of land, an attractive cross between African bush and English country garden. It's the home of a second-generation white Tanzanian family and they offer tourist accommodation within a working farm. We take a cottage which sits in a field of wildflowers on the edge of an orchard and it is so comfortable, and the weather so cool after all the heat, humidity and rain we've passed through, that we stay on a little longer than we had first planned. After two days we've still not ventured out to explore the farm, but are happy to just loll around the cottage, sit in deck chairs on the yellow-flowered lawn and wander up to the restaurant when the drums announce the next meal. Well, the warning from our hostess about the presence of many snakes on the property could have been a contributing factor.

Further down the TANZAM Highway is the town of Mbeya, where we'll turn off and head south for Malawi after an overnight stop. The English manager of the hotel we stay in has spent most of his working life in Tanzania but has been trying to retire to the United Kingdom for many years. He explains his prevarication by likening Africa to a worm that makes its way stealthily into your being. Sometimes it sleeps and sometimes it wriggles about, but it's there, just under your skin. He says that he's fought it, and tried to ignore it, but has had to accept his destiny, for now the worm is not only under his skin but also in his blood. Neil and I exchange a look — we've heard that one before, but now it's making a lot of sense.

The manager convinces us to visit Matema Beach on the northernmost shores of Lake Nyasa before entering Malawi. Hard to get to rather than remote, it really is a beautiful spot, with the Livingstone Mountains to the east, rising jagged and steep straight up from the water's edge, and the huge blue–green expanse of Lake Nyasa lapping on the beach where dugout canoes lie about and locals wade. The hotel, really an R&R hostel for the Evangelical Church, is staffed by young boys with little English but good intentions. They look after the place well. They rake the sand every morning and are continually cleaning, and they provide unexpected luxuries such as thick towels, good bed linen and the toilet paper folded into a V.

We've had to bring our own food and we eat light lunches and pasta for dinner, and the boys turn a blind eye to us cooking on a primus ring on the cottage floor. In the evenings the locals gather in little family groups at the water's edge to bathe, kids splashing about with the soap while the adults socialise and gossip. In the heat of the day the sand, shimmering big brown crystals, is almost too hot to walk on, and when we go for a swim the warm water sits on our shoulders like a favourite cardigan. We sit on deck chairs under a tree, trying to catch a breeze, dozing and reading, and the boys drift over to us from time to time with offers of fresh fish, cold beers or handmade pottery for sale.

With a little haggling and some difficulty because of the language problem we negotiate a price for a canoe trip to the pottery village, via the Saturday morning market in a village at the end of the beach. We're quite pleased with ourselves for getting the price down from 25 000 to 15 000 Tanzanian shillings, about US$10, which we feel is fair and just for a canoe trip for three to four hours.

At eight o'clock the next morning our canoe is waiting on the beach. Philip, its owner, is a thin, dignified man who speaks even less English than the boys, but he has a steady oar and a strong paddling technique and we steam across the mirror-clear water racing our reflection. The market is crowded and full of life: *Jambo, hello mama! Welcome and welcome again!* Big happy mothers breastfeed chubby babies; women looking expectant and bored at the same time sell onions and green tomatoes, fancy headscarves and bright *kangas;* and everywhere clay pots are stacked in neat piles forming great walls of pottery.

Back in the dugout, heading towards our next destination, Philip doesn't miss a beat and the rhythmic splash splash splash of his oar would have lulled us into a doze if it wasn't so uncomfortable sitting cross-legged in a little pool of water on the hard canoe floor. We disembark again at the village and lots of little children run down to meet us. They hang onto our fingers and jostle for prime position closest to us, but Philip turns around and scatters them with a few words. The tour of the village is a bit disappointing as Philip, without English, can't explain anything, and of course all the women who are the potters are back at the other village selling pots. Whenever we meet someone younger than Philip they are deferential, exchange very long courteous greetings with him, and the women curtsey. Young girls also curtsey to Neil and me. It appears that Philip is a man of importance, despite his ragged clothes.

After a good hour of solid paddling we're delivered back to our beach and Neil hands over the money. Philip accepts it quietly but politely, and as I walk up the beach I turn around to see him sitting on the lip of the canoe with his head in his hands. Either it's not the amount the boys had told him to expect or he was hoping for a much bigger tip. He looks *very* disappointed. Neil is philosophical and mutters something about people never being happy, but when Philip follows us to our cottage and hangs around outside we both begin to feel guilty, and then downright mean. We decide to give him one of Neil's shirts and I retrieve it from the back of the Troopy. It's accepted gracefully and Philip is obviously pleased, but then after a couple of minutes he calls one of the boys over and they hover around outside, deep in discussion. Neil and I are now seriously troubled but stay indoors, trying to ignore them. They drift off and we later see Philip walking off down the beach.

A couple of hours later Neil and I are out sitting on deck chairs under a tree on the beach. I read to Neil from a current guidebook, which says that a canoe trip to the pottery village should cost no more than 1500 Tanzanian shillings and we agree that, even allowing for inflation, Philip should have been more grateful. A well-dressed man walks up purposefully, and shuffling, half bowing, shakes our hands. *Thank you, thank you, Sir. Asante sana mama. God bless you. God bless you, Sir.* It's the shirt that makes us twig that this is Philip, scrubbed up, in clean trousers and his new shirt, and it takes but a moment to realise that we've paid him ten times the going rate and he's been wrestling with his conscience ever since, wanting to tell us but so needing the money. His solution is perfect for him, but it leaves me uncomfortable and embarrassed. It is more than simply feeling like the Queen dispensing waves and favours; it feels like paternalism of the worst kind, being able to determine a person's happiness with a cast-off shirt and a few dollars.

HE SAiD WHAT?

The road into Malawi and down to Lake Nyasa is spectacular. It descends quite rapidly from an altitude of 2500 metres to just a few hundred metres, and passes through tea plantations, fields of bananas and maize, and forests of pine and eucalyptus, all with the magnificent backdrop of steep mountain ranges. As soon as we enter Malawi I'm reminded of something from our last visit 30 years ago: umbrellas are very important to the Malawian psyche. Then, it was in imitation of British dress and the brollies would be black, always rolled up and carried by men in dark woollen suits. Now everyone carries one, on their bikes, hooked over one shoulder or balanced on the head. You see them for sale on the side of the road in neat colourful rows and in a great variety of sizes — there are ones with wooden handles, hooked plastic handles, small ones, checked ones and golf-course-strength ones. They're used as much as sunshades as they are to keep the rain off and many times we've driven past women walking in the rain with their umbrellas carried horizontal on their heads, still unfurled.

Mzuzu is the main city in Malawi's northern region, situated between the lake and the high Nyika Plateau to the west. Driving around the streets in search of an Internet café I notice a young thin boy running up the street behind us, but I'm distracted and pay him no attention. We drive to one location, find no café there so cruise around the corner to the next hopeful place. As we're peering into the shop a face appears at my passenger's window. He introduces himself as Peter, and although he's out of breath from chasing us, he explains that he and a friend make greeting cards and sell them to tourists to support themselves, so would I like to buy a card. No? Then would we like a tour guide to show us around the town? If not then perhaps he could guide us down the road to our next destination? He's eager and naturally friendly, and his eyes are trusting despite his sad life, which we learn about shortly.

Peter is an AIDS orphan and one step above being a street boy. He was taught to make greeting cards by some NGO, and he and his friend Elliot set up a little business. Elliot paints the scenes on the cards and Peter sells them about town. They make enough to afford a shared room in the township. Peter hustles for business relentlessly in a town where few tourists visit. Maybe because of their determination there seems to be a level of acceptance of the boys among the townsfolk and after we buy some cards from him we see Peter go into a 7-Eleven, buy a Fanta with the proceeds and sit on a bench alongside local businessmen eating their lunch.

We come across Peter again when we're passing through town a week later. He seems distracted and asks if we could lend him some money for a public phone call, about 2 cents. Someone he's been close to is being buried today and Peter is desperate to find out where and at what time the funeral is. He finds us later to give

Neil change and tells us that he got through with his call; although he was too late for the funeral, he's spoken with the family and so has done his duty. He's lost a bit of his spark so Neil buys him a Fanta and he comes with us to a café where we order lunch. The proprietor wants to kick Peter out, thinking that he is annoying us, but when we indicate that Peter is our guest, he sits sipping his Fanta with great dignity before thanking us and quietly slipping out the door.

Right up on the plateau in the north-west of the country, Nyika National Park is different to anything in Africa we've seen so far. It's at an altitude of over 2000 metres and strikingly attractive, with rolling green hills, bushlands of proteas, over 200 varieties of native orchid, pine forests planted back in the 1950s, and a few patches of original forest draped in moss and staghorns. It is home to plenty of animals, too, although not a great variety: roan antelope, eland, bushbuck, reedbuck and mountain zebra, and apparently the highest concentration of leopard in Central Africa, although we are not lucky enough to see one of these elusive inhabitants during our stay at Chelinda Lodge. The weather is cool, cold even, and a great relief to Neil from the humidity of the lake. But there's still plenty of rain about and that is the cause of the Troopy's first real challenge.

Late one morning we're driving on a firm, clayey track when we come to a bad patch, washed away by the rain. Neil thinks he'll go off-road to avoid it, but just as he starts to drive onto the verge the road gives way under the back wheel and the Troopy lurches over sideways, stuck. Luckily the wheel is sunk so deep, right down to the axle, that it prevents the Troopy from falling over completely onto the driver's side. Fearing that any shift in weight might topple us over we very gingerly vacate the Troopy on the passenger's side. Because of the tilt it will be too dangerous to use the Hi-Lift

Jack, and there are no trees and no rocks for miles around that we could use as packing. The Troopy is in a tight spot. By a stroke of luck we have the phone number of the lodge stored in the satellite phone, and it is even greater luck that Neil is able to connect and summon help.

We walk a kilometre or so in heavy rain up to the top of the nearest hill so that the rescue party can locate us, and three and a half hours later a battered Unimog, a big, solid and slightly lopsided rough-terrain vehicle, comes trundling along, loaded up with workers. Neil has slung a snatch strap around the Troopy and these guys all swing on it so that the Troopy doesn't fall over with any extra movement; we connect up to the Unimog's towline and in a flash we're pulled out. What an anti-climax. Neil and I are wet and muddy, but we're light-headed with relief and drive back to the lodge, where we eat a huge lunch at 4.30 p.m.

From its position on the fringe of a pine forest, Chelinda Lodge looks out over rolling grasslands of alternating green and amber. The buildings are constructed entirely of pine logs and stone, and each of the cabins has a log fire, and steaming hot water from huge beehive-like donkey heaters outside. Skittish, pretty bushbuck wander out of the thicket below the lodge to nibble thick grass by the walkways, and families of roan antelope graze the slopes beyond. Up here on the plateau the night sky is so clear that it could be a computerised image, and the stars so bright and so close that they seem to be hovering just above our head. From our first days of camping, when Neil taught me to locate the Southern Cross, we often sit outside in the still and quiet of night, marvelling that the African sky could be this perfect. With neither pollution to cloud it nor illumination to confuse it, the sheer volume of what can be seen is overwhelming. 'All the consternations of the Universe,' as one enthusiastic but misled guide once told us.

What interesting people we meet on our travels. An English honeymoon couple flew into the park on the day we arrived. They are young and in love, and probably still a little drunk after three straight days of celebrations and travelling. She is pretty and well-bred, with pale peaches-and-cream skin and vibrant blue eyes. When her husband complains that the tsetse flies and mosquitoes always target him she nuzzles his arm and murmurs, 'That's because you're delicious, darling.' On a game walk she is attacked by red ants so straight away pulls down her jeans. The African guide dutifully picks the ants off her hips and thighs while her husband laughs that it's just as well she's wearing her horse-riding knickers and not a thong. It turns out that he is Irish, a fact which becomes apparent when his accent drops from plummy English to lilting Irish after he becomes comfortable in our company. Down to earth but slightly eccentric, he's been a jackaroo in Australia and a cowpoke someplace in the United States. She's been around, and a more perfectly matched pair would be hard to find. Totally uninhibited and with the confidence of youth, the world is their oyster and their company brings sunlight into every day.

The road we take south runs parallel to the shoreline of the lake, now called Lake Malawi by Malawians, and passes through acres of rubber trees, spooky and sinister in the afternoon light. I've read that no native birds inhabit rubber plantations so this might explain the empty, lifeless feel to these woods. Unhappy-looking boys hold out handmade rubber soccer balls for sale, and as we approach they throw them on the road to demonstrate their perfect bounce. We're tempted to buy one just to cheer the boys up.

Makuzi Beach is a lovely spot. The lakeshore is very picturesque, the water's warm and calm and it's hippo and croc free, so everyone spends a lot of time in or on the water. Set in a little rocky cove between two fishing villages, the Makuzi Beach Lodge is very small and family run and we decide on the spot to stay a number of days. According to their passports the owners' two young boys are just the thirteenth and fourteenth white indigenous Malawians to be registered, which goes to show what the native white population is. We go swimming and kayaking every day and the young boys and their dog attach themselves to us, all three desperate for outside company. The oldest boy's hero is Steve Irwin and when he talks about Steve's adventures he unconsciously takes on Steve's persona and Steve's daring feats become his. His goal is to grow up quickly so that he can fill the gap by Terry Irwin's side made vacant by the untimely demise of her husband.

The parents get a kick out of Neil's unique interpretation of where we've been and what we've seen and their frequent '*What* was that again, Neil?' leads many times to splutters of laughter. Like Estonia National Park instead of Etosha, Neil has also been to Sangria Bay, not Senga Bay, but didn't have time to visit Fish River Gully (Fish River Canyon, just the second-largest canyon in the world), although at Lake Nakuru he saw plenty of flamencos on the shoreline. Our hosts are particularly tickled to learn that Japanese use shit cakes (shiitake mushrooms) in their cooking and all of us, including Neil, have a good chortle when Lake Chilwa becomes Lake Chowder. But Neil is unrepentant and says later that the obvious food theme must be a subliminal reaction to the general standard of dining we've experienced throughout our travels.

A half day's drive down the lake we find the Livingstonia Beach Hotel, a lovely old whitewashed colonial building, a poor cousin to the Victoria Falls Hotel in Zimbabwe. We're the only guests staying here and have the pick of rooms. We choose a cavernous one that has TV and a little garden and the staff fuss about fetching extra pillows and re-hanging droopy curtains. We return from breakfast one morning to find the room attendant has left 'Feel at Home' spelt out in little flowers on a napkin by our bed.

To get to and from the Livingstonia we must pass through the town of Salima, a dishevelled, bustling place surrounded by maize and tobacco fields. Its main road is full of donkey carts and bicycles jostling good-naturedly for space, and on the footpaths a number of coffin-makers compete for business. One has a selection of very expensive-looking lacquered and brassed coffins on display while another, the Comfort Coffin Shop, has a billboard offering 24-hour service and a cell phone number. It's noticeable here in Malawi that there seems to be no stigma attached to this most necessary of industries, or to the reason for having the industry in the first place. In other countries we've passed through the coffin-makers often run their businesses from behind other shops, or just have a display of their wares alongside more domestic furniture. One exception was in Uganda, where we were alerted by a slightly alarmed American Christian Aid worker that he'd seen coffins with windows. So what, I thought, until I too saw them displayed by the roadside. The windows are in the sides, not on top, and no one has been able to give a logical reason for this although I'm sure there is one.

Malawians seem a practical bunch. As well as embracing the coffin shops and umbrellas, they give their children descriptive but totally unromantic names. We've met Trouble, Simple, Danger and Memory, and when Neil asked Trouble's friend how he could have got such a name the answer was perfectly reasonable: he might have been sick or difficult as a baby and his parents foresaw trouble ahead. Reasonable as well as obvious, by the look on the friend's face.

Throughout our travels we've come across myriad objects carried on heads — umbrellas, hoes, metal beams, a halo of bananas, a Medusa spray of spinach, Bibles on Sundays, schoolbooks on school days, a suitcase, a metal bucket with a suitcase in it — but on the road out of Salima we come upon the best of them all: a shiny tin bathtub with a baby sitting in it. He's enjoying the ride and has a goofy smile on his face as he gently sways about to the rhythm of his mother's steps.

Our next stop is at the southern end of the lake in a very nice Italian-owned place, Club Makokola. With 36 rooms it's quite a bit bigger than we're used to, but because of the rains we're the only guests once again. The chalets are set in grassy flowering gardens under baobab trees, and there's a long white beach and a long white cloud that settles by lunchtime over the mountain ranges on the far side of the lake.

The managers are a white Zimbabwean couple, in Malawi to make some money and to escape the sadness and madness back home. They take us with them on a social outing to visit another Zimbabwean couple; these ones have left for good and are biding their time before migrating to Australia. They are a most eccentric couple. They live in a magical rustic cottage nestled on a peninsula in the lake, surrounded on three sides by water and on the fourth by an orchard carpeted in thick green grass. The house is under thatch and has leadlight windows and low dark rooms. And dogs. At present there are about twelve of them but the menagerie started at more than 30. There are little ones, big ones, smart ones, playful ones and a blind one, mostly strays or abandonees but all now living out a happy life. The owners brought some of them from Zimbabwe in a specially chartered plane but inherited the rest from the previous owner of the property, where the deal was that the dogs came with the house. When the dogs have all died the couple will be free and on the first plane to Perth. The family's devotion to the mutts is total, and the dogs are allowed to eat biscuits and scones and sit on the best sofas. It's a beautiful crazy household full of love and laughter.

Many people have sung the praises of Liwonde National Park and recommended that we visit it. They've spoken of its beauty and its position, bordered by the Upper Shire River and Lake Molombe at the bottom of Lake Malawi. With all that water around, it has swamps, grasslands, deciduous forests and, Neil's favourite, *mopane* woodlands. It's also reputed to be home to a great number of animals and birds. We couldn't let this one pass us by so we've booked in to Mvuu Camp, one of only two lodges in the park.

It's good and exciting to be back in a game park again. We leave the Troopy at the barrage where there is a transfer boat waiting to take us upriver to the lodge, and here we meet Angel, our guide. He takes us on game drives and river safaris and his turn of phrase enchants all of us aboard. He tells us that 'warthoggys do need to drink oftenly', and that the carcass of a young zebra was 'found deaded' yesterday. He has a sore on his shin and when someone gives him a bandaid he announces unselfconsciously that he doesn't know 'how to make it'. After he's shown how to apply it he wears his bandaid like a badge and it's still in place when we leave. Like many of the guides we've come across his knowledge of the local flora and fauna is self-taught but extensive, and he imparts it with generosity and humour. A bachelor herd of impalas, united in their inability to lord it over a breeding family, becomes 'a pack of losers', and he refers to a newly arrived group of middle-aged female tourists as 'the spinster herd'.

Accommodation at Mvuu is in roomy stone and canvas chalets (pronounced 'tchalettes' by the staff) and the only drawback is their proximity to each other. A small clique of Germans arrive on our second day and move in to the chalets next to ours, and in a couple of hours they quickly dispel the rumour I started in Namibia that German tourists travelled around moody and uptight. This pack goes to bed after midnight, laughing and calling to each other, waking everyone around them, then are up with the monkeys at dawn to continue the fun and games. Angel puts it down to the fact that they're noisy boozers, something he'd been before becoming a born-again Christian.

The crack–crash of thunder is so sudden, so close and so loud that for a second we lose all sense of place. Then hippos bellow and monkeys screech, and humans all utter the same expletive simultaneously. It's an afternoon thunderstorm, but Angel and his fearless followers venture out for a game drive in an open vehicle. With only thin raincoats we cheerfully predict an early break, a drizzle of short duration before the clouds clear. Time passes and game is thin on the ground and the folds of the raincoats channel water onto the cameras and into our shoes. Neil wants to turn back: he's already had enough and sits dispirited beside me. But he can see that I'm enjoying myself and so are our companions, a Dutch couple from Blantyre where the husband is a visiting paediatrician. This is a rare weekend of R&R for him and anything must be better than the dark pressures of the ward, so Neil hunkers down silent and resigned, looking very much like he did the last time the Australian rugby team lost to South Africa.

The rain intensifies, and the only animals we see are a family of waterlogged warthogs. On a steep incline the vehicle slides and lurches alarmingly then conks out altogether. Like rats we scramble out and head for higher ground, slipping and sliding in the mud. Angel looks worried. He revs the engine and burns up the hill with mud flying, splatting our arms and chests. We're out of danger but now we've all lost enthusiasm so agree to head back to camp for a hot shower. At least we get a round of applause from the rest of the guests sitting warm and dry at the bar and taking snapshots of our appearance, which is more New Guinea Mudmen than *Out of Africa*.

Malawi is a forgotten island stranded in the middle of the greatest welfare state of them all. Not well known for its wild animals or prolific national parks, tourists don't flock to Malawi, and with a peaceful history and relatively stable government, aid agencies don't feel the need to throw huge sums of money at the country. Sure there are many worthy projects that have only been possible through overseas funding, and the streets of Blantyre and Lilongwe are humming with the usual number of white and shiny four-wheel drives bearing the insignias of the World Health Organization or the European Union, but the cries of the rest of Africa — in more dire straights and in immediate need — must be a compelling priority. Most of the other tourists we come across are locally employed Europeans snatching a little R&R. They don't have a lot of money to spend and they certainly don't drive around in donated vehicles. The Dutch paediatrician tells of the frustrations of trying to get things done in an under-funded public hospital. He concedes that there have been giant leaps forward: from having one of the highest HIV-positive incidences of any African country, Malawi has got on top of the disease and now just 15 per cent of the population are infected. But the legacy is enormous; in a country of 12 million, 1 million are orphans, and these have medical needs that the health system is struggling to manage. The number of child rapes that his hospital deals with weekly is horrific, but there is no money for counselling, post-treatment care or follow-up. In a country of calm and industrious people, things aren't always what they seem.

PORTUGUESE TARTS

We're heading for Mozambique so get off to an early start from Blantyre, where we've overnighted. As we drive out through the hotel's gate the old security guard salutes, gives us a big smile and wishes us a very safe journey. It is hard to explain the warmth and sincerity of these oldies. They have a natural grace that wraps you in its kindness and puts us to shame. I run a theory past Neil, that somewhere along the way we in the First World have lost this generosity of spirit and the graciousness to accept life at face value. We've become materialistic and competitive, and the importance of friendship and family has faded as the star of consumer goods shines brighter. Neil is more circumspect and suggests that this attitude could be seen as paternalism, even racism, because it's seeing another culture from a perceived position of greater sophistication. He's right, of course. I'll have to work on that theory.

Poor, sad Mozambique. For over 200 years it was under the thumb of Portugal, which bullied the people with a racist system similar to South Africa's apartheid. This was followed by a violent independence movement, then after independence in 1975, the country was racked by civil war for another twenty years. During all this time the general population as well as the land suffered terribly and often villagers didn't know who was responsible for the atrocities carried out against them. On top of this, drought, floods and famine hit the country with cruel regularity. The land in some provinces has been devastated and the accepted social structure of the shell-shocked peasant population has disintegrated under these assaults from all sides. Landmines still lurk in many fields, and many villagers have yet to lose the siege mentality learnt from generations of fear and disorder.

At the border the Mozambican officials are surly, bordering on rude. We haven't encountered this before and it makes us wary. But the money they request is legitimate and we receive a receipt for all fees paid.

The contrast with Malawi is noticeable almost at once. The bad condition of the road for a start, then the huts and villages are of a different style and material, and the people react differently to the Troopy driving past them. Our early impressions are that the country is very, very poor; we drive through infertile, swampy land where villages are large and hunkered down in protective clusters, not spread out along the road. We see no churches, there's no waving from the children as we drive past, and road sense seems to be slightly askew, with people darting across in front of vehicles or, the opposite, not moving off the road at all as traffic approaches. Held up for sale are chickens, melons, a kitten, squash of all shapes and sizes. We're nearly wiped out by a big lorry taking a curve on our side of the road and unable to correct at the speed he's going. It's simply good luck that there happens to be a verge for Neil to swerve onto. I see a landmine sign for the first time but don't understand if it means that the land behind is clear of landmines or is literally a landmine.

When we get to Tete we stop for lunch at the motel we'd earlier considered overnighting in. Despite being right on the banks of the beautiful Zambezi River, the rooms have one small window each, heavily curtained and barred, and the restaurant is an inside room with no view at all. We sit with a couple of truckies and assorted hangers-on and watch English football on a snow-bound TV while we eat. The food is good and cheap and the staff patient with our lack of Portuguese, but we're glad that we're pushing on.

Back on the road and cruising along at 100 kilometres per hour we become aware of a deep whine, which gets more pronounced as speed increases. We're hundreds of kilometres from any town and the thought that the Troopy should toss in the towel here is too awful to think about. We pull over and Neil gets out for an inspection. Seeing him with his head under the bonnet, mouth open and a completely blank look on his face, is enough to lighten the situation for me. He looks accusingly at a connection or two and touches a couple of things, then drops the bonnet and dusts his hands like mechanics do. He tightens the roof racks, the Hi-Lift Jack, the shovel clamps, anything that could possibly have come loose, then off we go again. And back comes the whine. Stop, inspect, tighten, and this time to our great relief, the noise is no more. It turns out it was the shovel, slightly loose in its clamps, rotating in the wind and acting like a tuning fork as the air whipped over the blade.

Shortly afterwards we get a speeding ticket for 1000 Mozambican meticals, the local currency (equivalent to about $45), because Neil is going quite a bit over the limit through a village. The policeman shows printed proof that the fine is legitimate, and he doesn't nibble when Neil suggests that it was more like a 500 meticals fine, in cash.

Then we run over a chicken. Then we're involved in the apprehension of a criminal. Neil is once again driving a bit too fast through a village when we're slowed by an angry crowd of men swarming onto the road. The air is electric; there's a frisson that something is about to happen. In the midst of the mob is a policeman, gesticulating that he needs help and behind him in the melee a handgun waves about. Neil stops, saying that there is something in the policemen's body language that suggests a degree of anxiety and he doesn't think that his speeding is the cause. We reverse and see that the policeman clings to a desperado whose eyes are wide and frightened. Both men are out of breath and covered with sweat and twigs. Puffed, the policeman asks urgently in broken English if we would drop them in the next town and when we agree the mob visibly relaxes. They help the other two into the backseat of the Troopy and only then do we see the handcuffs on the felon. The crowd waves goodbye as we drive off, a strange and sudden about-face after the fierce hysteria of moments before. Judging by the conversation in the backseat, it's obvious that both men are mighty grateful to be away from that pack of vigilantes, and they both sigh and yelp with relief.

Twelve hours and 675 kilometres later we arrive at the unremarkable town of Chimoio, just after sunset. Finding overnight accommodation in this half-light, in a junction town of busy streets and jostling buses, makes us snappy, but we settle down when we see a sign, in English, for an executive hotel. This looks promising, and we honk the Troopy's horn at the gate for admittance. We're shown to a tiny, airless room with a big bed and just enough space for a chair to put our luggage on, but it has an en-suite, and breakfast is included. We're just settling in when there's another toot at the gate and a fancy car appears with two snappily dressed young men in the front seat. These must be the executives, we think to ourselves, and they seem to have brought their secretaries as well because two ladies get out of the backseat and accompany the men to their room, all four giggling and falling over each other. Soon afterwards another car with an executive and his secretary arrives, and Neil and I retire for the night with the sounds of loud music and bawdy laughter echoing around the corridors. It's been a long, long day.

Next morning we continue on the disintegrating road eastward, bound for the old port city of Beira. People had recommended we avoid Beira. It was a dump, they said, totally run down and not recognisable as the cosmopolitan European city of its Portuguese years. This is reason enough for us to visit, for Neil to witness the downfall of the playground of his teen years. Along with all the other young bucks from Rhodesia in the early '60s, Neil had piled into a clapped-out VW and driven down from Salisbury for a weekend of surfing and cheap wine. A 10-litre wicker basket of Portuguese wine was a couple of pounds and if you wanted to impress the girls you'd fork out for Mateus Rosé. Now we drive in to find a surreal city, a carcass of what it once was, with chunks dropping off classic Portuguese buildings and permanent dwellings on the median strip of tree-lined boulevards. We pass the shell of the once glorious Grande Hotel, where hundreds (some say thousands) of squatters now make their home. Everywhere decay and neglect — it's a Fellini movie of wasted dreams. Street boys with hopeful smiles volunteer small services for a coin, and a handsome proud young man with a leg blown off offers to protect the Troopy from theft while we lunch in comfort in the Club Nautico.

We are determined to eat at one of the famous old Portuguese restaurants still operating in Beira, and one lunchtime we drive slowly past Pique Nique several times before deciding to risk it. Well actually the security man sees us cruising by and waves us down. *Yes come in, the restaurant is open.* It just looks as though it's been closed for years. Inside it's all browns and oranges and we can't decide whether we've just walked back into the '30s or '50s. The '50s are probably when these waiters were first taken on and ours is a big black gentle hulk of a man whose sleeves on his major-domo jacket stop short of his wrists by many centimetres. We order an aperitif of chilled white port, then fried sardines and grilled tiger prawns to follow, and to Pique Nique's credit the dishes are prepared as if the chef has just perfected something new and exciting and this is their first day on the menu.

For the next few days we stay in an apartment in a small complex catering to Zimbabwean holidaymakers, and in the evenings, we eat at Club Nautico on the beach. This really is a club and non-members must pay a small entrance fee. Middle-class white Portuguese, Portuguese Mozambicans, blacks, whites, foreigners like us are all welcomed and occupy the plastic tables and chairs of the open dining verandah, fanning ourselves with menus and lifting sweaty T-shirts off our shoulders. Children wander down the steps and half-heartedly kick sand about; young macho men take off their shirts and stretch back in the sun, skin glistening, while waiters bring out plate after plate of fried chicken and chips. A family of golden-brown boys, the youngest no more than four or five, sits up to big bowls of minestrone and they tuck in with the genteel manners of a French count. But the chicken is what draws the crowds and it is moist and tender and tastes like chicken as we know it, not the stringy birds with a gamey flavour that the Ugandans and Tanzanians are fond of. *Pili pili (piri piri)* sauce is served on the side but only the innocent or the brave dip in a spoon. Neil, who has in the past asked waiters to bring chilli sauce to liven up anything from scrambled eggs to French fries, realised very early on in Mozambique that *pili pili* here is something else again. It's sold by the roadside, homemade in second-hand jars and empty Sprite bottles, all lined up in neat rows like scarlet piano keys on a vaudeville stage. The contents are so diabolical that we've been warned to never ever accept the offer of a sample tasting should we be so stupid as to stop and browse.

One night there's a wedding at Club Nautico. Music, noise and heat. It's hot in the reception room and guests spill out and onto the beach. Men unbutton shirts, take off their shoes and run their feet through the sand. Bridesmaids in silver dresses and tortured hair wade in the ripples, stilettos dangling from a hand. One of them becomes tired and emotional and is escorted sobbing on the shoulders of a relative to a quieter place. A straight-backed father and his little son shed their formal white shirts and sit bare-chested on the beach, legs out, side by side. There's a little girl in a pink frilly party dress just a couple of sizes too big, with shoes that flash lights when she walks, and a trio of boys catch handfuls of moths in the sand then throw them into the air, liberated. Later they sit in the dark and carefully pull the moths apart, fascinated by their smell. The dance floor is packed, mostly males, but a tall well-dressed man with one gold earring shuns the crowds and dances on the steps to his own beat. The music is pumping and a mother with her daughter tied on her back can't walk without strutting to the beat. Down to the beach goes a neglected man who looks like an interloper, tipsy with a plate of food, and he half tumbles as he sits to eat. On the plate is the skeleton of a fish and he holds it up, dusts the sand off and sucks on the bones. Shortly after a member of the wedding party goes down to him and shouts; he gesticulates back to the restaurant and manages to move the diner not out of the building in disgrace but back to join the bride at her table. It's hot, loud and chaotic, and I'd give my eyeteeth to be a part of it.

The morning we leave, loaded up with Portuguese tarts and cheese and ham croissants for the trip, we pass a thin boy on hands and knees over the swill of a blocked drain, extracting a rotting banana with a stick then stuffing it into his mouth unpeeled. Then another youth, black rags and open sores, sits in the gutter and uses a piece of broken glass to dig something from the sole of his foot. We can see no hope for these poor young men, trying to exist in the lost and found of a struggling city.

THE DOWNWARD SLOPE

On the road south of Beira we give a lift to a young Austrian hitchhiker. He's a music producer/documentary-maker currently living in Mozambique. We talk of many things to pass the time and the craziest thing he tells us about is the giant rats trained to detect landmines. Because the relationship relies on trust from both sides, the rats are treated like pets by their handlers and are fed and housed handsomely. For their part, they sniff out live mines and indicate their position then the handlers go in and detonate them before the rats blow themselves up.

Five hundred kilometres south of Beira is Vilanculos, a busy port and beachside tourist town. It's the stepping-off port for divers, anglers and honeymooners wishing to visit the islands of the Bazaruto Archipelago just off the coast, and it is bursting with restaurants, resorts and backpacker hostels. We find Casa Rex, another of those slightly eccentric guesthouses owned by an expat and run by friends or lovers. The room we are given looks out across a vivid blue sea towards the archipelago and below us a broad sweep of beach is patrolled every evening by a resident pack of curl-tailed dogs. The temperature is steamy and for most of the day we are content to sit in the breeze of our terrace or go on short excursions in the air-conditioning of the Troopy. Mornings and evenings we go down to the beach despite the fact that the sand has a suspicious texture and smells as your feet break the surface.

Soon after we arrive a trio of Italian girls checks in. They all work in Malawi and surprisingly not with an NGO or volunteer group, but on salary in the private sector. They're young and friendly and we get into the habit of chatting with them over breakfast coffee. At first just small talk, plans for the day, what we've seen and where we all are going. Then, as can happen on holidays when talking to complete strangers, more personal questions find their way into the conversation. The girl with the best English asks how long we've been married then apologises and says that they've been wondering and couldn't decide whether we were long-time married or newlyweds. 'You are the partners,' she says, and it takes a minute for us to understand that she means to each other. So after all those miles we've travelled through all those years, this is what Africa has given us in just a few months: the understanding that marriage isn't a competition but a partnership.

Two weeks later Vilanculos is flattened by Cyclone Favio and footage on the news shows Casa Rex looking like Pompeii after the eruption.

Further down the coast is Barra Beach and it would have to be one of the best beaches I've ever seen. Palm-tree lined, wide firm sand, no beach boys pestering us to buy crummy jewellery; there's good surf and clean clear blue water. This shouldn't warrant special mention but does, because in some of the coastal towns — Vilanculos for one — the plumbing infrastructure hasn't been replaced after the neglect of civil war and, out of necessity, people use the shoreline as a bathroom.

Driving out of Barra Beach we pass a middle-aged man standing on the side of the road. Straight-backed and in a shirt buttoned formally to the neck he holds a tin plate in one hand and a small bunch of bananas in the other. On the plate are two avocados, polished until they shine, and he holds his goods out for sale like he's holding the collection plate in church. His pride is clear and I try to imagine what it would be like to have to stand on the street for hours trying to sell the food off my plate.

Xai-Xai is another 500 kilometres further on, through dusty towns now looking more European than African, and on a road which improves the closer it gets to the national capital of Maputo. We book into a lodge for a couple of nights at Xai-Xai Beach, and it is here that we come across holidaying South Africans for the first time in a long time. They don't seem to venture much further north than the relatively safe countries of Namibia, Botswana and southern Mozambique, and many times when we've described our trip to a South African they've looked horrified and told us we are foolhardy and asking for trouble. I suggest to Neil that this reaction must be because they live with danger on a day-to-day basis and assume that it's worse in more 'uncivilised' countries, but Neil has a simpler explanation: the general population can afford neither the cost nor the time to travel to Uganda or Kenya. If they are going to fly to a holiday destination they're likely to choose Europe or Egypt or Madagascar, where they'll be able to have a new experience and a different culture to explore. This time I'm backing my theory.

Back at the Xai-Xai Beach Resort our neighbours unload iceboxes from their *bakkies* (utes) and talk to each other loudly with snapped grainy Afrikaans accents that I find hard to understand. The men are all big and noisy, wear flip-flops and short shorts and have unruly hair and straining beer-bellies. Their women wear tight Capri pants and glitter on their tops and sandals. They busy themselves wrapping potatoes in foil and making big spiralled coils with long links of *boerewors*, those thick, meaty sausages so loved by South Africans. In no time the group has taken over the pool and *braai* area and a ghetto-blaster is positioned in a strategic spot. The smell of frying *boerewors* and the pop of brandy bottles dances our way and the ghetto-blaster starts up. This music is a strange marriage of styles, half German oompah military and half country and western, but it's good. They are having a marvellous time and invite the rest of us to join them.

After Xai-Xai we drive straight down to Maputo and look for a hotel. We choose one on the beach, a little distance from the noise and bustle of the city centre but close enough to walk to restaurants and cafés.

Another deciding factor is the free Internet connection it offers, as it's time for Neil to start contacting all those to whom we've promised first option when it comes to selling the Troopy. Timing is now becoming an important issue. If the Troopy is sold, we'd like to hand it over as close to our departure date as possible. On the other hand if no one wants to buy it, we'll have to ship it back home, which means finding a sail date that corresponds more or less to our leaving, and then pre-booking container space on the vessel. Negotiations for both eventualities will need to start soon and they'll have to run in parallel until a cut-off date is reached. Neil sends off emails to five of the most promising interested parties and while we wait for responses to filter back we make forays to different parts of the city. Now that we're conscious of our days with the Troopy being numbered we become clingy and drive everywhere on these daily excursions, even though most of the places we want to go can be reached on foot.

The city seems to have been spared some of the destruction wreaked on the rest of the country during the independence battle and civil war. We find some beautiful old Portuguese buildings still standing and in good repair, although there are many that have succumbed to neglect. My favourites are the Natural History Museum, a perfectly proportioned confection of ornate white plaster, and a wonderful private home on a main *avenida*, its ornate façade heavily decorated and tiled. Neil's favourite by far is the railway station. It's still an imposing, well-maintained building, but the tracks terminating inside are rusty, and the numbers have long ago fallen off the arrivals and departures board.

The goal each day is to find somewhere serving coffee as good as we got in a café in Kampala and a restaurant with food to match Beira's. This becomes an uncontested challenge in a city now so influenced by South Africa that all we encounter are Wimpy outlets and cappuccinos made with boiling milk and burnt beans. The food in Mozambique generally has been pretty good. Apart from the chicken at Club Nautico and the grilled tiger prawns at Pique Nique, my favourite is sultana jam, which is *the* best thing to spread on toast and pastries. And at Barra Beach I had *matapa* for the first time, a southern Mozambique staple of peanuts, coconut and clams cooked up with pumpkin leaves. Sounds a ridiculous combination but the one I had, which substituted prawns for the clams, was out of this world despite looking like vomit.

By our own measure we've zoomed through Mozambique — 2000 kilometres in ten days — but there really hasn't been anything to tempt us to stay longer. Until the country sorts out its national parks it only offers beaches, islands, diving and fishing for tourists, and for us they aren't enough to make us stay longer.

Before we left Beira we thought about heading up the coast to Pemba and the Quirimbas Archipelago in the northernmost province, close to the Tanzanian border. We'd read that Ibo Island in particular would be worth a visit — an atmospheric, crumbling blend of Muslim and European in an unspoilt area of great natural beauty — and the island reef ecosystem in the surrounding Quilálea Marine Sanctuary is said to be the most significant in the Indian Ocean. However, the diversion would have involved a number of days driving through regions not geared to tourists, on bad roads, with few attractions along the way. Worth the effort? The truth is that our heart just wasn't in it. It felt wrong to turn around and head northward after being in a big clockwise circuit for so long; it would have been going backwards at a time when we were on the homeward run.

So now here we are at the southern tip of Mozambique, poised to enter South Africa again ten months after arriving in Cape Town last year. Then, we thought we were prepared for any outcome and had considered most possibilities on the practical side. And we had, as it turns out. Neil has been thrilled that the Troopy has performed so magnificently, and I'm impressed that we managed to pack the right clothes and the right equipment to meet all eventualities so far. What we couldn't have anticipated, however, was on a more personal level. The thrill we both continue to get from visiting national parks and seeing their wildlife, enjoying the hospitality and friendship of strangers and, more than anything, the satisfaction of travelling together and sharing experiences, both good and bad. Even though I was confident that our nation of two would be united and strong, I couldn't have anticipated that it would be this good, and feel this true. When

I've said from time to time throughout the journey that I've never been happier than doing what I was doing at the time, I meant that I've never in my life been happier.

Strangely enough, we weren't concerned about our personal safety before we arrived, and now that we're here and the months of travelling have rolled by we've become even less so. We've never felt wary of anyone, nor have we ever thought that we've wandered into a dangerous situation. We've taken few risks because few have arisen, and anything different, even confronting, we've chosen to see as an adventure.

But I think that, beyond the animals and adventures, it is the heart of the people of Africa that has affected us the most. Their infectious optimism, their stoicism and grace in the face of hardship, and their understanding and acceptance of life's calamities. Even though Neil has taught me to look beyond the pathos and to look for the rhyme and reason, I am still, every day, inspired.

A BiRD SHOW AND A BACKSTREET BRAWL

The South African border is just a short 100 kilometres from Maputo on a wide, multi-lane, tarred highway. It's good to be back on this sort of road, and after months of being in the Third World I'm excited when we reach the town of Nelspruit. It's modern and thriving, and we can stay in a stylish B&B and go shopping for familiar things in a well-stocked supermarket. As we first drive through the streets we can tell that here things are run efficiently, and rules and regulations are adhered to. The houses have been built by people with tastes similar to ours and there's a comforting amount of rage on the road as people speed around in expensive new cars.

The Troopy needs a service so we agree that while Neil takes it to Toyota I'll go window-shopping in the centre of town. I'm very excited and head for the first department store I've seen in many months. In Women's Wear there are new-season clothes and, even better, racks of sale items to browse through, and there's a

Homewares department with interesting things like slingshots and big plastic pestles. But something isn't right and I'm not really enjoying myself. In fact, I'm losing interest fast and getting anxious, wondering if Neil has found the right address and whether he's taken something to read while he waits. The time drags. We're both early when we meet up at the appointed café for lunch and chat away as though we've not seen each other in months.

It's in Nelspruit that it starts to sink in that we really are on the home stretch; that the hardest but more rewarding part of our adventure is coming to an end. The dream run has run its course and we'll soon be back to a world of responsibilities and obligations. As we've driven through country and village, and weeks have turned into months, we've begun to think of ourselves as free spirits, detached from everyday life. Now there's a time frame to consider and business to attend to — the despatch of the Troopy — that involves a certain amount of attention and forward planning.

Neil has received the first positive response from one of the people he emailed in Maputo. We never really doubted that we'd be able to sell the Troopy here when the time came — the possibility had turned into a given by the time we'd granted first option for the fifth time. We know that it's the sensible thing to do; we'll have no use for the Troopy back home and all indications are that we'll get a better price for it here, plus we won't have to fork out for the return shipping expenses. But now that the prospect is becoming a reality, not just something on the horizon to be dealt with later, the sense of imminent loss first experienced in Maputo sits permanently behind us on the backseat.

Regardless of what's on the horizon there's still a lot for us to discover over the next month or so. Places of history and nostalgia for Neil, and one of the most well-known national parks in the world just a stone's throw away. It's weeks since we've been in a wildlife park and the prospect of visiting Kruger National Park makes us eager to get moving. Neither of us has been to this park before and our expectations are high, for not only does it have a reputation for exceptional game viewing, but it will enable us to recapture the thrill of the wild that we've become addicted to.

Kruger, South Africa's largest game reserve, sits in the far north-west of the country, bordered by Zimbabwe to the north and Mozambique to the east. It's huge, nearly 2 million hectares, and is home to large populations of game as well as an impressive diversity of flora and ecozones. It has a reputation for responsible park management and is a leading participant in the world of endangered species protection and breeding. Kruger is now part of the Great Limpopo Transfrontier Park, a peace park that links Kruger with the Gonarezhou National Park in Zimbabwe and the Limpopo National Park in Mozambique. Combined, they will all form a truly monumental park once Zimbabwe's present woes are overcome and the depletion of Mozambique's game during the civil wars can be addressed.

Our plan is to enter Kruger roughly halfway up its western border, travel to the north then sweep down to the bottom in a big S. We've booked chalet accommodation in seven of the park's rest camps and bush camps, as Neil is convinced that rainy patches will prohibit camping. In truth we abandoned the idea of camping long ago, but we feel obliged to justify our extravagance with a token excuse every so often.

The road, which runs parallel to the western boundary of the park passes through townships, farmland and private reserves. The drive is uneventful until we hit a swarm of bees. Splat! Suddenly the windscreen is totally covered with yellow fatty bombs making visibility nonexistent. Luckily Neil knows what has hit us and straight away uses the windscreen wipers and water spray before the stuff sets hard. Other drivers aren't so quick off the mark and we see them swerving to a halt wondering what the heck has hit them.

Each day in the park brings something special and unexpected. Like parking by a riverbed at dusk to watch two fish eagles hunt using daringly executed teamwork. They launch themselves from a tree overhanging the river, trapeze artists calling to each other in their high, haunting language, swooping and dipping right over our heads. With one long shrill call the first one swoops down low and fast over a crocodile. As the croc snaps the air in annoyance, the second bird drops from the sky and whisks up a fish from right in front of the croc's jaws.

One morning we come upon two young bull elephants, sparring, practising for more serious times ahead. One uses a branch held in his trunk while the other repeatedly whacks his opponent over the head and shoulders with a trunkful of grass. He doesn't look as though he means real harm, more like a transvestite wielding a handbag in a backstreet brawl.

Overall though, our visit to Kruger has been a little flat. Try as we might, we can't shift that pesky feeling that we're in a large, wild but ultimately controlled environment. We try not to compare it with the raw excitement of parks such as Katavi but there is no ignoring the mass of visitors (6000 available beds at any one time), the tarred roads, and the atmosphere of a well-run metropolis that the main camps exude. In retrospect we've been a bit too ambitious in the distance covered, and it's been too much driving for Neil when you add morning and evening game drives. He's a bit gamed out at present, and even the sighting of three male lions gazing out over a waterhole from a thorn thicket so all-concealing that the cars before us have failed to see them receives just an 'Oh yes, good spotting', and a brief pause for photos before we're gone.

On our last day we're driving out of the park, having just left the night's camp, when we come upon cars pulled over, binoculars and cameras trained on the river below the road. 'Look, look at the crocs!' comes from the nearest vehicle. 'Oh yes, lovely,' replies Neil, then he rolls the Troopy past, intent on continuing on. 'No, the hippo!' insists our friend. We get the binoculars out to see what all the fuss is about: in the middle of the river are dozens of crocs feeding on the body of a hippo while 40 or 50 more are fanned out in formation, waiting for an opportunity to sidle in. I have just enough time to attach the telephoto lens and take a photo when I feel the Troopy moving off. 'But what about the lions?' our obliging neighbour whispers, pointing into the bush beside the road. A group of adult females has apparently just crossed the road in front of his car, heading for the river. 'Great, let's sit here and wait for them to move into that clearing,' I whisper to Neil, while I hurry to now remove the telephoto lens, but the Troopy is already slowly rolling away, heading for our next destination. I didn't think I'd see the day when there'd be no stopping for lions.

The tiny kingdom of Swaziland is a few hours' drive south from Kruger, bordered on three sides by South Africa and by Mozambique on most of its eastern front. It is a mountainous land, with bare rolling peaks interspersed with large-scale agriculture. Ruled by a unique system of dual monarchy, its king, the world's last absolute monarch, shares the balance of power with the queen mother. This is one of the places I've wanted to visit from the start, as I've always had in the back of my mind a newspaper photo of the colourful ceremony in 1968 when Britain granted autonomy to Swaziland.

What was I expecting? Intricately woven beehive huts and warriors in exotic costumes like the ones shown in the newspaper? Instead, what I see are people dressed no differently to those around them in South Africa, poor villages and a wealthy, Westernised capital. To the casual eye, it's a clone of South Africa, but here's a nation that's always been a kingdom and never had apartheid. It has its problems, though. It seems that the natives are restless, that the pro-democracy movement is alive and sometimes subversive and that there is dissatisfaction with the extravagant spending and lifestyle of the king, but he does have an expensive responsibility to bear. He must take many wives from across the kingdom in an ongoing quest to bring new blood into the royal family and to ensure national unity. Maintaining the hierarchical lineage while avoiding inbreeding has been managed through a brilliant but simply executed plan, but I still can't see how everyone isn't related to the royal family by now. And sadly, the king's subjects could be emulating his approach, as I see in a recent paper that Swaziland recently overtook Botswana as the country with the world's highest rate of HIV/AIDS. This might also explain the announcement in the same paper for the Swaziland International Trade Fair, proudly sponsored not by Telkom or Mercedes-Benz but by Trust Condoms.

There are many new and expensive cars on the streets of the capital Mbabane, and sophisticated men dressed in designer casuals frequent the bars of clubs and hotels. The traditional dress is nowhere to be seen except in photos of the king looking paternally down on his subjects from every hotel lobby and shop wall. In one or two of these he's draped in a colourful but decidedly unregal cloth and has cut-out red feathers on his head, a proud secretary bird trying to attract a mate.

By now Neil has had two more positive responses from prospective Troopy purchasers. The others have declined or moved on, so Neil becomes absorbed in reeling in one of the three interested parties. At this early stage he's still buoyant, sure of a sale and hopeful that it'll be at the price we're after. He's adopted the salesman's focus that I saw in him during campaigns at his work, and he's forever scheming, constantly looking at alternative ways of baiting the hook. He's in his element.

We stay overnight at a place called Nisela Safari Lodge, recommended by a local, and which turns out to be a hunting game farm. A game drive over its acreage is somewhat unique when the guide points to a handsome antelope and says, 'Kudu, 15 000 rand,' then at a female impala, '500 rand'. It doesn't take us long to work out that these figures are the cost of shooting the unfortunate animals, but the accommodation is good and very cheap, subsidised by the hunting season, I suppose. We're given the Impala Honeymoon chalet and it's terrific. Large, with a dressing room, a big bathroom decorated to give the impression that we're in the forest, and a wide, shady verandah where in the evenings we sit and watch the wildlife wander past. Incongruously, two donkeys graze nearby and the next morning the guide informs us matter-of-factly that the donkeys are purchased locally to feed to the lions. Yes, the lions. Unfortunately, there are only two males left because the females have recently been sold off. I tell myself that this is to avoid inbreeding, but deep down I know that they went to hunting lodges. We're taken to see the males and as our vehicle approaches their enclosure the guide whistles loudly and beeps a little tune with the car's horn. Time to perform. But this is Sunday, and on Saturdays the lions are given a quarter of a donkey so all we see is one magnificent mane in the long grass in the distance, a contented nod the only recognition of the paying public.

I'm not against farming wild animals and I can see the argument for breeding some species for the hunting industry, but it still irks me to know that there are people out there who get a kick out of shooting an animal that doesn't run away or that is confined in a cage. It's cowardly and unsportsmanlike and wealthy people do it just because they can afford to. Perhaps our stay at Nisela follows on too closely to footage shown on South African TV of the shooting in a hunting concession of a lioness, just separated from her cubs and put in an enclosure no bigger than the average Sydney backyard. Some big brave hunter shot her but couldn't even execute a clean kill with one shot. The force of his over-powerful gun threw the lioness into the air more than once before she mercifully died. Her cubs watched on through the fence. The scenes were so horrible that it forced the South African government to phase in legislation banning what's known as canned hunting. Then there are the hunters who can't afford a lion and just want to shoot something, so they'll kill a zebra or a hippo, both of which are hardly moving targets and present no sport whatsoever. The letters to the editor pages of hunting magazines I flip through are overflowing with explanations from shooters trying to justify their bent, and some of the reasons are so ridiculously philosophical that they inadvertently reveal the true nature of the writer.

Back in South Africa, we head for the Weavers Nature Park near Hluhluwe. It's advertised as being a secluded private reserve and the cottage I particularly like the look of is called The Canopy, another honeymoon suite as it turns out. The pictures on the website make it look comfortable and classy all at once, and the kitchen looks to be large and very well equipped. Neil isn't so keen and is unimpressed by the photos, the location and the isolation. He wants to be near an Internet café where he can keep his finger on the pulse of the Troopy's sale. We arrive at the managers' house and as we pull up a back tyre slowly hisses to a flat. We're parked in loose sand and at a slight angle, which presents a bit of a problem for changing tyres, so when we finally arrive at our little love nest Neil just wants to sit down with a beer and have a cool shower. I open the front door to a room dominated by a massive and over-dressed king-sized bed. 'Where's the chairs?' grumbles Neil. We look in the bathroom, which has a giant spa, twin basins and a whole wallful of storage space, but no shower. This is too much for Neil, particularly after the manageress wouldn't come to the party when he asked politely for stand-by rates. Luckily, I find a light switch and pull open the heavy curtains to reveal a wonderful lounge area with big comfortable-looking sofas on the verandah, and in a few minutes we discover an outdoor shower on the back deck. From then on it only gets better and we wander the reserve in the early mornings and late evenings, and are visited by monkeys, buck and bush pigs throughout the day. The seclusion is addictive and in a couple of days Neil stops talking about offers and counter-offers and can be found on the verandah dozing, an old copy of the *Economist* flopped open but face down on his chest.

We motor to St Lucia on the coast via Hluhluwe Umfolozi Park. This park is made up of two distinct game reserves and is managed not by SANParks but by the local provincial authority, Ezemvelo KwaZulu–Natal Wildlife. Although the park is said to have the Big Five (lion, leopard, elephant, rhino and buffalo) and to be well stocked with game, we catch only glimpses of small herds and lone animals so decide not to stay overnight.

St Lucia is a different matter, a town wedged between river and shoreline, where crocs sleep on the banks of the estuary and hippos wade in the swamp below our apartment window. It's a service town really, once just a base for rough and hardy fishermen but now the centre of tourism and the management hub for the surrounding iSimangaliso Wetland Park, a World Heritage site. The residential parts of town are green and neat but the main street has already outgrown itself with many accommodation options, and tourists busy with arrangements for estuary cruises, whale watching, deep-sea diving and game drives.

On our second day in town we drive into the park and are unprepared for this wonderful place. Very unprepared, as we've left cameras, binoculars and guidebook behind. After immediately spotting a glossy grazing hippo we turn a corner to see three whopping great white rhinos in a grassy field on our right. They wander around with massive heads to the ground, nibbling, kicking a sod, staring with little dumb eyes at the wildflowers for minutes on end. 'Would make a good photo,' we keep muttering to each other.

After that we come across a dazzling array of animals — large herds and an even larger variety of species — all scattered around, grazing the grasslands and wandering the vegetated dunes. One thing I had read in a Ezemvelo KwaZulu–Natal Wildlife pamphlet beforehand was that the driving force behind the ecology of these wetlands is the continual comings and goings of the hippos, estimated at over a thousand, as they move through the waterways onto dry land to graze. The pamphlet went on to say that park management has embarked on a huge program to rid the park of non-indigenous flora and the evidence of this is all around, with hundreds of acres of planted forests cleared to reveal coastal plains and river systems.

On the return road we call in at Mission Rocks, and apart from dodging little antelope, the shy red duiker, continually sneaking across our path, the highlight is a sign by the walking track to the beach from the car park:

Beware of Animals.
Hippos, Buffalos, Black Rhinos, Crocodiles and Leopards
Inhabit This Area.

What, no lions?

Neil's Aunt Elizabeth lives in Umhlanga Rocks, a resort town on the KwaZulu–Natal coast 20 kilometres or so north of Durban, the province's major city. It's a small-town Surfers Paradise with high-rise apartment blocks crowding the beach and large security-fenced residences in suburbs on surrounding hills. Most of the faces in the street are white, and there's a bright holiday feel to the place that must be a breath of fresh air to weekending Durbanites and Jo'burgers. When we arrive the town is jumping and it looks for a time as if we won't get accommodation. At the twelfth hour we book a unit in a big time-share beachfront property. It's okay but we want more, so after three days we move into an apartment on the thirteenth floor of a swanky place where we live like kings. Each day we collect Elizabeth and the three of us sit up in our eyrie, drinking tea, watching the sea and taking many photographs of ourselves and the coastline running all the way to Durban. Neil and I tell ourselves that the enjoyment she's getting from experiencing her town from a different perspective is worth the additional outlay.

The Troopy's sales campaign is stalling. One buyer has dropped out, one really wants it but can't afford it, and the third can afford it but is acting cool. Neil spends time each morning in an Internet café in an attempt to keep the dream alive, but negotiations are at that stage when it could easily become a nightmare. Although Neil is still optimistic, he's progressing the option of shipping the Troopy back home and makes a tentative booking on a vessel that departs Cape Town six weeks before we're due to leave. Not ideal, but the only berth available within our timeframe for a Troopy-sized container.

Elizabeth, tactful as ever, doesn't comment one day after Neil and I have a hairdressing session. Neil appears with a slightly patchy number three after I dropped the clippers, and I emerge as a brunette, although I was hoping for more of a Paris Hilton look.

One of the things that I insisted on packing in the Troopy before it left Sydney was a year's supply of my hair colour, but my calculations were out and the stockpile dried up somewhere in Kenya. Subsequently I've been reliant on local supplies, but I've discovered that what's in the box seems to bear no relationship to what the box says is in there. I've had colours that are totally different to the description (as in Umhlanga), colours that don't colour at all, and factory-sealed boxes that are missing one of the components. I strongly believe that manufacturers treat Africa like the Third World continent it is and, like drug companies, off-load expired and inferior stock here. Sick of my rantings on this subject, Neil suggests that I should take it up with the local MP, or the World Health Organization. They're sure to give it priority.

THiS iS THE LiFE

Port Edward is not a big port, it's not even a port at all but a green and leafy enclave for weekend Durbanites tucked away on the KwaZulu–Natal South Coast. We spend three nights at The Estuary Country Hotel, an estate built on grassy slopes around an old Cape Dutch manor house. It's very calming and pretty, with long views down the estuary to the beach and white Cape Dutch-ish cottages and palm trees reflected in the water. The beach is small but a good one for walking, and we are content to go down there in the mornings and afternoons then drive around the region on little excursions in between. Sometimes we have surprise visitors because the hotel has started on a refurbishment program and our room is the first to be completed. Staff, workmen and other guests are curious to see the glamorous new furnishings, so we get used to a light tap on the door, a head around the corner followed by, 'Oh hello, just looking.' Rather than being annoying it's kind of nice and friendly — we just have to remember to be appropriately dressed at all times.

The road south of Port Edward passes through a region that was once called the Transkei, but which now forms part of the Eastern Cape Province. When he was at boarding school Neil spent his short holidays here on the farm of a schoolfriend's family and he has a soft spot for this starkly beautiful place. Now it's famous as the home of Nelson Mandela, but for three centuries it's been a land of determined and resilient people, the Xhosa. Today it's cold, windy and spitting rain but the people don't seem to notice. We drive through high, rolling and treeless hills separated by grasslands and deep valleys. Homesteads are dotted about everywhere, the houses painted in cheerful colours like bright turquoise and lolly pink. Men carry a *kierie*, a short wooden club used as a walking stick in times of peace, and everyone wears a blanket. Neil remembers a time when these were always red and woollen, but these days brown is favoured and microfibre has been discovered. Men herd their stock on horseback and young ladies with white-painted faces walk along the road. These hills have only ever seen a handful of white farmers and now there is no sign of a European face. It's one of those areas in South Africa that could easily be a separate country, so detached does it appear to be in both place and time.

We arrive in Port St Johns under heavy rain and through the most spectacular of entrances. The road winds steeply down from the hills of the Transkei then suddenly crosses the Umzimvubu River and we're so awe-struck by the high precipitous cliffs through which the river cuts that we don't realise we've actually arrived. What a forgotten little town in such a memorable location. This stretch of coastline is known as 'the Jewel of the Wild Coast' and apparently Port St Johns jumps with holidaymakers during the school holidays, but now it is sleepy and slightly seedy, with low-key family resorts along the riverbank and old, poorly maintained cottages fronting the beach. It could just be the bad weather, but the over-riding feeling is of a place that has forgotten the magnificence of its surroundings.

We press on for another 20 kilometres or so to Umngazi River Bungalows, unconvinced that they'll offer anything more than we've seen in town. But first impressions aren't bad and they have a bungalow free for one night, and once shown to it we're immediately captivated. Someone with a bit of style has put some thought into the design and fittings and it is light and breezy, but the main draw card is the spectacular view over the river mouth and the pounding cyclone-driven surf beyond.

This place is advertised as a family resort and they take this claim seriously. Signs in reception advise that you must pre-book for day care, for nannies and for all sorts of fun-filled family activities. Young couples with pre-schoolers wander about, coddling and chastising and discussing the opening hours of the nursery. Lunch is a traffic jam of designer strollers and toddlers tottering around between the chairs. Even our bungalow has a cot in the spare bedroom and at the bottom of the king-sized bed stands a crib, which the porter immediately stores away when he sees the horrified look on our faces.

I can't shake the feeling that this is all a bit weird. It's a holiday in a giant nursery of strangers and something that I would have thought all sane parents would avoid. We leave the next morning and on the drive out we have to concede that no place is totally ideal. We might never find that perfect little haven where the accommodation is as wonderful as the surroundings and where we could happily melt into both for a week or two.

Further down the coast, East London is the port city where Neil went to high school, and we're here for old time's sake. We do a sweeping tour of the old school, the pool where Neil thrashed the opposition in swimming galas, and the movie theatre where he liked to scare himself shitless watching horror movies on Saturday afternoons. I like the place but he can't get over the fact that now the main street looks like one in any other scruffy country town and the department stores, which were once very classy, now have armed guards at the doors and iron bars over the windows.

Decent accommodation is scarce, as East London has become another place where government officials like to hold conferences, but somehow we manage a front room in a sea-facing hotel. Along with everyone else we're at our window watching the colossal seas demolish the beach in front, a result of extraordinarily high spring tides on top of the tail end of Cyclone Favio. That night we eat in a restaurant on stilts over the sea, with spotlit breakers crashing and white water foaming under the floorboards. A seal at the aquarium next door stretches out on his slippery-dip and as he succumbs to sleep he slides into a heap at the base, a contented flipper occasionally waving in the breeze. Outside, a barefoot old man with bright alert eyes asks for a coin. After Neil obliges with a few rand I think it a good idea that he also hand over the shoes he's wearing, which he intended giving away anyway before we go back home. We walk off along the promenade engaged in an animated discussion on the subject when the old man approaches, smiles and shakes his head. *No, you keep your shoes*.

Leaving East London, we detour inland to Grahamstown, where Neil spent some of his school holidays. Although it's a city it gives the impression of being a country town with leafy, gardened neighbourhoods and low-rise buildings. The streets are lined with quaint old cottages and grand town buildings, all in good nick and lovingly cared for, and right in town is a university which anyone would want to attend just because it's so beautiful. In a backstreet we find the little cottage where Neil stayed with an aunt and it's still exactly as he remembered it. If it was in Australia the whole town would be heritage listed. A shop on High Street has stained-glass trim on the awnings and the original timber counters are tens of metres long, while the polished wooden shelving extends to the ceiling. There's a famous observatory right in the city centre looking more like a neo-Greek theatre, and dapper young Xhosa men walk the streets like characters out of a '30s movie. Rhodes University *is* Grahamstown, and its streets and buildings merge with those of the town so effortlessly that we find ourselves trying to check into a college instead of a B&B. We might have had more luck at the college because there is no accommodation to be had anywhere in town.

So it's back down to the coast and Port Alfred, and The Lookout Guest House. It stands on a hill looking out over the town towards the sea, the apartment large and sunny and our hostess, a local girl, good fun. She and Neil engage in long conversations about the South Africa of their youth, the boarding schools, train journeys and childhood holidays. Neil has found someone who can relate to his life here, and I'm happy to sit back and listen to their reminiscing. In the mornings Neil and I take long walks on the beach and visit an Internet café to check the latest movements in the Troopy's Sales Campaign, but then we return to Louise and her cathartic conversations.

Port Alfred is where Neil's grandfather lived, and once or twice when Neil and his brother were very young the family made the long journey down from Northern Rhodesia to pay him a visit and to have a holiday by the sea. Neil thinks that he can just remember playing on the edge of the surf but it's more likely that he's relating to an old black-and-white photo in which the boys can be seen cavorting in nappies in shallow, low-tide ripples. They look thrilled and wary at the same time; all that water must have been overwhelming to toddlers from a dry, landlocked country.

After a couple of days Louise has to kick us out as The Lookout is fully booked, so we cross the river to a cabin in the Medolino Caravan Park. What a gem, not only because the owner's pride and joy is an Australian cockatoo but also because it shows what a caravan park can be with a little love and imagination. The log cabin we're given is comfortable and quiet, and overlooks a little lake where kingfishers, herons and Egyptian geese mill around. To be picky, the master bedroom is a bit on the small side and during the night I hear Neil cursing as he knocks his shin on the bed-end when he tries to move around it, but that's a small price to pay.

The grounds are grassy green and thick hedges between the sites give the sense that we are lodging on the manicured lawns of a swanky estate. Staff constantly tend the gardens, do the washing, and service the cabins and public ablution blocks. The floors of our cabin are mopped daily, the barbecue scoured and clean towels materialise.

I start passing the time of day with other couples who, like us, have the time to holiday at a leisurely pace. Taking a grey gap year, as one clown suggests. I walk past a couple sitting on recliners in front of their van enjoying sundowners and a bag of chips. The husband raises his glass in greeting. 'This is the life,' he says with great contentment and I find myself thinking, yes, this is the life — and it has nothing to do with nationality or wealth or age, but with your state of mind.

Both Neil and I have been insidiously gaining weight. Our excuse has been that we've been leading a sedentary life, sitting in the Troopy for long stretches and frequenting national parks where we've been restricted to our vehicle and just a small safe area to walk about in. There is truth in that, but deep down we know that the Cadburys Eclairs have been weaving their magic. We started a get fit campaign at The Lookout, and now it's just a short walk over the dunes to the beach so both morning and evening we go down, walking for a good hour. The locals are a friendly lot and we learn many wonderful things on these walks, such as why sea sand is better than river sand for making cement, and where you'd wash up if you got swept away while swimming in the bay. The morning we leave we come upon hundreds of sea urchins washed up at just one spot near the rocks. There are blue ones, large black spiky ones, ones with geometric mauve patterns and baby pincushion ones. Everyone stands around looking at them in wonder, silenced by the gifts nature constantly surprises us with.

On these beach walks and as we drive along in the Troopy we talk about this and that, Neil usually musing over the political situation while I worry about homeless boys or the availability of fresh milk. But something subtle has been happening and Neil has become interested in my chatter, can discuss everyday trivia with the same intensity as me, while I've begun to comment on governments and political personalities. With just each other to talk to, we've gradually become more tolerant of each other's point of view and more involved in the other's interests. We're no longer bickering over insignificant things, like who had the map last before it went missing, but are instead arguing about a country's policies and its future. Without even trying, we've become interested in what each other has to say and more accepting of the other's shortcomings.

CHARMED

We've booked the Zuurburg Mountain Inn in Addo Elephant National Park thinking that it will be bang in the middle of elephants and eland, and that we'll be game driving through the park to get to it. But it turns out that the park's borders aren't straight up and down, but a confusing pattern of indentations and bulges around railway lines, public roads and privately owned land, and that it's sectioned to accommodate the various biomes that it encompasses. Only one section, the one in the middle, actually has the famous elephants. This population of Eastern Cape elephants, now at over 400, has grown from just eleven in 1931 when the park was established to save the sub-species from extinction through poaching. The park has subsequently expanded to cover additional landscapes and biomes, and now a diverse range of species call it home. Because of its accessibility the park is popular and we've been able to book just one night's accommodation at Main Camp. We're disappointed that we'll only have 24 hours in what we think could be the last wildlife park we'll be visiting.

Well, it may be just 24 hours but it's an exceptional day. There are fields of eland and waterholes of buffalo, and all three types of warthog, namely brunette, blonde and redhead. And of course there are the elephants and, almost as precious as those, the dung beetles, and flightless ones at that. Signs all over the park warn that dung beetles have the right of way and on game drives you see cars erratically swerving or screeching to a sudden halt as they come upon a dung beetle rolling his perfect ball of dung across the road. Sometimes the road is scattered with dung beetles and it's only with some very fancy driving that they can be avoided. Even so we come across more than a few squashed bodies, not so much victims of a heartless motorist but unavoidable due to their sheer numbers.

On the afternoon drive we round a corner to see below us a fabulous sight. A series of waterholes surrounded by and filled with elephants, 60 or 70 of them, drinking, playing, larking about in the mud or wandering through the car park where some lucky people are parked, cameras working overtime and big smiles on their faces. Out of the bushes more herds wander in while others, slick with mud and dark with water, move off to make room. It's ordered and stately, and after what seems like just a few minutes they've all gone, engulfed by the surrounding bush. Twice more before we leave the park we visit this waterhole but there is no one there. Our earlier encounter could have been a dream, an illusory trick of the harsh African light.

As we continue towards Cape Town it becomes apparent that now we're heading westward, not south, as the coastline has flattened out and runs roughly from east to west. It's a concept that continually confuses me, as set in my mind is an image of South Africa with Cape Town sitting on a point at the southern extreme. When we were in Cape Town I assumed that I was looking out south towards Antarctica, but I must in fact have had my sights set on Argentina. My sense of direction has been thrown and I fear that from now on I'll be continually guiding us 45 degrees away from our destination.

Our initial intention had been to stay at Jeffreys Bay, home to the Billabong Classic of surfing fame, but it looks bleak and wind blown when we arrive, and we've heard bad things about property safety from previous visitors so we decide to push on to St Francis Bay. This little town looks as pretty as a picture on approach; all whitewash and thatch nestled into a gully amongst sand dunes and the low-lying coastal heath known as *fynbos*. We continue down the peninsula to Port St Francis and then, because we're almost there anyway, Cape St Francis. Not quite as quaint and ordered as St Francis Bay but arranged around a wide sandy beach that stretches as far as the lighthouse. This is the beach that attracts international surfers in winter when tides and winds combine to give a magic mile-long ride right across the bay from the rocks in front of the lighthouse. Now the sea just looks rough and there's not a surfboard in sight.

We choose a place to stay which meets only half of our requirements: there's no view, no international news on DSTV, no Internet facility to track the progress of the Troopy's sale, and what's more, there's an interconnecting door — but we like it all the same. We like it even better when the manageress gives us a discount and says she'll keep the connecting room vacant for the duration of our stay. We continue our get fit campaign with the bravado of the weak-willed, but do manage to stick to a loose regime of morning and afternoon beach walks.

I love this sort of walking — dodging waves, picking up shells, patting dogs. I think about why so many bluebottles have been washed up, and plan what we'll have for dinner. Why do some walkers greet you and others ignore you? And what could that lady have been thinking when she came to walk on the beach in high-heeled espadrilles? When I raise this last important issue, in fact have to repeat it twice, Neil looks suddenly askance and says, 'What?' He's been discussing with himself the future effects of South Africa's policy of Black Empowerment and Affirmative Action, and we laugh at the disparity in our thoughts. We may have, finally, learnt to respect the other's ideas and interests, but my froth and Neil's earnestness will always be there. Now we can appreciate that, underneath it all, we both whistle the same song. I think back to a night in St Lucia. We were sitting at a table in a restaurant and, in a heavy drizzle, a group of black entertainers sidled up to the owner and asked permission to busk. In imitation of the upmarket Khula Happy Singers who entertain tourists all about town, these were dressed in white tuxedos and white gloves, black and white minstrels in reverse, and they sang and danced their hearts out. I don't like to think what it cost them to put their costumes together but there they were, in the rain and with reserved reception, hoping to make a buck. Other diners sat at their tables, eating, drinking, some turning their backs to the boys. As the dancers hummed and clicked their boots I felt a sense of hopelessness for these earnest young men with big dreams but little future. I glanced over at Neil, who was staring into his plate, so wretched did he feel about their nightly humiliation. When they'd finished and the hat was passed around Neil emptied his pockets of change to try to make up for the indifference of others.

We've booked two nights in Tsitsikamma National Park, not really knowing much about it except that it is by the sea and has good walking trails. Ho hum, I'm thinking, as we approach through scanty pine forests and old maize fields. We check in at the gate, where we're given a key and a map, and head off for Storms River Mouth Rest Camp, immediately entering thick forest. There are a couple of marked walking tracks veering off into the undergrowth and through the trees are glimpses of water. The road continues and then in front of us a dramatic stretch of coastline is revealed. We notice tents and caravans and mobile homes spread along a grassy verge right on the rocky shore. Down a little track and we find our chalet nestled up against a ridge of *fynbos*, right on the rocks, 180 degrees of ocean staring back at us just metres away. Wow! Inside it's even better, with a lounge room designed for lounging and a big bed facing the water. Feng shui or whatever, this place immediately feels just right.

We sit on the deck in the sun, watching giant gulls weave, timing the breakers between sets, and above the roar of the ocean we can hear others oohing and aahing as waves blast like water bombs on hidden high-tide outcrops. We've been sitting there for some time when we realise that we haven't investigated the rest of the camp, so we wander over to the public areas. These turn out to be perched right on the mouth of the Storms River, which is pulled to the sea through a deep dark chasm. It's wild, wonderful and untouched, and the feeling that something special is happening here affects everyone.

During the day car parks full of visitors arrive, and some go walking and some go splashing about on the tiny perfect little beach. We go for long walks, a boat trip up the gorge, and on the last afternoon we cut short a three-hour waterfall walk so that we can spend more time on our deck. As the last of the day-trippers disappear up the hill and the afternoon shadows grow longer and darker, a quiet, peaceful mist descends and the dassies come out on the grass to catch the last of the sun. They squeal to each other and race about the rocks, and later when it's dark and cold, their calls carry over the thunder of the sea.

Sometimes it feels like we're leading a charmed life. So much has fallen our way and so little has gone wrong that we've come to believe that all those warnings of doom and disaster were delivered out of jealousy, not concern. But there have been many near misses. As we approached Port Elizabeth we thought we'd drive in to Marine Drive to check out the beach and to look for a shopping mall with an ATM and Internet café. At the last minute we decided to drive on, and a couple of days later we read in the paper that a family of four were held up at knifepoint on Marine Drive and their car stolen. The perpetrators were later caught in a police sting, as this was their modus operandi, high-jacking fancy vehicles on Marine Drive. Then on page three is the news that a gang, again in Port Elizabeth, has been robbing people at ATMs and the last victim got shot in the stomach. Add to this, the plane crash in the Selous in Tanzania, the closing of the Serengeti due to flooding days after we were there, and Cyclone Flavio leaving Vilanculos flattened in our wake. The tail end of another cyclone hit Durban and Umhlanga Rocks four days after our visit, and all this on top of high autumn tides causing windows in Neil's aunt's apartment block to blow out and the road south being closed due to flooding. You have to admit that we're leaving behind a trail of devastation.

MAD, BAD AND DANGEROUS TO KNOW

The press here carries daily articles and letters to the editor about Mugabe and Zimbabwe's slide into insanity. The statistics are sometimes incomprehensible. An inflation rate of 3000 per cent; four out of five people out of work; life expectancy one of the lowest in the world at 37 years for men and 34 for women; 3000 deaths each week from AIDS; and so it goes on. Some of Mugabe's edicts are barely believable, like Operation Nyama announced early this year. In tacit acknowledgement that his people are starving, his cunning plan is for them to go out and kill the wildlife. *Off you go — an elephant should keep you going for a week or two.* Never mind that without animals there will be even fewer tourists, many of those lucky enough to still have work will be jobless and the input of foreign currency to the street economy will dry up.

The man has been out of control for years and any hope of him seeing reason has long gone, so now the South African press has turned their attention to his best mate, their own leader Thabo Mbeki. This man must have had some very good spin-doctors when he took office after Mandela. He was heralded as a quiet academic, a deep thinker who would, through diplomacy, honesty and subtle cleverness, take South Africa to further greatness. His performance since has been underwhelming and has disappointed both blacks and whites. Not only disappointed but embarrassed. Take the AIDS issue, for example. First, he proclaimed that AIDS wasn't an issue at all, then that it may exist but wasn't a problem in his country, and then his Health Minister got up in front of a world AIDS conference in Canada and told delegates that the disease can be cured with lemons, garlic and beetroot. As we travel through South Africa, it's evident he's becoming a joke and can't control his party, the African National Congress, any more than he can break the ties that bind him to Mugabe.

As we head towards Knysna, the newspapers are full of the Zimbabwean police beating up Mugabe's main opposition, Morgan Tsvangirai. Mugabe is unrepentant and somehow uses his tried and true argument of Britain not honouring its land reform obligations as an excuse for the beating. Similarly, Mbeki constantly plays the racist card whenever criticised, no matter that racism has nothing to do with the point at hand. It could be union corruption, government incompetence or a health issue, but you can be sure that white racism is the cause. When recently asked a question by a journalist regarding the culpability of one of his ministers, the response, wrapped around the statement that there are still whites who refer to blacks as *kaffirs*, left everyone scratching their heads.

Great news! Donald, one of the Troopy's admirers has agreed in principle to buy. There has been much to-ing and fro-ing, the price has been reviewed, things excluded being included, convincing, cajoling, but now our friend in Namibia has come good. It's not quite a done deal yet, as he'll have to establish the legalities of buying an Australian-registered vehicle that is travelling on a *carnet*, while at the same time trying to minimise the high duties that will apply. But he wants it, and badly. Neil's confident enough to abandon the plan of sending the Troopy home and cancels the shipping container, but still, in the back of his mind is that old salesman's maxim of waiting until the money is in the bank before acknowledging that it's in the bag.

Everyone who mentions Knysna speaks of it in glowing terms and confirms that it is a place where we must spend several days. Brochures show trendy shops, a beautiful wide blue lagoon and people canoeing through secret peaceful inlets. An image of a tranquil but upmarket holiday town has lodged in my head and I advocate staying a week, at least five days. We approach from the east and drive through a neat township with unruly shops, and a not-so-neat informal settlement. There are people all along the road hailing taxis, selling carvings, wanting lifts or handouts. A bustling place full of life and music. Up and over a hill and the first view of the main town shows a large lagoon with new, soulless estates on the shores and a low sand island jam-packed with uniform houses, and no greenery in sight. We can see a railway line running right across the water below, and up on the hills are massive, over-the top mansions that South Africa is so good at. These would easily house a dozen township families (let's face it, they'd house two or three Australian families), but are most likely the home of one lone retired couple.

We've lost some enthusiasm for the place and head straight to Knysna Quays at the North Wharf. There take a small apartment overlooking a canal and settle in. It's quiet and the outlook is pretty but what sells us on the place, after weeks of hand-washing, is the presence of a washing machine and dryer. Downstairs in the complex there are boutiques, jewellery shops, an Internet café and restaurants, and an elegantly dressed transvestite is doing a roaring trade at a tarot table. Another time and we'd love it here, but we both seem to be unsettled, our mind on the immediate future and looking for something without being sure what it is. After just two days we pack up and move on.

The road westward out of town winds around the north shore of the main lagoon. It passes family bungalows with little dinghies in front and inlets with fishermen in tinnies floating in the reeds. This must be what people were talking about, a lazy fishing village before the developers and architects came to town.

The town of Wilderness sounds like it could offer what we're seeking so we drive in with high hopes. Expecting a wilderness, we find a busy little hub squashed between the sea, the highway and the railway line. The beach foreshore is lined with those same grand houses that turned us off Knysna, but here they don't dictate the heart of the town. We drive around for a couple of hours, looking for accommodation near the beach, but it's school holidays and two days before Easter, and we get turned away time and time again. As a last resort Neil phones a place that I've seen an ad for, not on the beach but off in the bush somewhere. Yes, they have a cottage and off we go into the hinterland, expecting a log cabin with a view of trees.

What we find is Clairewood, a wonderful, peaceful haven with a stylish cottage looking out over valleys of mist and blue tall mountain ranges. We've just walked in and we know we want to stay longer. It has everything; besides the view there are friendly dogs, a visiting old horse, well-thought-out interiors with the best bed we've slept in so far, a considerate host who very soon becomes a friend, a pack of marauding black baboons, and neighbours so far away that they might not be there. It's so quiet that noise carries kilometres across the valley and the sound of someone calling in their dogs at a farm two hills away drifts across and weaves into our sitting room as if the dogs are here at our feet. Each day we ask to stay a day longer and each day we hang around the cottage, forgetting the walks and canoeing we'd talked about doing the night before.

Sweetness comes each day to clean and she embarks on a project to teach us Xhosa. Basic grammar and common nouns are interspersed with stories of her family and we gradually learn a little of her life. She left her husband when she discovered he was playing around, and she is training to be a natural healer because it's a way of helping her people. She's very religious. Easter Friday she spends six hours at the Zionist church, praying and singing to the beating of drums. When asked how far she must travel to the church she answers that it's about an hour's walk but if it's raining she runs. No one could have been better named. Her gentle nature warms the days and generosity flows around her like a sea mist in a secret bay.

One morning there's a hue and cry in the garden and we go out to find our host, garden boys and dogs trying to catch a runaway piglet. With the little pink porker in front they all hurtle about in diversionary directions, down a grassy slope one minute then into the undergrowth, followed by shouts and the sound of branches snapping and dead leaves cracking. But the funniest participant in the chase is the old horse who, tail out and neck arched, canters around behind the little pig, not letting anyone or anything else get close to it. No one's seen him move like this in years, and afterwards he's very pleased with himself and prances and dances about like a three-year-old.

The southernmost tip of the African continent lies in the Agulhas National Park, 170 kilometres south-east of Cape Town.

It lies on the meridian of 20 degrees east and this meridian also marks the official division between the Indian Ocean and the Atlantic. Neil and I decide that we'd like to see this point, if for no other reason than to photograph each other with one foot on either side of the divide. When we arrive in the settlement of Cape Agulhas it's sunny but blowing a gale. The town is treeless, under siege from the elements, only a place that fishermen would love. And fishermen there are, dozens of them lined up on the rocks, leaning into the wind with the spray whipping into their determined leathery faces. We head straight for the most solid-looking accommodation in town, the Agulhas Country Lodge, nestled into the *fynbos* in defiance. The wind is so strong that each time we venture outside we find another piece of hardware lying in the car park, blown off the exterior of the building. We take a drive to nearby Struisbaai to visit the National Heritage–listed thatched fishermen's cottages, but it's blustering too much to get out of the car. Instead we go to the harbour where we struggle against the force of the wind into a bar full of locals watching a Springbok–Wallabies match. No English spoken here. Neil goes to the bar and orders a beer in a low voice, trying to cover his Australian accent in a room full of Springbok supporters. I'm offered a stool by a gentlemanly young Afrikaner and I can't figure out if it's because I'm female, older then him, or if he's picked up on my nationality and feels sorry for me.

Around the corner and beyond a lighthouse lies the national park, a broad coastal plain that looks stark and windswept under these conditions, and down on the nearby shoreline are ancient fish traps where some smart Khoisan generations ago worked out a method of stranding fish in a series of stone corrals after they'd been borne in on incoming high tides. We like this battered, historic corner of the country and despite the wind and the

Wallabies' loss we leave town the next day with a positive feeling, a sense that here is a place still connected to its past and a people who have learnt to live with the elements and thrive.

Our last port of call before Cape Town is Hermanus, one-and-a-half hours' drive away. It's a favourite seaside destination for Capetonians in search of a weekend away, but is more famously known as offering the best land-based whale-watching opportunity there is. Tourists from all over the world flock to these shores around the month of August to view the southern right whale at very close quarters. The town's bays and inlets become one giant maternity ward as they harbour cows calving and mothers with their young, and cliff paths and vantage points overflow with expectant observers watching life played out in the waters just metres below their feet. One local puts a slight dampener on it though when she confides in us that, yes, it is wonderful and the whales are truly awesome, but *ag*, the noise, the crying and moaning as they give birth is heart-wrenching. She also tells us that the first of the northward-bound whales have been recently seen, four months out from the peak of the season. Just two on two separate days, but that's enough to give us the whale-watching bug. From the verandah of our flat we gaze out to sea, hopeful of a splash and a flash of white, and we walk the cliffs daily peering down into the lonely inlets. But for the duration of our stay, the whales aren't cooperating.

FULL CiRCLE

We're back in Cape Town, this time staying in the suburb of Hout Bay on the Atlantic seabord while we wait to hear from Donald with confirmation that all is in place for his purchase of the Troopy. The little flat we've taken is away from the bustle of Hout Bay's busy streets but close enough to pop down to the activity on the seafront. One of Cape Town's major fishing fleets is based at the harbour here, and the red and blue boats of the Cape Coloureds, who have dominated the industry in the past, dot the water in this sweeping broad bay of great natural beauty.

On the way to most places we drive past Imizamo Yethu, a controversial informal settlement that has grown rapidly over the past few years to cover 18 hectares slap in the middle of luxury retirement homes and million-dollar mansions. As many as 20 000 people are said to be living here in makeshift shanties with little or no infrastructure such as plumbing or roads. A more striking example of the haves and have-nots living in precarious harmony would be hard to find.

In emails from home we're often asked about the safety issue in South Africa, whether we've ever felt threatened or been in danger. I would have to say never, disregarding the credit card theft in those first days in Cape Town — and Neil has always put that down to a lapse in concentration on his part: he'd disregarded the first rule of drawing money from an ATM anywhere. The need for security is hard to ignore, with armed security guards, high fences and razor wire protecting everything from shops and car parks to public buildings and private homes, but you soon learn to look beyond that. On the surface, day-to-day life in South Africa is so like Sydney that it's easy to miss the undercurrents. Passing through the country as visitors, we've been impressed by the infrastructure. The roads are excellent and we've found the post reliable. But when we read the papers and speak to people on the street we can't ignore the fact that things are falling apart. The country has the second-highest murder rate in the world; hospitals are closing because they're a danger to the public when they treat patients; and billions of rand are lost or stolen from government at all levels due to incompetence and corruption. Every day we read about another huge loss of public funds — recently one local government body made 1000 employees redundant, but their remuneration bill went up by over a billion rand because the council officials rewarded themselves for achieving such wonderful savings. The ANC government is trying to take control of the judiciary, and the country experiences blackouts because the state-run electricity network receives very little maintenance and has no forward planning. With so many other pressing issues facing the government, security seems to have been left in the hands of the individual.

We're happy to be here in Cape Town, in what is arguably one of the most beautiful cities in the world, but it's a far cry from watching the sun go down over an endless yellow plain and waking to the warm embrace of the bush. We're both feeling slightly odd; we're in a neverland of neither coming nor going. Neil begins to talk of farewell lunches with relatives and friends and he starts thinking about the practicalities of going home. The floor of the flat is strewn with dog-eared airline print-outs and paperwork we've not looked at for almost a year. We have to remind each other that, although we've come full circle, the journey hasn't come to an end.

To convince ourselves of this we plan a little trip, visiting the sights that we were too preoccupied to see when we were here the first time. The thought of this perks us up considerably and we set off for a few days down the Cape Peninsula to the Cape of Good Hope in a good mood but grey, drizzly weather.

The first stop is Simon's Town. Although a naval base, it's nevertheless a very pretty town in an old Victorian English seaside sort of way. The architecture is all sandstone, weatherboard and wrought-iron verandahs, and the original naval buildings look more manor house than institutional. Nearby is an African, or jackass, penguin colony on the shoreline at Boulders Beach, and the breeding season is in full swing. The surrounding *fynbos* is a hive of activity, with mating, nesting and home-building going on, and the sand is covered with happy families socialising and sunbaking with heads back, flippers open to the rays. Every now and then there's a commotion in the undergrowth. The bushes quiver and shake and jackass brays start up, rise to a crescendo then die down as peace is restored. There are around 3000 little waiters here now, a far cry from the original two mating pairs of the early 1980s.

Next we visit the Cape of Good Hope in Table Mountain National Park. We're told not to expect to see much wildlife, as the little there is is spread out and tends to prefer the areas away from access roads. But we're not worried because even the road into the park is spectacular, with sweeping views of False Bay and unexpected inlets and coves. It's also a perfect day for this park — sunny but cool, with very little wind and great visibility. Although the coastal *fynbos* has been flattened and battered by gales over centuries and there are few trees, the park is starkly dramatic, and in flower.

Days before, a tourist was lost when he went swimming at Diaz Beach, between the Cape of Good Hope and Cape Point. Today we walk the path above the beach and look down over the wild seas where a visible rip, the culprit, moves like a sinister shoal across the bay towards the rocks. Even from way up here it looks hostile and forbidding, and you feel for the family who watched helplessly as a happy lark turned to tragedy in a minute.

On the way back to Cape Town we stop off at Kalk Bay, a little village tucked between the railway line and the shoreline. Standing patiently in the car park is a lady holding up appliquéd wall hangings for sale. As we admire the designs and workmanship of her craft we learn a bit about her. Winnie is her name, and she is totally without pretence, rooted to the pavement like a big warm shady oak, one that you'd like to shelter under. She's proud of her work and spends a little time explaining the scenes depicted and the materials she uses. She is from Zimbabwe but, unlike the recent refugees, she has been moving around all of southern Africa for many years, selling her work. Her husband is dead and her three children are scattered here and there. Winnie speaks softly and with great warmth and you come away feeling richer just from spending five minutes with her. She is everything I want to remember about Africa and one of many I'll never forget.

Waiting for us in Cape Town is the email we've sweated on: Donald has confirmed that the official paperwork is in his hands: he's drawn up a contract of sale and has arranged for money to be transferred to our account. The Troopy is soon to drive new roads, traverse new highways and bear proudly the number plates of Namibia. We start on a frenetic sorting and packing program and parcel up things to send back home, and this brings on twinges of nostalgia when we uncover safari khakis, dried baobab petals, a carving from Vic Falls which we discover has stained my underwear with boot polish. But we're in high spirits. Not only has the worry over the Troopy's fate lifted but we're also about to start on one last journey: we will deliver the Troopy in person to Windhoek as part of the sale agreement, and we will drive there via places that have lodged in a special part of our hearts.

The route north we've chosen this time is up through the Karoo, a semi-desert that stretches across the middle of South Africa. We set out from Cape Town and have been on the road for only fifteen minutes when we pass a body in the middle of an exit ramp. It's near the airport where the huge squatter camp envelops the freeway, and the poor soul must have tried to cross from one side to the other in the early morning traffic. It's awful and sad but eerily peaceful — the police have cleared a big area around the body and there is no one near it; he's just lying there while commuters go on their way on either side and his down-at-heel shoes lie empty on the road 10 metres behind. He could be sleeping were it not for his limbs akimbo and the stillness that has permeated the scene.

We can't resist a stopover in Stellenbosch to re-acquaint ourselves with some half-decent wine. The heart of South Africa's wine industry, Stellenbosch is also a university town and it's a place of tradition, culture and great scenic beauty as well. Camberley

Cottage is our home and Blackie, a rolling black Labrador with loose eyes and long wet jowls, is our host. The cottage sits by a vineyard and we look out over rows of maroon and mustard leafage along the dramatic Franschhoek Valley, its slopes and floor a chequerboard of orchards and vineyards. The owners of Camberley, Blackie's masters, are away and he's attached himself to us for company and handouts. The first night he retires to our bedroom along with us and I fall asleep with my hand held soft and warm in his mouth. He spends the night alternating between Neil's side of the bed and mine but by morning he's gone.

Next day at lunchtime we eat in a restaurant in town which has a novel way of billing customers — you help yourself from a buffet, the plate is put on a scales and you're charged according to weight. Good fun and fast service, and everyone walks away content as they believe they've eaten exactly what they paid for.

We visit Lanzerac, an old French Huguenot wine estate. With a whitewashed, elegant Cape Dutch manor house surrounded by ruler-straight vines, it's the holy grail of a gracious Cape wine estate. Our goal today is to taste five wines, after which we'll each be given a Lanzerac-etched wineglass free of charge. No matter that we'll soon have no use for them. On arrival we're told that we must have read about this offer in an old wine magazine as it no longer applies, but we enjoy the tasting nevertheless, particularly when a group of young glamourpusses arrive. After confidently asking to taste a sweet wine, they are prepared to settle for a semi-sweet when their first choice is not forthcoming. No semi-sweet? 'Well, where do we have to go for a good sweet wine?' When told Robertson, a town many kilometres away, almost in the desert, they decide to make the best of it and sample what Lanzerac has on offer. Reading off the list one says she'll try chardonnay, another, 'cabenette'. A third, still holding on to a dream, asks if magnum is sweet. We could easily stay a week here, but after four days we are forced to leave Blackie by the need to push on to Namibia.

The road across the Karoo is long and the distance between towns far, but I'm just happy to be heading north again. I can see that Neil has mixed feelings: sad that we'll soon be parting with the Troopy, happy that he's sold it for a good price, but anxious that the final handover proceeds without a hitch. We overnight in Beaufort West in a guesthouse surprising for its class and style in the heart of the desert, then the next day we reach Upington and annoy ourselves by driving around the streets, lost, in a town we thought we'd remember. But Kgalagadi Transfrontier Park is now just a day away and even a mediocre B&B can't dampen our rising excitement.

COMMAND PERFORMANCE

Driving into Kgalagadi once again, our anticipation is high. Now we know what to expect and we think we know where to head for the best wildlife viewings, but once on the access roads we're struck by how it's changed in ten months. No wildlife congregating where they were before and no recognisable landmarks. What's up? Of course, it's now autumn, another season, and summer has been harsh and long. Where before tall yellow grasses covered the dunes and dry riverbeds, now there is brittle brown stubble scattered across a loose sandy expanse. Before, big herds of antelope stretched along the rivers, but now we find them crowding around permanent waterholes or walking towards them in long dusty lines.

This park is remarkable. On our first day we come across two big black-maned lions by a waterhole. We're sure these are the brothers from our previous visit until a ranger points out that these are new to the park, spotted a few weeks ago trailing in from Botswana. They are so fat and full they don't move all day except to follow the shade. We go back to the waterhole three times and they are always there, once lying in the shadow of an onlooker's sedan; another time, on their backs asleep under a camelthorn tree, manes unruly and matted with twigs and large padded paws pointing to the sky. Then one afternoon we're on a sidetrack that looks as if no vehicle has passed along it for some time when, right beside the road, there stands a magnificent leopard who gazes at the Troopy with lazy Adonis eyes. He runs off, not because he's frightened but because he has a female waiting in the bushes. We just catch a glimpse of her svelte young body before they get down to some serious mating in the long grass.

Staying once again in Kalahari Tented Camp we're visited by a snake, a jackal, a genet and two yellow mongooses by the time we've downed sundowners. Anything more and we'd have to charge admittance. The snake, long but thin, appears on the ground under the Troopy and the camp attendant thinks that it would have ridden into camp with us on the Troopy. Neil, remembering the experience in Ruaha National Park, tries to convince me that it's a mole snake, living harmlessly underground, but I've no doubt that we carried this one in on the Troopy as well. Our two experiences mirror a story told to us 30 years ago by friends who had lent us their army-green Peugeot stationwagon. They were working in Jo'burg and Neil and I had been travelling on the cheap through southern Africa. Our friends very generously lent us the Peugeot to complete our journey to Cape Town, but it came with this warning: never leave the parked vehicle with the windows open. Some months before, they had been doing a tour of Rhodesia and when they got to the Great Zimbabwe ruins they were hot and tired and annoyed with each other. Robbie refused to get out of the car and sat in the passenger's seat sulking, window down because of the heat. After a couple of minutes Lyle coaxed her out and she slid across the bench seat to exit on the driver's side. Then she remembered the opened passenger's window and leaned back to wind it up just in time to see a deadly black mamba sliding down from the roof of the car, in through the open window and down onto the floor under her seat. If she'd not glanced back at that particular moment she would have wound the window up then afterwards got back into the car, oblivious to the danger coiled under her seat.

Although it's been less than a year since we were last at this camp, the wear and tear is showing. While still spotlessly clean and well serviced, things like broken tent zippers and unmended Velcro window seals have changed the camp from stylishly rustic to 'bush condition'. This is borne out when we chat to the camp attendant and he tells us that headquarters never seem to get around to sending replacement zips and new Velcro; he hints at under-funding and corruption in low places and refers to similar neglect in the wildlife management area as well.

Then it's on to Namibia, through the same border post as before but this time we're held up not by having our firewood confiscated on the South African side, but by Neil getting involved in a long conversation with the Namibian officials on soccer, South African roads and how the Troopy's fared on its long trek. These men are in the back of beyond and would have only a handful of customers each day, but their uniforms are pressed and crisply white and their shoes polished. The Customs team check the Troopy's fridge and drawers for contraband with great thoroughness all the while arguing whether the World Cup in Cape Town in 2010 will be successful (*No, there is too much crime in that place*) and which African country will be able to beat Namibia (*Sadly, I think, Sir, all of them*).

The red dunes are beckoning, so after a forgettable night in a plain, gritty highway town we're back in Sesriem. Not the campsite this time but a kilometre or two away in the middle of a tussocky, rocky dry plain. Desert Camp. The reception desk is manned by a thin, slightly scary, young lady who announces that she does not have our booking and knows nothing about us — and who was it anyway that Neil thinks he spoke to when making the reservation? I can see his hackles rising as he over-politely explains the phone conversation and tries to say without saying it directly that the person he spoke to was black. 'It was me!' she cackles just in time. This is Gizella, making a joke. 'Oh, I'm a bad girl. Hello and welcome.'

While checking us in Gizella tells us that she's on a self-improvement kick. Before, she smoked and drank and was cheeky to everyone. She was always fighting and getting into trouble. 'See this?' she asks, pointing to a round mouth-sized skin graft on her forehead. After a heavy bout of drinking she started fighting with another girl who jumped on her and bit a piece out of her. 'Oh, I was bad news then.' When asked how long she's been off the alcohol she proudly tells us one month, so Neil and I tacitly agree to give Gizella a wide birth for the duration of our stay. But we find ourselves gravitating to her and her exuberant personality and by the time we leave the camp we've learnt more of her wayward past. No husband, two children, one living with her mother and one with her uncle. She's working towards becoming a better person, leaving the desert and getting her children back. Two years is too long in a desert she declares, partly in English and partly in Italian, her favourite language. If we buy her a ticket to Italy she can marry a wealthy Italian, sit by the sea and drink and smoke. Her children seem to have been forgotten in this optimistic but flawed plan.

Last year we thought the Sesriem public camping ground was in a great location but this is even better. Gizella has given us the end tent and we sit on the verandah and look out across endless desert. I could stay here forever. The colours change with every whim of the sun and a landscape that is red and glowing one minute becomes soft lilac the next time I look. The worst time is in the heat of the day when everything is stark and flat, shimmering in and out of focus, washed out by too much light. The mornings and evenings are magical. Then, the light sits on the landscape and sparkles like a pastel jewel, and the stillness goes on as far as the eye can see. This is heaven. We go to bed with the soft sounds of the night in our ears and in the morning we're woken by the busyness of birds and low African words as staff start their day.

On our last night in camp we're having a drink at the bar under the stars when a horned adder comes sidling in out of the gloom. The black staff are very frightened — they want to kill the 'horny adder' — so Neil finds a cardboard box and with the help of the bravest barman he captures and relocates the intruder. We return to our tent and there on the steps is a scorpion, shiny and arched in our torchlight, and we congratulate ourselves that we didn't change out of our walking shoes before going to the bar. As we've learnt to expect of Africa, its beauty can often hide its wild heart.

GOODBYE MY FRiEND

We've a day or two to fill in before handing over the Troopy, so a detour to Swakopmund seems like a good idea. The Troopy can have one last service and the windscreen replaced at the auto service centre we used last time, and we can walk and shop in familiar surroundings while repacking drawers and bundling up unwanted clothes. We arrive late in the day under heavy skies and have trouble finding an estate agent still open, let alone one who has a rental property available. We're referred to an agent who comes up trumps with a small flat near the centre of town. It's cosy and quiet, unlike our agent, who is strung out, edgy and brittle. Over the next 48 hours we have contact with her several times and her demeanour shifts from rude to harried to nervous breakdown. Her dark personality and the coastal fog clinging to the shirt-tails of the town every day we're there creates a completely different impression of Swakop to the one we left with last year.

The grey mood follows us to Windhoek. We book into a cabin in a holiday park, right next to the runway of Windhoek's airport, and spend hours cleaning the Troopy and polishing the duco. We give boxes of clothes, first aid supplies and kitchen utensils to the staff to distribute amongst themselves. On the afternoon before the handover we drive out into the bush, a final voyage and farewell to our home and safe haven for the past eleven months. We're as taken with the Troopy now as we were the day we collected it and settling into the front seat is like nestling up to a favourite aunt for the last time. It hums over the tarmac and hugs the curves as confidently as ever, and the late desert light shines off the chrome work while those on the roadside look on with wide admiring eyes.

The handover is long as the papers are checked and contracts signed and Neil lovingly explains every quirk and attachment. Then Donald drives away and the Envy of all Africa gets smaller and smaller though it still stands out like a bright morning star.

So it's come to this. It's over, and all that is left is the journey home. Without our anchor we feel alone and directionless, the rest of the day passing in a blur of long silences. Night comes, and I lie in bed listening to Hadeda ibis calling from the runway and low African voices moving along the footpath. They remind me of other places, other nights. The cry of jackals on a moonsoft plain and the humphing of hippos across a still lagoon. I want to hear again soft voices in gentle conversation and bask in the warmth of people like Winnie. I want to sit on a stoep in Kenya, hearing stories of leopards and brave dogs, and laugh with new friends in the glow of a bush campfire. Most of all I want to be back on the road with Neil, driving through a landscape of unexpected beauty where every day reveals a secret and every corner hides a promise of things new and improbable. I miss Africa and I haven't even left yet.

I tell Neil how I feel: how I could easily do our journeying all over again, I *want* to do it all again, just find the Troopy and head north like before into the wild blue yonder. Neil turns to me and the look on his face says it all. *Oh god. I'm hooked.* I've become one of those people who have let Africa get under their skin. From now on I'll see Kilimanjaro in every mountain and the Zambezi mirrored in every sunset. In my dreams I'll journey to my favourite places and in my mind I'll hear the language of an ancient landscape where fish eagles cry at dusk and the innocent laugh under white flowering baobabs.